For Brooke

" Make your life something
beautiful for God! "
— Mother Teresa

God's First Book

Jon Leuer

ISBN: 1439239169
ISBN-13: 9781439239162

For my three nephews, my three Godsons,
Colton, John, and Thomas

Table of Contents

Part I
Truth, Goodness, and Beauty

Part II
Faith and Reason

Part III
A Reading from the Physical World

Part IV
A Reading from the Human Person

Part V
The New Heavens and Earth

Acknowledgments

I would like to thank my parents, Richard, Susanna, and Paul, for exposing me to the treasures of the Rocky Mountains and the Hawaiian Islands. I would also like to thank my nurturing mother (*alma mater*) Franciscan University of Steubenville and the four professors who became my mentors: Dr. Regis Martin, Dr. Mark Miravalle, Dr. Scott Hahn, and Dr. Patrick Lee. Anything insightful written on these pages should be credited to them, anything misleading to my own shortcomings, and anything inspiring to the Holy Spirit. Finally, I would like to thank all the little ones who have given me so much joy over the years, as well as my guardian angel, without whose help this project would never have come to light.

Preface

In the eleventh century, St. Anselm of Canterbury insisted that there is no bigger thought than that of God. If that is true, then it seems a good thing to think about and think about well. One of the great privileges of being Catholic is that you don't have to wake up everyday and try to figure out who God is and what God wants: the most generous and loving people in the history of the world, the saints, have already done that. This book, then, is little more than an attempt to canvass a view of creation which is consonant with the Catholic faith, building upon that great heritage of saints in a manner which responds to the needs of the modern world. Youth especially need weapons to protect themselves from those persuasive but poor thinkers of our time, that is, those who advocate skepticism, relativism, and atheism.

The word catechist is derived from a Greek word meaning to echo or resound. Thus, the goal for a faithful catechist is to stay out of the way and let saints, shepherds, and scriptures* teach the wisdom of the ages. As St. James tells us: "not many of you should become teachers, my brothers, for you realize we will be judged more strictly, for we all make many mistakes." (James 3:1-2) With that in mind, I have tried to keep things simple without watering them down. It is not within the scope of this book, for example, to separate metaphysics into ontology and natural theology, to distinguish induction from deduction, to illustrate the three degrees of Holy Orders, or to explore all the dimensions of beauty, art, and love. What is attempted here, rather, is an overview of reality which lays an *objective* foundation for clear thinking and right

---

* Scripture quotations are from one of three translations: The New American Bible (used for Mass and the Liturgy of the Hours); or The Revised/ New Revised Standard Versions (both used in the Catechism of the Catholic Church).

living. If I have quoted others too often, it has only been to show that the ideas contained within are not my own; they belong to that luminous "cloud of witnesses" who have expounded truth, goodness, and beauty in their thoughts, actions, and lifestyles.

Footnotes have been included (in a familiar rather than formal style) for the sake of emphasizing this great treasury of wisdom accumulated by those closest to God. My own stories serve only to provide context, to be the binder of those sacred pigments, and my own words are of no importance unless they resonate within a soul in a way that brings them closer to God and His Church.

Finally, this publication is unedited, and I would like to apologize in advance for any and all errors in spelling, punctuation, and grammar. Please feel free to contact me at *jonlewer@wyoming.com* and may God's peace be with you always.

Introduction

Growing up where the Great Plains meet the Rockies meant that wide open spaces and giant mountains were in my blood from the beginning. Three 14,000 foot peaks – Long's Peak, Pike's Peak (which inspired *America the Beautiful*), and Mount Evans – dominated the 150 mile skyline of my youth. I was also deeply influenced by the roses and butterflies of summer, so much so that when I was six years-old my Mom and Grandma made me a birthday cake in the shape of a yellow swallowtail.

My grandparents were all from cow towns, and my parents' deep appreciation for natural beauty was passed on to me and my brother during our frequent camping and fishing trips. My uncle, Dick Megill, was likewise a profound influence as he is a committed and refined outdoorsman.

Additional formation was provided by two great calderas, two great national parks: Yellowstone and Hawaii Volcanoes. From the time I was twelve years old, every Christmas vacation began on the champagne powder slopes of Steamboat Springs, Colorado, and ended on the Kona coast of the Big Island of Hawaii; and every summer vacation was highlighted by a trip to Yellowstone. And though foundations were being laid all along, the inspiration for this book came in a rush, a wave of overwhelming enlightenment, as I was hiking alone during my annual retreat into the most remote wilderness in the lower forty-eight – the upper Yellowstone River.

Known as *The Thoroughfare* since the days of the mountain men, it is an unforgiving land. Help is so far away that one serious mistake and prayer is your best chance of survival. I always have my rosary in hand. But is also a place of Edenic beauty. On the seventh day of what turned out to be a nine day trip, I was passing through a section of river meadow we later named "The Garden", when suddenly I was staggered by the loveliness of it all. And I was filled with light: God wanted me to write about the book of creation. He had been leading me to that moment in such a way that it could not be anticipated yet came as no surprise. Still, I began to weep with gratitude. For not only had He dispelled the darkness, He had gathered together an entire lifetime of dreams and disappointments then poured them into a single moment of superabundant meaning.

My annual wilderness retreats began after a defining conversion my freshman year of college, when the life of St. Francis of Assisi inspired me to emulate his love for the poor by working with special needs children and later volunteering at the Samaritan House homeless shelter in Denver. Shortly after I began at the shelter, however, I found it increasingly difficult to see God in the impoverished faces of the inner city, even though I could still find Him in the riches of nature. I wanted to serve the homeless, but the ugliness of alcoholism, trash, and widespread mental illness proved a recipe for confusion. (Years later I learned from Mother Teresa that without being able to recognize and draw strength from Jesus in the Eucharist, I would not be able to recognize Him for long in "the distressing disguise of the poor.") I needed clarity, and when I asked myself where the most beautiful place on earth might be, the answer was immediate – Jackson Hole, Wyoming.

Jackson Hole is a valley surrounded by mountains, making it look like a hole to the early trappers. The northern half of the valley has been preserved as Grand Teton National Park, which sits just south of Yellowstone National Park. Since my family always entered Yellowstone from the south on our summer vacations, we always passed through Jackson Hole. And on our very first trip, during the summer of our nation's bicentennial, I had come to the conviction that this was the most beautiful place, for the impression it left changed my heart forever.

The day my stepdad, mom, brother, and I packed into our Volkswagen bus, finally ready to leave the suburbs of Denver behind, was a day charged with excitement and resolve. We had come to believe that no vehicle ever made was better suited for creating vivid road-trip memories than a geared up VW bus; but since we had also come to believe that no vehicle ever made was slower than a VW bus (especially one hitched to a tent-trailer choked with said gear), our plan was to drive all night and arrive at Yellowstone in the morning. About an hour from the south entrance, my brother and I were asleep in the back when our mother's voice drifted from the front seat: "Boys, look outside." I remember her tone being firm enough to preempt all debate (I was, after all, on the threshold of my teens), yet there was something else: her voice was soft, serene, as if she had been grieving but then found peace. I propped myself up on one elbow and pressed my forehead to the window – it was around 2 a.m. The full moon had by then risen high in the sky, and was casting shadows so distinct they seemed to protest belonging to darkness. And there, before an audience of applauding stars, the glaciers and granite of the most celebrated mountain range in the Rockies, the Tetons, were quietly humming in the moonlight. In retrospect, the Grand Teton itself, towering above the rest, seemed to be performing a duet with the moon, harmonizing praise. And though I can't say exactly what happened during that first encounter with Jackson Hole, I do know that God was speaking to us, that somehow my own heart had expanded; and that throughout those lingering moments, when the line between time and eternity had blurred, no one had said a word . . . . . . except Him.

Part I

Truth, Goodness, and Beauty

CHAPTER 1

The Book of Creation

I was raised on the long rolling divide which separates the South Platte River from Cherry Creek, and my high school sat upon a hill with a panoramic view of the Front Range of the Colorado Rockies. And every spring, as the sweet fragrance of hope returned to the high plains, our track team would train at Cherry Creek State Park, which bordered our campus to the east. We would all run down the valley for a few miles then turn around and begin to trudge back, barely able to find the breath to complain. But often I found the thought of returning on the same worn pavement uninspiring, somehow without merit, and instead preferred to take a game trail back to school that cut right through the prairie. No one ever went with me.

The narrow path gradually ascended a small butte, then winded along a ridge and traversed a ravine until it faded near a fence across the street from our campus. I don't know why no one else liked to run on the soft earth rather than the jarring asphalt (perhaps it was too muddy or they would rather engage in the inventive and slashing banter that faithfully accompanies groups of young men), but I do know that for me running went beyond the physical: it was a time to be alone with God, to enjoy the clean air, and to dream of an Olympic gold medal – and my heart leapt whenever I left the main road.

My dad and I had discovered the trail when I was 13 and he was my track coach; and over time it became my favorite run because of the wide open spaces, the vigilant prairie dogs, and the ever present hope of seeing a badger. And even though I possessed an undefined yet certain sense that this gentle slope on the banks of Cherry Creek was sacred, I could not begin to imagine that half a million youth – from the ends of the earth – would one day gather on that butte to be inspired by Pope John Paul the Great:

> Young pilgrims, the visible world is like a map pointing to heaven, the eternal dwelling of the living God. We learn to see the Creator by contemplating the beauty of his creatures. In this world, the goodness, wisdom, and almighty power of God shine forth, and the human intellect . . . can discover the Artist's hand in the wonderful works which he has made. Reason can know God through the book of nature.[1]

By saying that we can read nature like we read a book, John Paul II was simply reiterating an ancient perspective – God wrote the universe with creatures the way we write a book with words.

Mankind has always and everywhere believed that nature speaks to us and has a story to tell, but becoming literate in this "universal language of creation" is a process much like learning our native tongue.[2] We all begin to read God's first book from the moment we are born, but fluency in any language involves persistent study. Perhaps, then, by briefly examining our own use of words in books we can improve our comprehension of God's use of words in nature.

Words Are Signs

Think about what a word is and about what we are doing when we read and write them. For example, the page you are currently looking at is composed of letters of the alphabet. Each letter is a little symbol or character that has been assigned a common value and then combined with other letters to form a word. Each word is a sign that communicates a specific idea. To express the idea of countless or immeasurable in English, we write the following sequence of eight symbols or characters: i-n-f-i-n-i-t-e. To express the same idea in Spanish or French, we would use different letters and a different sequence. Creation, however, is a

---

1   Pope John Paul II, *World Youth Day: Vigil of the Assumption of Mary*, August 14, 1993; Cherry Creek State Park, Colorado.
2   *Catechism of the Catholic Church*, #2500

universal language, so when God wanted to convey the idea of infinity He wrote with universal words by simply creating "the stars in the sky and the sands of the sea shore."[3] In the thirteenth century, St. Thomas Aquinas discussed how man-made words correspond to the words of creation: "Just as words formed by a man are signs of his intellectual knowledge; so are creatures, formed by God, signs of His wisdom."[4]

Every bug is a little word of God, every flower a phrase, every mountain range, beach, or biome a paragraph; and every sunrise a new chapter. The universe contains as many songs as there are children, as many poems as there are sunsets. Every element . . . color . . . sound . . . and fragrance . . . is a sign written by God in His literary masterpiece, "the great book of creation".[5]

The Main Theme

As with any great book there is a main theme of creation, a "thesis" as it were. So before we examine some particular messages of creation, it will be of great benefit to define the general message.

If we identified what all existing things have in common, it would be the simple fact that they exist, they have *being*. When we inventory the universe we also discover that no thing has caused itself to exist. If nothing inside our material universe has the power to cause its own existence, there must be a non-material power outside of the universe that has caused material things to be. As St. Augustine wrote in the fourth century, the very existence of creatures is in itself the most persuasive argument for the existence of an all-powerful and eternal Creator:

> But there is a great book: the very appearance of created things. Look above you! Look below you! Note it! Read it! God, whom you wish to find, never wrote that book with ink. Instead, He set before your eyes the things He had made. Can you ask for a louder voice than that? Why, heaven and earth cry out to you: 'God made me!'[6]

---

3   Genesis 22:17
4   St. Thomas Aquinas, *Summa Theologica*, III.12.3.2.
5   *Catechism of the Catholic Church*, #2705
6   St. Augustine, *Sermo Mai*, 126.6.

Created things speak to us with such conviction that St. Augustine rightly assumes that God's first book is written for us. Since it would be meaningless to write anything at all if it wasn't legible and intelligible, and since we alone are capable of reading and understanding, we must be the primary audience for whom all the words of creation were intended.

Other animals certainly have various degrees of intelligence, but let us recognize for the moment that only the human animal can read a book and understand the idea of God. Thus, the existence of every creature, including every human creature, is a proclamation that: (a) there must be an all-powerful Creator because they did not create themselves; and (b) the existence of the Creator is being proclaimed to the one type of creature with the capacity to comprehend such an idea. Simply put, the main theme of being is that God exists, and is speaking to us: "God speaks to man through the visible creation. The material cosmos is so presented to man's intelligence that he can read there traces of its Creator. Light and darkness, wind and fire, water and earth, the tree and its fruit, speak of God".[7]

The Transcendentals of Being

By reading carefully, we can also perceive three sub-themes of being – truth, goodness, and beauty. These "transcendentals" are like echoes resounding from within the main theme; for while each one speaks of God existence, it at the same time articulates more. An analogy between the universal language of being and the universal language of music may help elucidate this point.

When a melody is sung in tune by three different persons, all three are singing the same notes but the quality or "timbre" of each voice remains unique to each singer.[8] Likewise, truth, goodness, and beauty are interpenetrating voices which are both unified and distinct, both one and three. All three are singing to us the main theme of being, though each has a timbre which reveals something deeper. The main theme of being is not altered by the transcendentals, but rather is expanded, amplified, and clarified so we might discover the basic philosophical principles that God has written within the universe.

---

7   *Catechism of the Catholic Church*, #1147
8   pronounced "tămber"

The Human Soul

At this point, it is important to emphasize that human nature is part of the book of creation – we can read ourselves and each other like we do any other creature. Human beings possess a natural openness to truth, goodness, and beauty that is manifest in our abilities of thinking rationally, choosing freely, and creating artistically. If we are honest about how unique these gifts really are, we have come upon the evidence of our spiritual soul.

The extraordinary spiritual powers of the intellect, the will, and the heart cannot be traced to physical processes alone, demonstrating that we are neither purely physical nor purely spiritual, but both body and soul. Also, since these powers go beyond a physical source they must originate from a spiritual source beyond the physical universe. As such, they are further indications of the existence of God and our special relation to Him. We'll discuss this more in a later chapter, but for now let us simply recognize that these unique spiritual gifts, which allow us to read and respond to God's text, are also part of the text.

First Principles

Whether we are reading what is written in other creatures or what is written in us, the Creator is teaching us Philosophy 101 – the first universal principles of being.[9] These principles can be difficult to grasp because they are implicit in our thinking, choosing, and creating. For the remainder of Part I, therefore, we will explore this *implicit philosophy* by carefully reflecting on truth, goodness, and beauty from "a twofold point of departure: the physical world and the human person."[10]

---

9   A "first principle" is an endowment, law, or cause of being.
10   Catechism of the Catholic Church, #31 (While we are part of the
     "physical world" in that we have bodies, this term refers to all non-human
     creatures of the physical universe.)

CHAPTER 2

Truth

Truth in the Physical World

To begin with, let us distinguish between objective and subjective truth. Subjective truth is where we determine for ourselves what is true or not true; like our favorite color or who we think is the greatest quarterback of all time. We can change our mind from red to green, or from Johnny Unitas to John Elway, at any time and still be correct simply because it is a matter of personal opinion. This kind of truth is called subjective, because we are the *subject* who gets to decide what is true. Objective truth, on the other hand, is truth which is true for all people at all times: the earth has one moon, the interior angles of a triangle equal 180 degrees, do good and avoid evil, etc. If we do not believe these things are true it's not just a difference of opinion, we are flat-out wrong, because truth is a reality or *object* which remains true apart from whether or not we as the subject give our assent.

Realism vs. Skepticism

There is a deep reality to the things that exist in the physical world: a truth that they are really there in an objective and understandable way. This is the philosophical perspective known as realism. Unfortunately, much of the past three hundred years of philosophical thought has been

9

obsessed with whether we can know anything about reality with certainty. This is the philosophical perspective known as skepticism.

Shortly after my freshman year of college at UCLA, where my thoughts about reality had been "liberated" by skepticism, I was sharing with my dad a new found certainty about reality being uncertain. He responded in a tone that was mildly irritated (I'm sure with how his hard earned money was being spent), and mildly threatening, (again I'm sure from a loving desire to knock some sense into me). "Well pal," he said, "I'll guarantee you that if I slap you in the face right now you'll be 'absolutely certain' that I slapped you in the face." Hmm, I thought to myself, had Descartes and the other fathers of skepticism ever stood toe to toe with such a challenge? And from a veteran of war no less?!! I delighted for a moment in the idea of Descartes, Hume, and Kant standing before my dad, speculating about whether they would know for sure if they were slapped, only to be silenced by the crystalline knowledge of a stinging cheek. I even imagined some of them being so arrogant that they needed Dad to provide more than one "proof" of his argument. (Needless to say, no demonstration was necessary in my case.)

Skepticism seemed to have been dealt a death blow from a combination of corn-fed common sense and Marine Corps pragmatism. With one incisive statement, my dad had reduced the volumes of these highly intelligent men to the theoretical speculations of guys who got stuck in their own minds. That is not to say that we can't learn anything from these philosophers, but just that we shouldn't spend too much time engaged in their hypothetical debates over epistemology (the study of how we know things). Why? Because it is much more difficult to prove that we *don't* know what is really real than it is to prove we do. For instance, how do the skeptics know with certainty that "we can't know anything with certainty"? At the very least they are saying that we can know one thing with absolute certainty, that is, their basic tenet that "we can't know anything with certainty". But how do they know that we can't know? Where is the proof for their one objective truth which claims there is no objective truth?

Right Reason

I later learned that over three hundred years before Jesus was born, certain Greek citizens began to think about things apart from the influence of mythology so as to arrive at objective truth about reality.

They called it right reason. Perhaps the most famous of these men was Aristotle, (a student of Plato, who had in turn been a student of Socrates). From his great masters and through his own natural genius, Aristotle developed a gift for identifying things that are so simple, so fundamental, and so implicit in our thinking and acting that they often go unnoticed and undefined. He saw how we can survey the physical universe, including ourselves, and then use our ability to reason to discover the general laws or "first principles" which govern the objective realities of truth, goodness, and beauty.

One of the first things Aristotle noticed was straightforward: "All men naturally desire knowledge."[11] We all seek to understand reality, to know the truth about the way things are. Notice that we do not naturally desire to know what is false, except to distinguish it from what is true. As St. Augustine noted, "I have met many who wanted to deceive, but none who wanted to be deceived."[12]

By definition, knowing truth is a conforming of the mind to reality; that is, attaining a correspondence between what we think is true and what is actually true.[13] In his book entitled *Metaphysics* (the branch of philosophy that studies first principles), Aristotle identified the "first principle" which is implicit in our pursuit of truth.[14]

The Principle of Non-Contradiction

The words of creation, much like the words we write, must be understandable if our desire to know truth is to be fulfilled. In order to be understandable, words must have an identity, that is, they must be what they are and not something else. And it was precisely here that Aristotle was able to see and define the under-girding rule of reason and reality: the principle of non-contradiction.[15]

When we examine this principle as it is revealed in the truth of the physical world it is sometimes called the principle of identity. This objective law states that something cannot both *be* what it is and *not be*

---

11 Aristotle, *Metaphysics,* I.1.
12 Saint Augustine, *Confessions*, X.23.
13 Cf. Saint Thomas Aquinas, *Summa Theologica*, I.16.1.
14 What is learned through the intellectual reading of being is still called metaphysics, but should not be confused with an alternative meaning often found in bookstores where metaphysics is defined as anything spiritual. This broader definition includes new age spiritualities, witchcraft, and the occult.
15 Cf. Aristotle, *Metaphysics*, IV.4.

what it is at the same time and in the same sense. A tree is knowable as a tree because it has a non-contradictory identity as a tree – it is what it is. A tree cannot both *be* a tree and *not be* a tree if we are to know it as a tree; a bear cannot both *be* a bear and *not be* a bear, etc. If a tree suddenly became a fish, then a bear, then a cloud, the universe would not be a harmony of distinct beings but a chaotic swirl of confusing images melting into one another. The universe only makes sense to us because it is filled with various types of things that have a distinct identity. If things were not identifiable types of things, nothing would seem real and nothing would be reasonable because *nothing* would be *something* long enough to be known. It would be like trying to read a book where the letters were constantly being rearranged; there would be no identifiable words and therefore no way to understand the book.

Whenever we try to identify a creature, we are assuming that it cannot both be what it is and not be what it is. The non-contradictory identity of each creature is what renders it understandable as a certain type of creature – and what gives it a distinct identity is its essence.

Generally speaking, the essence of a tree is to have roots, leaves, and a trunk. The essence of a bird is to have wings, feathers, and a beak. Since a tree has an essential identity as a certain type of thing, we are able to identify it as a tree. In the same way, we are able to identify a bird. If a *prairie cottonwood* was simultaneously flying around as a *mountain chickadee*, how could we think of it as a tree? How could we have formed the idea of treeness? How could we see the essence of roots, trunk, and leaves if it was co-mingled with wings, feathers, and a beak? It may be difficult at first to conceive, but the *truth of being* in the physical world is that things are what they are and not something else. We are able to know things as certain types of things, that is, as real and understandable words of truth, because they have an identifiable essence.

Eventually, we all come to learn the difference between a tree and a bird, but let us now consider the spiritual gift of the soul which allows us to attain that knowledge.

The Human Intellect

As children, we are taught what things are by having particular examples of those things pointed out to us. Our parents and grandparents point to the roses in the garden, the daisies on the table, or the lilies in the mountains and say, "Look at the pretty flowers. Can you say flower?"

Eventually the child sees what is essential to being a flower and forms an idea of "flowerness". Then one day, maybe while out for a stroll, the child points to something they have never seen before, an iris perhaps, and says, "Flower." Why? Because the child has seen what is essential to being a flower: stem, leaves, petals, etc. The spiritual gift which allows us to form one universal idea from the many particular instances of a thing, that is, to see the essence or "whatness" of a thing, is called the intellect.

The word *intellect* is a compound of the Latin prefix *inter* (between), and *lectum* (reading). When we are learning to identify what something is, we are literally *reading* what is common *between* the individual examples of a thing. This process is known as abstraction. Once we have read what is essential, by abstracting the essential qualities out of the non-essential or "accidental" qualities of size, shape, color, etc., we have formed a universal idea. Whenever we encounter that type of thing, we can then identify *what it is* no matter how different the accidental qualities might be. An iris is not the same size, shape, or color of a daisy and yet the intellect of a child is able to see the essence of "flowerness" nonetheless. Moreover, once we have formed a universal concept of something, we can identify any drawing or other artistic image as a representation of that thing.

One of my favorite people in the world is named Kyle Dockter, but I just call him Doc. He has the mind of a two year-old but is now in his mid-twenties. He can't speak anymore, but when he was a teenager it was my joy to care for him and call him my friend. One morning as we walked by the front desk of his school for kids with special needs, I noticed a *paper-Mache* bird in a cage hanging from the ceiling. At first, it was hard to tell what it was because the student that made it had a "special need" of further training in arts and crafts. In any event, one of the ways to get Doc to think about things (or any two year-old mind for that matter), is to leave the subject blank and give him time to process. So I said: "Oh look Kyle, it's a . . . it's a . . . um . . . . . ." "It's a zoo!" he said excitedly. Then he started jumping up and down and clapping his hands wildly, as was his custom. When we both had stopped laughing, I realized that even though in Kyle's mind any animal behind bars was a zoo, he had displayed the gift of forming universal ideas, albeit in a limited and general way. He had been to real zoos and had seen pictures and drawings of zoos in books, and by *reading between* those particular images he had determined what was essential then formed a general concept of "zooness". Even though it was a poor representation, when

13

he looked at the bird in the cage he was able to do something that went beyond the physiology of instinct and the mental organization of sense perceptions; he could remove the accidental qualities of shape, size, and color, and abstract the essence.[16]

Before we know *what* a thing is, however, we know *that* it is. Being is the first thing we apprehend. When we are unable to identify a thing, whether it's an odor, noise, or movement, we commonly ask, "Do you smell something?" "Did you hear that?" "Did you see that?" Consider also how common it is to hear someone ask the more general question, "*What* is *that?*" Initially, we only know *that* some thing exists, but then we desire to know the basic truth of that thing, its "whatness". As we gather information from our senses, we apply our ability to reason and form categories by reading similarities and differences, and then we make more and more distinctions to determine what type of thing it is. We might first only detect that some *thing* is out in a meadow. We might think it's a bush, but then it moves and we know it is an animal. Then we see it walking upright and know it is a certain type of animal, a human. As the person comes closer, we see that it is a woman, then a young woman, and finally that it is a particular young woman, our friend Amanda.

I became acutely aware of this after my freshman year in college, when I set out on my first solo retreat into the Yellowstone backcountry. I chose an area known as the Pelican Valley for simple reasons: it had the best trout fishing in the park; and the highest concentration of grizzly bears. Perhaps it is needless to say, but wherever there is an abundance of cutthroat trout and griz, there is also pristine wilderness.

A solo retreat has the immediate effect of awakening the senses to all that is out there – and this is especially true when the largest predator in North America is on the list. During my first night, the sounds of the forest conspired with my imagination to produce sleep-depriving thoughts of a grizzly special-forces unit strategically closing in on nineteen year-old human tenderloin (or at least my canned pudding). I could hear them creeping up on me, inching closer all the time . . . and something kept clawing at my backpack. I was wide-eyed and terrified. Several times I sat up and yelled, only to have the silence broken by the stealth maneuvers of bears on a mission. At first light, which in mid-summer is around

---

16 Notice that recognizing something in abstract artistic form is possible because we have first intellectually abstracted the essence of that thing, forming a universal concept.

4:45 a.m., I finally caught one of them in the act. A beetle, no larger than an almond, had been trying to crawl up the side of my pack and slipping down. The sound of his legs scratching the nylon, along with the other little noises, had been so amplified in my mind that I invented a sinister plot of assassins. (I won't say if I smashed the poor creature out of anxiety-induced grumpiness . . . but even with a good night of sleep I've never been much of a morning person.)

The next day, after hiking 10 miles of my scheduled 17, I again heard something peculiar, this time up ahead on the trail. The sound was deep and rhythmic. Initially, I thought it might be a bison or bear snoring and my pace became cautious, but as I entered a clearing I found a geothermal mud pot, about the size of a pool table, boiling and gurgling intermittently. In my hyper-awareness of being, of the certainty *that* some thing was out there, I had again exaggerated the possibilities of *what* that something was.

The cosmos is made up of things which have a non-contradictory identity, and the human intellect is equipped to know the "whatness" or essence of those things. The principle of non-contradiction is the foundation of truth in the language of the physical world. Let us now examine the same principle as the foundation of truth in the language of the human person.

Truth in the Human Person

In addition to being the under-girding principle of reality, the principle of non-contradiction is the governing law of rational discourse. Just as God's words in creation are non-contradictory, if our own words are to communicate something meaningful they cannot both be *true* and *not true* at the same time and in the same sense.

For example, if I honestly said my favorite color is yellow, that would be true for me at that time; but if I changed my mind and said my favorite color is not yellow but blue, then that would be true for me, yet at a different time. Furthermore, if I said that blue is my favorite color of clothes (which is one sense), but yellow is my favorite color of flowers (which is another sense), then both blue and yellow would be my favorite color at the same time but not in the same sense. What is important to see here is that when I assert that my favorite color is yellow,

I cannot mean that my favorite color is *not* yellow at the same time and in the same sense or else my statement is meaningless; because no one is any closer to knowing my favorite color.

In order for us to learn a human language, the words used to identify things must be consistent. Imagine a child trying to learn what an apple was if sometimes their parent held one up and said, "This is an apple" and sometimes said, "This is *not* an apple." The mental confusion that would ensue would numb the child's mind.

The Assumption Behind Every Assertion

When Aristotle looked at the principle of non-contradiction in the context of interpersonal communication, he found that it was the assumption behind every assertion. All rational thought and conversation is based upon the idea that a thing cannot simultaneously be affirmed and denied in the same respect: left cannot simultaneously be right, north cannot be south. Without this starting point, there is no objective ground from which to communicate rationally.

He also saw that by denying or challenging this principle one is confirming it, because in the very act of arguing that contradictory assertions *can* both be true, one is assuming that each word used in the argument is to be understood as a specific word with a non-contradictory meaning. Perhaps an imaginary dialogue between Aristotle (whom St. Thomas Aquinas honored with the title "The Philosopher") and a challenger to the principle of non-contradiction will help clarify:

The Philosopher: Do you believe that something can be *true* and *not true* at the same time and in the same sense? Or to put it another way, that it is possible for something to be affirmed and denied at the same time and in the same respect?

The Challenger: Yes, I do.

The Philosopher: Are you saying that you *do not* believe that the principle of non-contradiction is true.

The Challenger: Yes, that is correct. I do not believe the principle of non-contradiction is true.

The Philosopher: If I can prove the principle is true by examining our assumptions whenever we communicate with one another, would you believe it then?

The Challenger: Certainly.

The Philosopher: Alright. You just responded to my question by saying, "I do not believe the principle of non-contradiction is true", correct?

The Challenger: That's correct.

The Philosopher: And by stating that you *do not* believe it to be true you expected me to understand that you were not also saying that you *do* believe it to be true, right?

The Challenger: Obviously, but I don't understand what you're getting at.

The Philosopher: When you assert, "I do not believe the principle of non-contradiction is true", you are denying that the principle is true, and implied in your assertion is that you are not at the same time and in the same respect also affirming that the principle is true.

The Challenger: Again, that's obvious, but I still don't understand what you're trying to say.

The Philosopher (thinking to himself that he needs to try a different approach): Well, I'm glad you finally understand what I'm trying to say.

The Challenger: Wait a minute, I said I *don't* understand.

The Philosopher: You *do* understand then?

The Challenger (with irritation): No! No! I said I *don't* understand.

The Philosopher: I'm sorry to have aggravated you, but I was only trying to illustrate the assumption which proves this principle. By saying "I *don't* understand", you assume that your assertion cannot also mean "I *do* understand" at the same time and in the same sense. If I said to you, "Let's

17

go have lunch", and also meant the opposite statement, "Let's not go have lunch", we would not be able to communicate because no statement would have any real meaning. I wouldn't even be able to learn your name if when you said "My name is Jack", it could mean at the same time and in the same sense, "My name is not Jack." Rational discourse would be impossible if every statement could also mean something contradictory.

The Challenger (after a moment's reflection): I think I understand now. When I said, "I don't understand" I expected you not to think I was saying the contradictory statement "I do understand". I cannot simultaneously affirm and deny something at the same time and in the same sense, so whenever I try to communicate anything meaningful I am assuming and proving the principle of non-contradiction.

The Philosopher: That's correct . . . now let's go have lunch.

God has written truth in the book of nature: in both the physical world and the human person. The principle of non-contradiction is the format by which words of truth are presented to the human intellect. God's words in creation, and our own words, are meaningful to us because they maintain a non-contradictory identity.

CHAPTER 3

Goodness

Goodness in the Physical World

For the past thirty years or so, I've had the privilege of vacationing with my Dad on the Big Island of Hawaii, where he is now retired. During one spring break when I was in college, I was struck by the diversity of produce at the local grocery store: bananas from New Zealand, corn from Nebraska, pineapples, peanuts, grapes, mangoes, carrots, peaches, peppers, potatoes – all gathered from different parts of the world into this one little store in the middle of the ocean. It occurred to me that almost everywhere people lived God created conditions where plants could grow and provide sustenance, and that this was a testament to His loving concern for us. When the Apostle Paul addressed the men of Greece in the first century, he tried to draw their attention to just a few of these *substructures of sustenance* in order to show how they reflect God's good will: "In bestowing goodness, He has not left himself without a witness, for He gives you rain from heaven and fruitful seasons – satisfying your hunger and filling your hearts with joy."[17]

It's a simple idea really – food and water – but a complex reality. Think about all that needs to happen for rain to fall and for plants to germinate, mature, reproduce, and bear fruit. Without gravity, rain would never reach the ground. Without the slight tilt of the earth as it

---

17   Acts 14:17

orbits the sun, there would be no seasons. Without the laws of heat and light, or force and friction, the intricate processes of photosynthesis and pollination could not take place.

Laws of Nature

God made a universe which can at least temporarily satisfy our hunger, our thirst, and our desire for joy. The more we become aware of the various laws of nature which make "rain from heaven and fruitful seasons" possible, the more we should be able to read the *goodness of being* from the physical world. In the first century, Pope St. Clement emphasized that God has enacted these laws as a testimony to His providential care:

> By his will the earth blossoms in the proper seasons and produces abundant food for men and animals and all the living things. . . The seasons – spring, summer, autumn, and winter – follow one another in harmony. And the ever-flowing springs created for our health as well as our enjoyment, unfailingly offer their breasts to sustain human life.[18]

Sustenance, however, is only an initial witness of goodness, for whenever we build, play, or experiment (just to mention a few) we are able to do so because the universe following laws. Imagine trying to build a house without the properties of metal and wood being stable, or trying to throw a frisbee without consistent air pressure and gravity, or trying to conduct medical research without the reliability of the periodic table of elements. A universe where water sometimes put out fire and sometimes exploded would not be good, but terrifying and uninhabitable. Instead, water has consistent properties which allow it to evaporate, forms clouds, cool, and fall as rain.

Laws of nature are good because they make life on earth possible. They are good rules willed by a good ruler. The fact that the Creator has "arranged all things according to measure and number and weight", and established an environment in which we can farm, fish, hunt, build, play, experiment, and cook is a testament that He is a lawmaker who

---

18   Pope St Clement, *Letter to the Corinthians*, 20. (Office of Readings, Thirtieth Sunday in Ordinary Time)

wishes us well.[19] The physical world communicates the transcendental of goodness through laws of nature, and at the core of this transcendental lays our next principle.

The Principle of Finality

Goodness has been written into creation by a benevolent lawmaker. By making things act and react consistently, God has legislated that each creature has an orientation toward the goal or *finality* for which it was made. For example: birds hatch, fledge, and fly; plants germinate, grow, and reproduce; fish eat, swim, and spawn; gravity pulls; light diffuses; the earth rotates, etc. Notice that each creature moves toward what is good and fulfilling for it – not what is bad. Unless there is something out of order, birds do not try to swim in lava, plants do not uproot themselves and try to flap their leaves, and fish do not try to nest in trees. Since the goal of a creature is to act according to its nature (which is its good), every creature communicates the principle of finality simply by doing what it was created to do. It was again Aristotle who recognized that the Creator was the cause of order in the universe, and then defined this primordial principle in a succinct manner: "the good has rightly been declared to be that at which all things aim."[20]

Although it is easier to understand when applied to living things that grow, move, or choose (i.e. plants, animals, or humans), aiming at the good also applies to creatures like rocks, chemicals, and sound waves because they too act and react according to fixed laws. The general law of finality gives consistency and direction to the specific laws of physics, chemistry, and biology. It is a non-physical law which orchestrates the physical laws of nature to each play their part so that the universe has harmony and, therefore, goodness: "When at the beginning God created all his works and, as he made them, assigned their tasks, he ordered for all time what they were to do."[21]

Each type of creature, therefore, has been made to have an identifiable truth (to be what it is according to the principle of non-contradiction); and each type of creature has been made to have an orientation toward goodness (to do what it does according to the principle of finality). At the most fundamental level, the principle of finality is the foundation of

---

19   Wisdom 11:20 (cf. CCC #299)
20   Aristotle, *Nicomachean Ethics*, I.1
21   Sirach 16:27; Cf. Job 28:26 "He made rules for the rain".

how God wrote goodness on the pages of the physical world. Now we'll examine this principle as the foundation of how God wrote goodness on the pages of the human person.

Goodness in the Human Person

As with other animals, the principle of finality can be read from the human person in that we instinctively seek what is good and fulfilling for our bodily life: food, water, shelter, etc. Unlike other animals, however, this principle can also be read in us because we seek what is good and fulfilling for our spiritual life: justice, fairness, faithfulness, etc. The law which orients us to freely pursue that which is good for our soul is called *natural law*. And whereas laws of nature are physical manifestations of the principle of finality, natural law is a non-physical manifestation of the principle of finality.

Natural Law

Natural law is the universal sense of justice and fairness written within each human soul. In other words, our innate sense of right and wrong: "The natural law is nothing other than the light of understanding placed in us by God; through it we know what we must do and what we must avoid. God has given this light or law at the creation."[22] Consider how common it is to return what one has borrowed or refute a lie out of a natural sense of justice. From a very early age we don't need to be taught that if someone pushes us off our bicycle and rides away that it's just not fair.

The human person is partly fulfilled by being honest, fair, and faithful; in a word, by being just. Justice, by definition, is to give each being their due. Another way of putting it is to give God, neighbor, and other creatures what they deserve. God deserves our thanks because He created us and gives us good gifts; our neighbors deserve to have their spouses, religious beliefs, and property respected; animals deserve to be treated humanely, etc. Could anyone be taken seriously who claimed to be fulfilled by being ungrateful, disrespectful, or inhumane? Or by being dishonest, unfair, or unfaithful?

As a young man, I was part of a committee which established the rules, privileges, and consequences of a residential public school. What

22   St. Thomas Aquinas, *Decem praeceptis*, 1.

we came up with was three imperatives under which every expectation could be categorized: Be Safe. Be Respectful. Be Responsible. I was not just a little proud of our achievement until about a decade later when I volunteered to teach at St. Ann's Native American school in the Turtle Mountains of North Dakota. Above the entrance to the gymnasium, in paint that was clearly more than a decade old, were the words: Be Safe. Be Respectful. Be Responsible. I realized like never before that we all have the same basic idea of what is fair and just. Natural law not only gives us grounds to set limits and expectations for children, it also forms the basis of civil law . . . but more on that later.

Because we naturally see that certain actions are always wrong, the natural law is also called the *objective moral law*. As Aristotle observed, the objective moral law is "natural" because it is part of human nature to reason; and reasoning is how we discover it: "[T]here is in nature a common principle of the just and unjust that all people in some way divine [understand], even if they have no association or commerce with each other."[23]

Like the principle of non-contradiction, the principle of finality is verified whenever someone tries to refute it. What goal could one have in objecting to this principle except to right a wrong, to pursue the good of preventing others from the "injustice" of being deceived? Even if one's sole purpose is to convince others that there is no natural law, the point has been made: the human person strives to be just. Perhaps another dialogue between The Philosopher and The Challenger will prove useful:

The Philosopher: I believe we can recognize within the human soul a principle or law which summons us to pursue what is just and shun what is unjust.

The Challenger: I disagree. There is no principle of justice written on the human soul, and there is no common goal toward which we strive in order to be fulfilled.

The Philosopher: Does it bother you that I spend my life trying to persuade others to recognize natural law?

---

23 Aristotle, *On Rhetoric*, I.13.2.

The Challenger: Yes, it does. I believe people should be warned that you are deceiving them.

The Philosopher: Would you call it an injustice that I am deceiving others, as you say?

The Challenger: Certainly.

The Philosopher: Good, I think we finally agree.

The Challenger: What do you mean? I think you are wrong, and that it is wrong for you to be drawing others into your error.

The Philosopher: Precisely, and by trying to right that wrong you have demonstrated that there is a law within us that pursues justice and seeks to rectify injustice; in this case, the injustice of deception. Otherwise, why would you even care? If there is no law of justice, no fundamental orientation to pursue what we perceive to be good, why would you be challenging me except to correct my mistake? Why would you object unless you believed that truth is good, and falsehood is not good?

The Challenger: I'll have to think about it some more, but I really must being going. I have appointment in five minutes and I don't want to be late.

The Philosopher: Why don't you want to be late? What's wrong with that? Why do you feel obligated to even show up at an appointment?

The Challenger: Obviously, because it wouldn't be fair to make an appointment and then be late or not show up at all.

The Philosopher: That is precisely my point. We all believe that it is good to be fair and not good to be unfair.

The Challenger: I really have to go.

The Philosopher: Well, be good!

Conscience

Part of hearing the voice of goodness in creation is hearing the inner voice of conscience. Conscience is the gift which helps us apply the objective moral law to a particular situation, that is, to weigh options and then do the right thing under the circumstances. It is the arbiter of natural law.

Since the sixties revolution, much has been made of the *right* to follow one's conscience regarding sex, drugs, abortion, and the role of God in the public arena. However, it must be emphasized that each of us first has a *duty* to form our conscience according to the dictates of right reason: "Although each individual has a right to be respected in his own journey in the search of the truth, there exists a prior moral obligation, and a grave one at that, to seek the truth and to adhere to it once it is known."[24]

For example, one has a right to follow their conscience and believe that God does not exist, but to believe something does not make it true. The very existence of conscience is, ironically, yet another proof for the existence of God; because such a universally binding law must come from a legislator powerful enough to engrave it within each and every person: "When he listens to the message of creation and to the voice of conscience, man can arrive at certainty about the existence of God, the cause and the end of everything."[25]

The Human Will

Even if we disagree on what is truly good and what is truly evil, everyone has the ability to look within themselves and read the first precept of natural law: do good and avoid evil. The gift which allows us to *read* natural law is the ability to reason with our intellect. The gift which allows us to *respond* to natural law is the ability to choose with our will.

Free-will is required for a creature to choose right over wrong, to be moral. Other animals are neither free nor rational in the sense that we are because they only act and react according to programmed instincts. We don't put grizzly bears on trial for eating backpackers or lecture puppies on why it is not fair that they chewed up our favorite sandals, because being held morally responsible presupposes that there was both an understanding of fairness and a choice in the matter. When we praise or punish our pets to teach them what to do, we are programming them to respond in a desired way without asking them to understand the

---

24   Pope John Paul II, *Veritatis Splendor (The Splendor of Truth)*, #34
25   *Catechism of the Catholic Church*, #46

concept behind the lesson. No matter how complex and adaptable an animal's instincts, asking it to sincerely apologize, make restitution, or explain why certain choices are wrong is absurd because it does not have the intellect to understand and the will to freely choose. We are held responsible for our actions precisely because we are capable of so much more than responding to sensory and memory data.

Unfortunately, some mock right reason by denying that we are actually free to choose good and not choose evil. This can lead to the philosophy known as materialism. There is no right or wrong according to materialists because we are animals without free-will or a spiritual soul. Instead, humans are simply material beings with highly evolved psychological instincts conditioned by social stimuli. In order to refute these specious arguments against God given free-will, one should simply appeal to common sense:

> The great truths without which man's moral life is impossible – for example, knowledge of God's existence, the freedom of the will, etc. – belong to this domain of common sense . . . All men, unless spoiled by a faulty education or by some intellectual vice, possess a natural certainty of these truths.[26]

Others mock right reason by granting the existence of free-will but then denying the existence of natural law. This can lead to the philosophy known as existentialism. There are no objective moral norms according to existentialists because we do not share a common human nature which is fulfilled by objectively good choices. Instead, we are free to invent our own individual nature through choices which are neither right nor wrong. Since there is only subjective freedom (or more accurately, the license of doing whatever one pleases), there is no such thing as a good conscience.

The natural law which the Creator has written on our souls, however, is like the laws of nature He has written into the physical world: both must be respected to avoid personal injury or death. For example, to avoid injury or death to the body we must respect the law of gravity. A person may claim that gravity is subjective and doesn't apply to them, and they may freely choose to jump off a cliff, but that does not make the law less

---

26 Jacques Maritain, *An Introduction to Philosophy*, 134-135.

objective, nor is it a choice without serious consequences. Likewise, to avoid injury or death to the soul we must respect the law of human life. A person may claim that the natural law's prohibition against intentionally killing innocent human life is subjective and doesn't apply to them, and they may freely choose to have an abortion, but that doesn't make the law less objective, nor is it a choice without serious consequences.

The fact that we have free will does not mean we can disregard *laws of nature* or *natural law* with impunity. Exercising our freedom by choosing not to believe them proves we have free-will, but does not in any way repeal their objectivity.

Fifty-four years before Jesus was born, the Roman philosopher Cicero wrote a comprehensive definition of natural law which illustrates its accessibility to all free and rational creatures. It is worth noting that he is the only non-Christian quoted in the *Catechism of the Catholic Church,* because it shows how God's existence and adhering to natural law are not primarily matters of faith, but right reason:

> True law is right reason in agreement with nature; it is of universal application, unchanging and everlasting; it summons to duty by its commands, and averts from wrongdoing by its prohibitions. And it does not lay its commands or prohibitions upon good men in vain, though neither have any effect on the wicked. It is a sin to try to alter this law, nor is it allowable to attempt to repeal any part of it, and it is impossible to abolish it entirely. We cannot be freed from its obligations by senate or people, and we need not look outside ourselves for an expounder or interpreter of it. And there will not be different laws at Rome and at Athens, or different laws now and in the future, but one eternal and unchangeable law will be valid for all nations and all times, and there will be one master and ruler, that is, God, over us all, for he is the author of this law, its promulgator, and its enforcing judge. Whoever is disobedient is fleeing from himself and denying his human nature, and by reason of this very fact he will suffer the worst penalties, even if he escapes what is commonly considered punishment.[27]

27   Cicero, *De Republica (On the Republic),* III. 22. (cf. CCC #1956)

The "worst penalties", of course, are the regrets and emptiness of a life which wandered from the path of goodness and fulfillment, the path of happiness. When our founding fathers drafted the *Declaration of Independence*, they too recognized that we can arrive at the objectivity of "the laws of nature [natural law] and of nature's God" if we are truly honest about what we read from creation:

> We hold these truths to be self evident, that all men have been created equal and have been endowed by their Creator with certain unalienable rights, and among these are life, liberty, and the pursuit of happiness.[28]

Recognizing and responding to the unalienable rights and duties of the objective moral law is simply a matter of being faithful – faithful not only to our gift of reason, which reads the statutes written on our hearts, but faithful also to the divine Author of those statutes.

Faithfulness

Goodness can be read from *the human person* because God consistently writes finality within us through natural law. The principle of finality does not start and stop. For our part, whenever we consistently follow that principle, being fair and faithful to others, we echo God's faithfulness to us. A faithful employee, a faithful spouse, or a faithful friend can be counted on to do the right thing and not betray us as much as we can count on spring to follow winter.

Goodness can be read from *the physical world* because God faithfully writes finality through laws of nature. The creatures of the universe display the good will of the Creator by moving in a consistent and orderly progression through time and space, making life on earth possible. The sun rises and sets, the moon waxes and wanes, the tides ebb and flow, wood and water are abundant, and so on. As Pope Benedict XVI has noted, through these many "goods" we receive day after day, we learn that God's goodness is tantamount to God's faithfulness: "Thus, a divine message exists, secretly engraved in creation and a sign of the *hesed*, the

---

28 *Declaration of Independence of the United States of America,* July 4th, 1776. (In the past, the phrase "laws of nature" was often used interchangeably with "natural law" without distinguishing laws of science from laws of justice.)

loving fidelity of God who gives his creatures being and life, water and food, light and time."[29]

The physical world is overflowing with ordinary examples of faithfulness, some so common they are easily taken for granted; but there is perhaps no more *extra*-ordinary symbol of God's fidelity than the Yellowstone geyser appropriately named "Old Faithful".

Clearly the most famous geothermal feature in the world, Old Faithful received its name from the remarkable predictability of its eruptions (currently, about every 90 minutes).   A few summers ago, I woke before sunrise and immediately hiked along the Firehole River toward Old Faithful, hoping to enjoy the morning with prayer and a cup of jo. Just as I arrived, the incomparable symbol of wilderness began to erupt and, as if on cue, the sun peeked over the great continental divide. What appeared before me was a sparkling fountain that gushed 100 feet above the earth and created a billowing steam plume which borrowed shell-pink hues from the dawn. I marveled at God's goodness for the laws of thermo, hydro, and aero-dynamics that made this spectacle possible . . . and then it hit me. If Old Faithful never erupted again, not one person would die of hunger, thirst, or exposure; it was not useful for sustenance or shelter. Nonetheless, it seemed to have tremendous value, but why? Simply by evoking awe and wonder, something about this particular word of creation had gathered up the realms of thinking and choosing – of truth in identity and goodness in finality – and then had somehow transcended those first two transcendentals. Here before me was an aspect of being that was more than stimulating to my intellect and appealing to my will. Here was something that went deeper and stirred my heart . . . something that was beautiful.

---

29   Pope Benedict XVI, *General Audience*, November 9, 2005. (emphasis in original)

CHAPTER 4

Beauty in the Physical World

In many ways, beauty is the most transcendent transcendental, and therefore the most difficult to corral. Yet for all its elusive and ethereal aspects, it remains an objective reality. Every right-minded person agrees that the geysers and other geothermal features of Yellowstone are extraordinarily beautiful; after all, it was the beauty of these geyser basins that inspired and sustained the idea of establishing Yellowstone as the world's first national park. But what is it that makes something objectively beautiful? How do we ever arrive at a consensus? And why, at times, does beauty seem so subjective?

Objective Beauty

According to St. Thomas, objectively beautiful things have three components: integrity, proportion, and clarity.[30] At first glance this definition may seem simplistic or even vague, but perhaps a few examples will prove its usefulness.

One winter I had the opportunity to lead a youth retreat on the Big Island. The theme for the first day was beauty, and my intention was to focus on the colorful reef fish that congregate at Kahaluu state beach

---

30   St. Thomas Aquinas, *Summa Theologica*, I.39.8.

park. The Creator, however, had other plans and opened up one of His art studios for an interactive seminar.

After snorkeling for an hour or so, we were all sharing our thoughts about how beautiful the fish were, but without getting any closer to understanding what made them beautiful. Then one of the students was approached by an old man who kept repeating something in Japanese and pointing to a tide pool about the size of a basketball court. We all looked but saw nothing besides the knee-deep pool dotted with several large rocks. Our curiosity grew, however, when a small rock floated to the surface beside one of the big rocks. Since most of us were certain that rocks don't float, we eventually realized that we were really looking at green sea turtles and one of them had just raised its head to take a breath. Immediately we ventured out for a closer look and soon the experience became surreal. We had entered a living art museum; and the twenty-two turtles on display could not have cared less that we had joined them.

Each turtle had distinctive markings on their head and shell, and we naturally began to rank their beauty by way of how "cool" each one was. There were personal favorites to be sure, but we were unanimous when it came to which ones belonged at the top of the list and which belonged at the bottom. But how was it that we were all in agreement? What had we seen that led to this consensus? I drew our attention to the three components of beauty and we began to revisit each turtle: some shells were chipped, therefore lacking *integrity* or wholeness; some shells were whole but had patterns that were not symmetrical or didn't fit the turtle's head, therefore lacking *proportion*; and some were whole and proportionate but had been blurred by algae, therefore lacking *clarity*. Each of our top choices, however, had all three.

Later that day, as we were returning to our condominium, another example presented itself. Several plumeria trees had dropped dozens of flowers on the ground. Each one that we labeled "pretty" and picked up to take with us was whole, symmetrical, and vibrant. Those that had been rejected either had petals that were missing, disproportionate, or had begun to brown and wilt. Again we had established which ones were beautiful and which ones were not according to St. Thomas' definition of integrity, proportion, and that radiant splendor known as clarity.[31] We had found that identifying elements of objective beauty in the physical world was not that difficult after all. But when it came to identifying objective beauty in the human person, things weren't quite so simple.

Beauty in the Human Person

St. Thomas' definition can be applied to the physical appearance of a human person just as it is to the physical world. For example, we would all agree that a beautiful smile is composed of a complete and proportionate set of shiny white teeth; thus, integrity, proportion, and clarity. The difficulty arises in that we have spiritual souls in addition to physical bodies. When someone who has crooked, missing, or discolored teeth is so kind, courageous, or generous that their interior beauty illuminates their exterior, the whole person radiates from an inner light . . . as if their soul had a beautiful smile. That's why Mother Teresa of Calcutta, who wasn't that physically attractive (and had the most deformed toes I have ever seen), could still be considered the most beautiful person of the twentieth century. But what precisely made her soul so beautiful? Well, the same things that make a physical being beautiful except on the spiritual level. First, she possessed integrity in that there was no disparity between what she believed, what she said, and how she lived. Second, she had proportion in that she worked and prayed, laughed and cried, talked and listened, led and followed, etc. all according to the needs of the moment. And third, she had clarity in that she radiated love for others through her smile, her eyes, and her manner of working with the poorest of the poor.

During my only personal encounter with Mother Teresa, inner beauty was never more evident or more moving. I was working at the Samaritan House homeless shelter in downtown Denver and we were asked to help organize a food drive for the occasion of her visit. I remember a lot of little things about that day, like gathering truckloads of canned goods, listening to a young misguided street preacher condemn Catholicism, and running into my cousin whom I hadn't seen since I was a boy; but

---

31   Integrity, proportion, and clarity are not the final word on beauty, but they are a solid introduction. Consider how these attributes apply, for example, when one imagines a beautiful Christmas tree, or Tutankhamen's burial mask.

more than all that, I remember the impact of her presence. Denver's sports arena was packed with 17,000 fans and when this diminutive Albanian nun walked out on the stage, rosary in hand, I began to weep, as did everyone around me. There was just something about her. Whether it be the heroic virtue of a great saint, a child overcoming a disability, or a grandma who tends her rose garden with joy, our hearts are moved by interior beauty.

In one sense, everything that is good is also beautiful, but in another sense beauty is something more. A person can be good if they say and do the right thing, but if their words and deeds are not beautiful, their example is usually uninspiring. Consider how making dinner or doing the dishes for one's family can be done out of a sense of duty, and is nonetheless good, but when carried out with a joyful levity, a light-heartedness perhaps accompanied by singing or humming, these simple acts become beautiful. Consider also how donating money to an orphanage for a tax break or for recognition is still a good thing, but when it is done without counting the cost or anonymously it is more than just good . . . it's beautiful.

Something as simple as picking up a piece of trash or correcting a child (or as complex as laying down one's life for another in marriage), can be done in beauty if it entails an inspiring way of doing it, a way which rises above plain truth and mechanical goodness. Beyond the black and white of doing what's right, there is the way we color things.

Subjective Beauty

A popular maxim states that "beauty is in the eye of the beholder", and this is partially true. The beauty of the human person can be subjective and objective at the same time, although not in the same sense. Clearly, some men and women will never be supermodels or be featured on the cover of a magazine, and yet they may have a spouse, fiancée, or parents who believe they are the world's most beautiful person – simply because they have been appreciated beyond their physical appearance, that is, as a whole person. To the eye of the lover, the beloved possesses some inner beauty so wonderful that it illuminates their entire being and overshadows any physical disproportion or disfigurement. To see this point, one has only to think of how often a young woman is pursued by a man whom she initially finds physically unattractive but eventually is captivated and falls in love. Some kindness, trait, or talent, leads her to appreciate him in a new way and she becomes enraptured, caught up in the beauty of his person as a whole. She then gives herself to him from the innermost core of her being, her heart.

The Human Heart

The spiritual gift which allows us to give of ourselves, both in works of art and in the art of living, is the same gift which allows us to receive inspiration from created beauty. When we receive beautiful words from another (whether it be a song or sunset) we perceive this spiritual gift expanding within us, for just as truth sparks the intellect and the good ignites the will, "the beautiful goes straight to the heart."[32] Our creative response might be a love letter, a prayer, or a gift of one's entire life to "whole-hearted and free service to the poorest of the poor."[33] That is not to say that the intellect and will are not engaged when we encounter and respond to beauty, but rather that, in a certain sense, the heart is greater than the sum of intellect and will, just as beauty is a synergism of truth and goodness.

Whenever we are inspired by beauty in the physical world or the human person, we are moved to imitate God's creative power of gift-giving. Beauty transcends the intellect's knowledge of truth and the will's pursuit of goodness, and summons the depth of a person to reach out with their own gift of artistic creativity, that is, with something personal. The more personal the gift the more meaningful it is. Flowers, poems, paintings, resolutions – even cookies – have value to the degree they come from the heart. Doesn't every grandparent prefer to receive homemade birthday cards from their grandchildren to ones that are store-bought? Moreover, an email can be personal because of what the words convey, but *consider how a simple thank you changes when it is handwritten with fine penmanship. The same words have been employed but because the writer has adorned those words with a personal touch they have more meaning.* Beyond the obligation of sitting down to the task of writing and clearly expressing thanks, beauty comes from a deeper place, a personal place of creativity, a place where we offer the gift of self. And it is precisely here, within the idea that beauty is freely and intelligently caused, where we can best situate our final universal principle.

---

32   Jacques Maritain, *Art and Scholasticism*, endnote #56.
33   Mother Teresa of Calcutta, *Total Surrender*. III.

The Principle of Causality

The principle of causality merely recognizes that *everything which comes into existence needs a cause to account for its being.* In a certain sense, it belongs to the primary message of being that we discussed at the beginning of Part I: that since no creature in the ever-changing universe has caused itself to exist, there must be an unchanging being who has always existed and has the power to bring creatures into existence. Discussing the principle of causality within the context of beauty, however, highlights how beauty, more than anything else – more than the truth or goodness of a creature – engages the intuition that there is an eternal and all-powerful Creator:

> Question the beauty of the earth, the beauty of the sea, the beauty of the air around you, the beauty of the sky. Question the order of the stars, the sun whose brightness lights the day, the moon whose splendor softens the gloom of night. Question the living creatures that move through the waters, that roam upon the earth, that fly through the air. Question all these and they will answer you: "See, we are beautiful." Their beauty is their confession of God. Who made these beautiful changing things, if not one who is beautiful and changes not?[34]

Any encounter with beauty, in divine or human works of art, stimulates the heart and the self-evident insight, "Someone made this." For some, however, the truth that human art has been caused by an artist exists alongside the belief that nature's art has not. Certainly no one in their right mind ever considered that Michelangelo's *Sistine Chapel* or Leonardo's *Mona Lisa* could have happened by chance, but isn't it just as unreasonable to suggest that the mosaics found on butterfly wings were not caused by an artist?

Most of us can see that things like a mosquito or a computer keyboard have been designed for a purpose without being moved by beauty, but whenever we perceive things saturated with the fragrance of self-gift, our hearts leap. Why? Because we are drawn to what beauty proposes: transcendent communion.

---

34   St. Augustine, *Sermo,* 241. (cf. CCC #32)

As human beings, the summation of all our longings is to love and be loved. We seem to know intuitively that beauty offers fulfillment and we wish to embrace those who create it. We want to know more about our favorite musician or the Missionaries of Charity because something about their song is so appealing. We want to join the band, if you will, because we desire some type of communion with that human artist. Likewise, we yearn for personal communion with the Divine Artist when "from the greatness and beauty of created things comes a corresponding perception of their Creator."[35]

God writes beauty in the language of the heart so that it may captivate us, plumb the depths of whom we are, and evoke our own gifts of self. Above all, then, beauty is meant to inspire love and creativity.

---

35 Wisdom 13:5

CHAPTER 5

Natural Revelation

The Creator has composed the universe as a great symphony, and right reason is its overture. The existence of God, the principles of non-contradiction, finality, and causality, and the spiritual gifts of the human soul, are all metaphysical truths which can be unveiled through our natural ability to reason; therefore, they are called *natural* revelation. These philosophical truths are universally and perpetually valid because they are derived from common sense; however, since they are often difficult to corral, the following outline may prove helpful in summarizing what we have covered thus far:

I. The main theme of the book of creation, whether it is read from the physical world or the human person, is that *God exists and is speaking to us.* The three sub-themes of creation are known as the transcendentals of being: truth, goodness, and beauty.
  A. God writes *truth* within creation according to the principle of non-contradiction.
    1. In the physical world, we read that creatures are real and knowable because they have been given an identity, an essence.
    2. In the human person, we read that our words are meaningful primarily because they are non-contradictory.
      a. Our intellect allows us to form universal concepts.
      b. Objective truth is known when one's thoughts reflect reality.
  B. God writes *goodness* within creation according to the principle of finality.

1. In the physical world, we read that laws of nature are consistent.
2. In the human person, we read that natural law, our universal sense of fairness, is also consistent.
   a. Our free will allows us to respond to laws of nature by giving God thanks, and to respond to natural law by pursuing justice.
   b. Objective goodness is pursued when one's conscience dictates a choice which is really good, not just apparently good.
C. God writes *beauty* within creation according to the principle of causality.
1. In the physical world, we read that creatures have been given existence and artistically designed.
   a. Objective beauty is achieved when creativity has integrity, proportion, and clarity.
2. In the human person, we read that we can emulate God's creativity through gifts of self, either works of art or the art of living.
   a. Our heart allows us to love and be loved, to communicate and receive beauty.

Behind everything that is true there is an intellect, behind everything that is good there is a will, and behind everything that is beautiful there is a heart. Many first principles of being were defined by philosophers who lived before Christ, especially Plato and Aristotle, and then polished by philosophers enlightened by faith, especially St. Augustine and St. Thomas Aquinas. Unfortunately, since the age of the so-called enlightenment, the explosion of science and secular humanism has led to an overemphasis on faithless contemporary thinkers.[36] Faith and antiquity are now seen as impediments to truth. The philosophy of any great thinker who was Catholic is discredited because of his religious beliefs, and the philosophy of any great thinker who lived before Catholicism, like the ancient Greeks, is discredited simply because he lived before the scientific revolution and is not "enlightened". Ironically, science is always discarding old theories (which in their own time were seen as irrefutable) for new theories which now disprove past scientific conclusions and may eventually be discarded themselves.

Advances in science and technology are impressive; however, scientific progress cannot become the criterion for judging the validity

---

36 Secular humanism focuses on our physical needs and potentialities, and should be distinguished from Christian humanism, which also takes into consideration our spiritual needs and potentialities.

of first principles. Why? Because first principles are not physical matters (which fall within the domain of science), but metaphysical matters (which fall within the domain of philosophy). In addition, they are so fundamental there is little room for new developments. We'll discuss this thoroughly in Part II, but for now let us simply assert that neither scientific discovery nor the passage of time will ever, even slightly, erode the objective nature of the first universal principles of being.

"Implicit" Philosophy

The universal principles of truth, goodness, and beauty can both prevent and cure the thinking errors of skepticism, relativism, and atheism (the cancers of modern thought and secular education). As a former college professor with a doctorate in both theology and philosophy, Pope John Paul the Great was particularly qualified to speak about the value of deriving objectivity from natural revelation. In his encyclical letter Faith and Reason (*Fides et Ratio*), he provides a syllabus for Philosophy 101, the perennial philosophy of being:

> Although times change and knowledge increases, it is possible to discern a core of philosophical insight within the history of thought as a whole. Consider, for example, the principles of non-contradiction, finality, and causality, as well as the concept of the person as a free and intelligent subject*, with the capacity to know God, truth and goodness. Consider as well certain fundamental moral norms which are shared by all. These are among the indications that, beyond different schools of thought, there exists a body of knowledge which may be judged a kind of spiritual heritage of humanity. It is as if we had come upon an *implicit philosophy*, as a result of which all feel that they possess these principles, albeit in a general and unreflective way.[37]

The pope is not saying that the first universal principles of being need to be understood or defined explicitly for a person to base their

---

37   Pope John Paul II, *Fides et Ratio*, # 4, emphasis in original. (* "subject" in this sense means one who is capable of loving and being loved: the concrete "I" or "You" whose value cannot be diminished.)

thoughts and actions upon them. Rather, they are implicit, that is, embedded and assumed in our dialogue with God, the physical world, and each other. When they do become explicit, however, they serve as the bedrock of objectivity. He continues:

> Once reason successfully intuits and formulates the first universal principles of being and correctly draws from them conclusions which are coherent both logically and ethically, then it may be called right reason or, as the ancients called it, *orthos logos, recta ratio.*[38]

Notice that what is implied in the term "right reason" is that reasoning and choosing can be wrong. Anyone who denies first principles is using their ability to reason and choose, just not correctly. Skeptics, relativists, and atheists (not to mention racists and child pornographers) all employ reason to justify their beliefs and behavior, just not in a way which is consonant with the message of creation.

But if to exercise right reason is to comprehend and apply objective truth, goodness, and beauty read from God's first book, why is it so difficult? Why are there so many contradictory interpretations of what creation says? Why do so many deny the existence of God? Why is there so much deception, darkness, and distortion in the midst of all this honesty, light, and clarity? And why, if nature is such a wonderful book, do we need a Bible? The answer is simple . . . . . . something is horribly wrong with us. As the author G.K. Chesterton once remarked, "Whatever else men have believed, they have all believed that there is something the matter with mankind."[39]

What Went Wrong?

We have all been created for truth, goodness, and beauty – ultimately, to find fulfillment by loving and being loved. But along with this innate inclination toward being, there is a disordered tendency toward falsehood, evil, and ugliness . . . an inclination toward nothingness.

Everywhere we turn, whether we survey current events or our own experience, we find our relationships with each other and the rest of creation are strained. From the time we can walk and talk, we reveal that

---

38 Ibid., emphasis in original (*orthos logos* is Greek, *recta ratio* is Latin).
39 Chesterton, G.K., *The Everlasting Man*, I.2.

something within us is engaged in a dramatic struggle between good and evil. For example, who has not witnessed the tantrum of a toddler who wants to hurt their parent that is keeping them safe but in the child's eyes is only preventing them from having their way? The parent is usually not injured by the child, but it "is not for the lack of will to do harm, but for lack of strength."[40]

As a young man, I had to come to grips with our disordered nature when I worked at a children's treatment center in Denver. Originally built as an orphanage by the Sisters of Charity, it had been turned into a home for boys and girls with special needs. It was a magnificent facility, and I was always impressed that through the generosity of benefactors, as well as the generosity of the nuns who had given up their lives to serve others, many young people were being loved and cared for.

One little girl who lived there was particularly adorable – new blond hair, bright blue eyes, and a wonderful sense of humor. When she was just five years old, her job was to serve the guests at her mother's parties. She would carry around a tray with lines of cocaine on it for anyone who wished to indulge. Frequently, she was raped by one of her mom's many boyfriends. Betrayed by her own mother, this beautiful little girl was a cocaine waitress and sex slave before she entered kindergarten. That's the human condition: we are beings capable of heroic virtue or cowardly vice, of staggering beauty or repulsive ugliness.

Our freedom is truly a blessing which allows us to love others, but it carries with it the curse of being free to hate. We are free to adopt unwanted babies or throw them in a dumpster; free to pull strangers from a burning building or endorse genocide; free to restore wolves to native lands or poison a river. The inclination to be self-centered rather than self-giving exposes the war being waged within us, a war that is anything but natural. Thus, we speak of our "fallen" human nature.

The reason that God wrote a second book, the Bible, was to explain what went wrong and what He plans to do about it. In other words, since God's first book speaks only of the existence of evil, His second book is a revelation of how evil poisoned the universe, and how someone has the antidote for its venom: "There is not a single aspect of the Christian message that is not in part an answer to the question of evil."[41] Evil, then, is what must be overcome if we and the rest of creation are to be restored.

---

40   St. Augustine, *Confessions*, I.7.
41   *Catechism of the Catholic Church*, #309

Part II

Faith and Reason

* * *

Prologue

At this point, let us map out where we have been and where we are going. In Part I, we saw how creation reveals the objective principles of *implicit philosophy* by means of the transcendentals; in Part II, we'll look at the similarities and differences between God's first and second book[1]; in Parts III and IV we'll begin reading the theological meaning of various creatures; and finally, in Part V, we'll examine the ultimate goal of the physical world and the human person – covenant communion with God in the new heavens and new earth.

---

1   Referring to Sacred Scripture as God's second book should not be taken to mean that the book of creation has a higher rank than the Bible but merely that it came first. We can distinguish here between primacy (first in importance) and priority (first in succession).

CHAPTER 6

God's Second Book

Supernatural Revelation

When God reveals things that are beyond our natural ability to reason it is called *supernatural* revelation, from the Latin *supra* (above). For example, many passages of God's second book reiterate the *natural* revelation that men and women were given "the power of their own free choice"[2]; but the Bible then goes further to supernaturally reveal that by abusing free choice we turned away from God's plan and now struggle to live as we should. Notice that we can discover our power of free-will without the Bible, but we cannot know why we abuse that power or how evil entered the world.

Sacred Scripture begins with the story of Adam and Eve, which tells us not only how evil entered the world, but also how it affected our ability to read. Originally, human nature was equipped to understand God's will because we were fluent in the symbolism of creatures. In a certain sense, creation was the only book we would ever need. Our original state was free from suffering, ignorance, and disordered instincts (like viewing others as mere objects of pleasure). Now that the astigmatism of sin has clouded our vision, we suffer and die, we must overcome ignorance through rigorous study, and we strain to read the inherent value of persons and other creatures, often failing to give God thanks. Now we need a second book to help us translate the first:

---

2   Sirach 15:14

It is certain that as long as man stood up [i.e. before the fall], he had the knowledge of created things and through their significance, was carried up to God – to praise, worship, and love Him. This is what creatures are for, and this is how they are led back to God. But when man had fallen, since he had lost knowledge, there was no longer any one to lead creatures back to God. Hence this book, the world, became as dead and deleted. And it was necessary that there be another book through which this one would be lifted up, so that it could receive the symbols of things. Such a book is Scripture, which establishes the likenesses, the properties, and the symbolism of things written down in the book of the world. And so Scripture has the power to restore the whole world toward the knowledge, praise, and love of God.[3]

After we lost our fluency in reading God's words in creation, God had to literally spell it out for us with human words in Scripture. He also needed to correct our vision with supernatural prescriptive lenses so that we could comprehend His supernatural text and thus bring His natural text back into focus. In other words, since our *natural* power of reason could no longer read the symbolism of creatures, we needed a *supernatural* power to read Scripture and overcome that illiteracy. The supernatural power which restores our sight is the gift of faith.

Faith

The word "faith" can refer to either the gift which allows us to know and assent to God's supernatural revelation, or to the supernatural teachings which God has revealed to the Catholic Church. The latter, however, is usually called "the faith". In either case, faith is not an obstacle to right reason but an aid, a guardian, a catalyst.

Without the confidence that God has made a map for us to follow, and provided light from above to dispel the darkness of sin, we can easily become disoriented and lose our way. Therefore, in an attempt to restore confidence in the objectivity of first principles, and to highlight the harmony between faith and reason, we have thus far quoted three popes, four saints, the Bible, the Catechism of the Catholic Church,

---

3   St. Bonaventure, *Collations on the Six Days*, XIII.12.

two Christian philosophers, and two pre-Christian philosophers. The pre-Christian philosophers, Cicero and Aristotle, located and defined certain aspects of first principles but they are the exception which proves the rule: those who also have the light of the Catholic faith are able to see those principles with greater clarity and hold them with greater certainty because they have the advantage of knowing both of God's books.

Frequently, any discussion of the existence of God or the spiritual soul is seen as a matter of faith rather than right reason, and is therefore disregarded as subjective. This is partly due to a failure to distinguish between natural and supernatural revelation. One source of confusion is the idea that if something is written in the Bible it must be purely a matter of faith. Indeed, the Bible is an incomparable source of what God has supernaturally revealed, *but it also reiterates the principles of right reason we may still discern naturally.* For example, the existence of a Creator is natural revelation that is first written in the book of creation, and then rewritten in the Bible; but that God is a family of three persons is supernatural revelation (which is beyond reason). Moreover, as we saw above, the existence of free-will is natural revelation that is first written in the book of creation, and then rewritten in the Bible; but that we abused our freedom and shunned God, thereby infecting the cosmos with sin and death, is supernatural revelation (which, again, is beyond reason).

Though we still have the natural power to understand first principles by reading creation, original sin has made it difficult. Therefore, God has also written these truths in Scripture and given us the gift of faith, so we might learn them "with ease, with firm certainty, and with no admixture of error."[4] And because God is a good author, His second book begins by affirming the basic truths of His first.

---

4   St. Thomas Aquinas, *Summa Theologica*, I.1.1.

CHAPTER 7

Genesis 1&2

In the following section, we will expand on how specific phrases in the first chapters of the Bible reaffirm God's existence and the unique capacities of the human soul. We will also look at some similarities and differences between God's attributes and our own, so as to establish guidelines for comparing an intelligent, free, and creative Creator to an intelligent, free, and creative creature.

"In the beginning"[5]

When we survey the physical universe, we discover that things come into existence and go out of existence; they come to be and cease to be. While it is harder to recognize contingency in inanimate things like rocks or the sun (even though we know the sun and the other stars are slowly burning up), we see living things die with regularity. When we look at ourselves and other persons, we find the same thing – death and decay are a certainty. As we discussed above, the principle of causality merely recognizes that *everything that comes into existence needs a cause to account for its being.* Since every person and thing in our physical universe has come to be and will one day cease to be (in other words, since no creature has the power to cause its own existence), we must acknowledge an Uncaused Cause "through whom all things are and through whom we exist".[6]

An ancient maxim states that no one gives what he does not have *(nemo dat quod non habet)*. If one does not have knowledge he cannot

---

5   Genesis 1:1
6   1 Corinthians 8:6

impart knowledge, if one does not have the power to forgive sins he cannot forgive them, etc. Likewise, if one does not have the power to cause and sustain existence, he cannot impart being. But the objection could be raised, "Then what created God? What gave Him existence?" The answer is that God did not come into existence, but has always existed without beginning or end. Existence is not something He was given, its part of who He is eternally.

The following diagram illustrates how radically different an eternal Creator is from temporal creatures. Let the arrow represent the forward movement of time, the stars all the caused and contingent creatures within the cosmos, and the overlapping circles the timeless, all-powerful, uncaused Creator who is without beginning or end, alpha or omega:

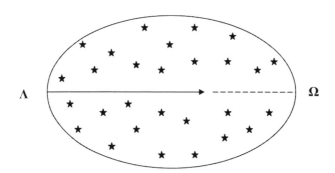

Two important concepts are brought to light by this drawing. First, the Creator is a being who is not limited in any way by time and space, and who encompasses both the beginning and the end. God lives beyond the stars, so to speak, but without being excluded from having a presence among them. Second, if time is the measure of motion and change within the physical universe, then outside of time and space there is neither motion nor change. So if someone were to ask what God was doing before He created the universe, the answer would be that since there is no "before" or "after" in eternity, God was, and is, and will be doing everything . . . simply because He has all the time in the world.

"when God created the heavens and the earth" [7]

Human creative power is in some ways the same as divine creative power and in some ways different. The *most notable difference* is that we create out of things that already exist, that is, out of pre-existing things; whereas God "calls into being what does not exist."[8] He did not have any materials to begin working with. He created every force, every potential to diversify, every atom and molecule, and every property of every element ex *nihilo* (out of nothing). Regardless of what scientific hypothesis about the beginnings of the physical universe is being discussed, all creatures resound this absolute, metaphysical, pre-scientific fact:

> All these things proclaim your glory as their Creator, O God, but how do you create them? How did you make heaven and earth . . . because until the universe was made there was no place where it could be made? Nor did you have in your hand any matter from which you could make heaven and earth, for where could you have obtained matter which you had not created, in order to use it as material for making something else? Does anything exist by any other reason than you exist? [9]

We should be able to read this truth from the book of nature, but with the confusion that resulted from original sin God knew we needed Him to rewrite this truth in the book of super-nature: "Look at the heavens and the earth and see everything that is in them, and recognize that God did not make them out of things that existed."[10]

On the other hand, the *most notable similarity* in God's act of creating and our own is that what was first in intention was last in execution. This is not to place a "before" and "after" within the eternal creativity of God, but merely to show how His creative process is in some ways like our own. For example, when a human artist decides to create a portrait of a family, he first gathers canvass, paint, and brushes. Then he paints the background. Finally, he paints the father, mother, and children. Painting the family was the first thing he intended to do but

---

7   Genesis 1:1
8   Romans 4:17
9   St. Augustine, *Confessions,* XI. 4.
10   2 Maccabees 7:28

the last thing he accomplished. In much the same way, what was first in intention for God (albeit eternally) was to create creatures who were creative – creatures in His own image and likeness – but this was last in execution within time and space because He first wanted to canvass an environment upon which to paint them.

"the earth was without form and void"[11]

The six days of creation reveal how God overcame formlessness and emptiness if we consider how days one, two, and three, correspond to days four, five and six. During the first three days, God gave "form" to the universe by establishing the realms of Day and Night, Sea and Sky, and Land and Vegetation, respectively. During the next three days, He filled the "void" by establishing rulers for those realms: the sun, moon, and stars "to rule over the day and over the night"[12]; fish and birds to rule sea and sky; and animals and humans to rule land and vegetation.

Day 1 Day and Night	Day 2 Sea and Sky	Day 3 Land and Vegetation
Day 4 Sun and Moon/ Stars	Day 5 Fish and Birds	Day 6 Animals and Humans

This view, known as the framework hypothesis, helps us to see the theological meaning of Genesis 1 – God has designed and set in motion a cosmos, an ordered environment in which His children can live and love.

Unfortunately, this unique account of creation is often juxtaposed with ancient creation myths. The similarities are then exaggerated to the point that Genesis is portrayed as one myth among many rather than as a distinctive literary masterpiece. While it's true that the human author employs imagery that can be found in other ancient writings, the following differences set the book of Genesis apart and preclude its categorization as myth:

---

11   Genesis 1:2
12   Genesis 1:17

1) God is the one, eternal, and all-powerful Creator of the universe, not just one of many "gods".
2) The sun, moon, and stars are creatures that light the day and night, not gods that are to be worshipped.
3) God creates man in a father-son relationship, denoted by the biblical phrase "image and likeness".[13]

"and darkness covered the face of the deep"[14]

The poetic language of this phrase from Genesis highlights how God is ultimately shrouded in mystery. A being that is unchanging, uncaused, omnipotent, and omnipresent is impossible for us to totally comprehend with our intellect. In general, the human intellect is designed to abstract the essence of a material thing, and then reason about concepts, relationships, and causes; however, to totally comprehend a spiritual being who is pure and eternal existence is beyond us. It is like trying to explore the depths of the sea by breathing water and seeing without light, we are simply not equipped for the task.

Whenever we begin to think or speak about the mysteries of God, we are confronted with the limitations of our intellect and language, "for between Creator and creature, no similarity can be seen without acknowledging an even greater dissimilarity."[15] The more we learn about God, the more we see that we can't see. Since He is both mysterious and knowable, we should be careful not to think we know things about God which we can't, while remaining certain of those things which we can.

"the wind of God was moving over the face of the waters"*[16]

Whereas "darkness" safeguards the mystery or transcendence of God, "wind" represents His accessibility to reason. When invisible wind makes its presence known by causing visible water to move, it is analogous to how an invisible Creator can be known to exist through the visible effects He causes.

---

13   The phrase "image and likeness" occurs both when God creates man in Genesis 1, and in Genesis 5, where it explicitly refers to a father-son relationship: "Adam . . . became the father of a son in his own likeness, after his image, and named him Seth." (Gen.5:3) Thus, we can conclude that God's relationship with us has always been familial.
14   Genesis 1:2
15   *Fourth Lateran Council*, II. (1215 A.D.) cf. CCC #43
16   Genesis 1:2 (* or "Spirit")

On a deeper level, since the Hebrew word for wind, *ruah*, also means *Spirit* or *breath*, "the wind of God" also represents His life-giving power. These complementary meanings are found in the following verses from Psalm 104: "You take back your Spirit, they die, returning to the dust from which they came. You send forth your breath, they are created; and you renew the face of the earth."[17]

Most of my personal retreats into the Yellowstone backcountry have been either solo or with my lifelong friend, Charles "Bud" Page. Over the years, we have developed certain responses or *antiphons* to various words of creation. Some are simple acknowledgements of God which were born out of the humility that deep wilderness engenders. Perhaps our favorite is to simply say *Ruah* whenever the wind picks up. Our little prayer is always spoken with thankfulness and reverence for many reasons. On a backcountry retreat, where so much is depending on God's providence (and one is continually faced with the reality of not being at the top of the food chain), the whispers among the treetops and the fanning of the fire are comforting reminders of His presence. Also, since Bud and I are often near the Yellowstone River inlet during early summer, when the sloughs and side-channels become prime habitat for breeding mosquitoes, our gratitude extends to relief from bugs . . . merciful relief, to be more precise. From our many trips back to *The Inlet*, we've learned two very important things: (1) bugs can really bug; and (2) bugs hate wind. So when the Almighty breathes on our little camp it is nothing less than a direct gift from heaven. A mysterious word that says, "I am here for you . . . Do not be afraid . . . Trust me."

"God created man in His own image" [18]

Whenever we make an analogy between God and ourselves, we are comparing things that imperfectly exist in creatures within time and space to things that perfectly exist in the Creator beyond time and space. We can apply terms like "patience" to God because we have formed an idea of patience insofar as it exists among men and women, but we can't know patience as it perfectly exists in God because no man or woman is perfectly patient. The language we use to refer to any attribute of God is always imperfect because it is limited by our less than perfect

---

17   Psalm 104:29-30
18   Genesis 1:27

knowledge of less than perfect examples. When we predicate terms of God, therefore, it is "only by taking creatures as our starting point, and in accordance with our limited human ways of knowing and thinking."[19]

The words we use to express our spiritual attributes, like "intelligent", "free", and "creative", are neither applied in the exact same sense nor in a completely different sense when the same words are used to express attributes of God. Rather, there are *both similarities and differences.* For example, when we think about God "creating" the universe there is a similarity in that God made a plan and put it into action, but there is a difference in that we cannot even begin to fathom creating something out of nothing. As St. Irenaeus explained in the second century, this distinction is crucial for us creatures made in God's image, because it guards His incomparable greatness: "Men, indeed, are not able to make something from nothing, but only from existing material. God, however, is greater than men first of all in this: that when nothing existed beforehand, he called into existence the very material for his creation."[20]

"the breath of life" [21]

After revealing that we have been made in His image and likeness, Genesis goes on to reveal that God has imparted to us the gifts of thinking, choosing, and creating, by infusing our physical body with a spiritual soul. Unlike other animals, we are matter *and* spirit due to these powers we have received from the Spirit or "breath" of God:

> The human person, created in the image of God, is a being at once corporeal and spiritual. The biblical account expresses this reality in symbolic language when it affirms that "the Lord God formed man of dust from the ground, and breathed into his nostrils the breath of life."[22]

By continuing to read Genesis 1 and 2 carefully, we can locate the phrases which demonstrate that God gave us intelligence, freedom, and creativity, so that we could read His truth, respond to His goodness, and emulate His beauty.

---

19   *Catechism of the Catholic Church,* #40
20   Saint Irenaeus, *Adversus Haeresis (Against the Heresies),* 2.10.4.
21   Genesis 2:7
22   *Catechism of the Catholic Church,* #362 (cf. Genesis 2:7)

"The man gave names to all" [23]

After Adam received a spiritual soul, he had a gift for reading or "naming" creatures. It would be simplistic to think that they were not just lined up and paraded by as he assigned each one the next name on the list, Aardvark through Zebra. Rather, the theological meaning of naming them was that he could read them as words of God's truth and understand them with his intellect: "In biblical language, 'naming' the creatures is the sign of this mission of knowing . . . created reality."[24]

"You are free" [25]

In general, to love is to will the good of another; therefore, free-will is a prerequisite of love. Offering a gift of goodness to another has meaning precisely because it was offered freely. Would any sick person who was being nurtured back to health find it meaningful if those actions were not freely chosen but merely bio-chemical responses? Would anyone be satisfied with the thought that the words "I love you" exchanged with their children were only the result of highly evolved instinct? Or that the communion shared with their spouse could be reduced to pheromones, endorphins, and psychological conditioning, having no spiritual and transcendent import? If the response to another is purely instinctual, and we are not free to choose otherwise, it is not a free and creative gift of self and, therefore, not an expression of love.

The objection might be raised that we are not free since God knows every choice we will ever make. If He knows what I am going to decide, how am I not predestined to choose one way rather than another? How can I remain free if He knows all my decisions before I make them? The problem of free will and divine foreknowledge is another example of our thinking we can know more about the Creator's perspective than we are able.

Because God is outside of time, He has an infinite amount of time and can eternally choose to respond to every choice we will ever make without imposing on our freedom. Every decision and every prayer, by every person who has ever lived, can be addressed without one tick of the clock. We see things as they unfold over time, God sees Alpha and Omega simultaneously.

---

23   Genesis 2:20
24   Pope John Paul II, *General Audience,* January 17, 2001.
25   Genesis 2:16

"Be fruitful" [26]

It is striking that the first words spoken to man in Sacred Scripture refer to his creativity. One way to interpret this proto-mandate is from the now familiar two-fold point of departure: our relationship to human persons and to the physical world. First, we are fruitful and creative when a man and a woman "become one flesh"[27] and procreate another person. To give the gift of one's entire life in marital communion produces the most beautiful fruit in the universe, a newborn child. Second, we are fruitful and creative when we "till and keep"[28] the garden which has been entrusted to us. The art of developing and preserving the environment requires that we become artists in our efforts to provide for the needs of others, both now and in the future. The cultivation and protection of both our offspring and our environment requires a creative self-giving, a self-donation which comes from the heart.

Let us now examine a final phrase from Genesis: one which is repeated so often it calls for special attention.

"And God saw that it was good" [29]

Creatures within time and space undergo change, yet remain what they are long enough to be identified. If creatures moved or changed too quickly, it would be like trying to read words on a rapidly scrolling computer screen. Also, if the sentences of creation were not in a coherent and meaningful order, it would be like trying to make sense out of a story where sentences were randomly being cut and pasted. It would neither be a good story nor the work of a good author. In fact, it would not be a story at all, just random nonsense.

The "book" of creation, in a certain sense, is more like the "movie" of creation, because scenes change and move through time. If the world was a static picture we still might be able to form the idea of *treeness* by reading the truth of a tree and abstracting what is universal from the many particular pictures of trees.[30] But since the universe is in motion we can know the germination, growth, and fruit bearing properties to

26   Genesis 1:28
27   Genesis 2:24
28   Genesis 2:15
29   Genesis 1:10,12,18,21,25
30   A picture tells a story only because we know stories as series of events and can see what came before and what might follow (i.e. we can imagine the precedent and antecedent.)

see how a tree moves through time and thereby arrive at a fuller sense of a tree. That is, we can see it as a being which is good as well as true. Seeing the way a tree acts and reacts with other things teaches us how good they are for fuel, shelter, and sustenance; which, in turn, reveals the goodness of the one who made them that way. Thus, after the Director of the cosmic movie set yelled "Action!" the universe was made to move at an understandable pace and in an orderly fashion so we could read its truth *and* its goodness.

From another perspective, if one's favorite movie were to be spliced and the images presented in no particular order, you could still identify the images (because of the principle of identity) but you would no longer call the movie "good" because it violated the principle of finality: it was not directed toward a goal in an organized progression. Imagine, for example, watching *Raiders of the Lost Ark* out of sequence. We would recognize men, women, snakes, spiders, whips, airplanes, trucks, etc., but without seeing them in a logical order we wouldn't say it was a good movie because it would no longer be a coherent story. The refrain in Genesis, "And God saw that it was good", indicates that creation's reasonable tempo and orderly sequence are both signs of the goodness God has willed to us.

CHAPTER 8

Faith *or* Reason?

Faith is a free assent of mind and heart to things that are beyond right reason, and at least an implicit assent to the principles known by right reason. First principles are reiterated on the first pages of scripture because they are presupposed in an act of faith. In a certain sense, an act of faith needs first principles to lay the foundations of objectivity, intelligibility, and possibility for "the obedience of faith".[31] That is to say, faith assumes that: (a) God is real and understandable; (b) that we have the freedom to respond to His revelation; and (c) that we may do so in a creative way. Since natural revelation is implicit when we place our faith in supernatural revelation, first principles are called the "preambles of faith" (*preambula fide*). That is not to say first principles must be understood or defined explicitly for an act of faith to take root in the human heart, but rather that when natural revelation *is* understood and defined explicitly it is a richer soil for the seeds of supernatural revelation.

When I first began to study for the priesthood I was surprised by the amount of philosophy required, and later by how disjointed it all was. At the time, the 10 philosophy courses required by the American bishops were in no particular order (e.g. Ancient Greek philosophy was not required before medieval philosophy and first principles were not required to be mastered before special courses in epistemology or ethics). The vibrant young men I was studying with were around 10 years younger than I, and whenever we began a philosophical discussion they would inevitably regurgitate difficulties posed by various philosophers

---

31   Romans 1:5

(perhaps to practice what they believed would be on the final exam) or become mired in speculations regarding how we speculate; but rarely did they make any sense. Gradually, I began to realize that a philosophical curriculum of 30 credit hours in preparation for the study of theology would only bear the desired fruit if those courses were grounded in right reason.

Rational thought about God and our spiritual powers of knowing truth, practicing goodness, and emulating beauty has been shrouded with difficulties by modern philosophy. Even though nothing in our life is more accessible than *being*, nothing more universal than the universe, few things are more neglected today than first principles. Most people just don't seem to care about right reason. It is no wonder that without the principle of non-contradiction so many succumb to the creed of skepticism: "Nothing is certain."; or without the principle of finality so many surrender to the creed of relativism: "That might be true for you but it's not true for me."; or worst of all, without the principle of causality so many yield to the creed of agnosticism: "God's existence cannot be known." As John Paul the Great noted:

> Abandoning the investigation of being, modern philosophical research has concentrated on human knowing [epistemology]. Rather than make use of the human capacity to know the truth, modern philosophy has preferred to accentuate the ways in which this capacity is limited and conditioned. This has given rise to different forms of agnosticism and relativism which have led philosophical research to lose its way in the shifting sands of widespread skepticism.[32]

It wasn't until I befriended a young man from a farm in Idaho (who was not studying for the priesthood and was not a philosophy major), that I was able to see and define the "implicit philosophy" that JP II would later identify in *Fides et Ratio*. My young friend had simply taken a course that discussed first principles for a few weeks as a foundation

---

32   Pope John Paul II, *Fides et Ratio*, #5. (nota bene: an atheist asserts that God does not exist, whereas an agnostic asserts that God's existence cannot be known one way or the other.)

for the study of political science. Not surprisingly, armed with such confidence in right reason and its relationship to faith, he entered St. John Vianney seminary in Denver shortly after graduating from college.

After my own graduation, I also began attending a major seminary but at a location which was less than faithful to the teachings of the Catholic Church. During my first week of classes, I was attacked by my *Theological Foundations* professor for agreeing with the Church that "God, the source and end of all things, can be known with certainty from the things that were created through the natural light of human reason"[33]; and then by my *Old Testament* professor for believing that the Exodus was a real historical event in which Moses actually led the people of Israel out of Egypt. The philosophy professor said I put too much faith in reason, and the scripture professor said I put too little reason in my faith. At that moment, I realized how important it was to maintain the proper relationship between the two. In spite of their advanced degrees and shelves of books, both professors had become confused and had lost confidence in God's desire to unambiguously reveal Himself through natural and supernatural words. I stayed at that seminary for only six weeks (which in hindsight was about five weeks too long).

The ultimate meaning of life and death is hidden from reason alone but is accessible through faith. Nonetheless, right reason is indispensable as the objective foundation of faith. All forms of skepticism, relativism, and atheism undermine the truth, goodness, and beauty which God's supernatural revelation builds upon. There is simply no room for objective supernatural revelation in a philosophical system which claims there is no objective natural revelation to begin with. As the philosopher Dietrich Von Hildebrand clarified, "the very nature of the Judeo-Christian revelation makes for an absolute incompatibility with any epistemological, metaphysical, or moral relativism."[34] Simply put, any philosophical system which denies that there is objectivity in what is real and knowable, in what is right and wrong, or in what is verifiable regarding God and the soul is not correctly interpreting what God has revealed in creation, and should be considered incompatible with what God has revealed in Scripture.

---

33   First Vatican Council, *Dogmatic Constitution on the Catholic Faith (Dei Filius)*, II. (Cf. Fides and Ratio, #21-22; CCC #286)

34   Dietrich Von Hildebrand, *Trojan Horse in the City of God*, 62.

Theology is the study of who God is and what God wants, and both of His books form the content and curriculum. If God and His will are to be known, He must be knowable. To be knowable one must communicate with reason, truth, non-contradiction . . . in a word, with *logos*: "God acts with logos. *Logos* means both reason and word – a reason which is creative and capable of self-communication, precisely as reason."[35]

As we have seen, meaningful self-communication presupposes that words are intelligible, at the most fundamental level retaining a non-contradictory identity according to the principle of non-contradiction. Since God created us to understand things primarily through reasoning, His revelation is reasonable. In other words, because theology is "a work of critical reason in the light of faith . . . theology needs philosophy as a partner in dialogue in order to confirm the intelligibility and universal truth of its claims."[36] It is no accident that Jesus established His Church at a time when reflection on His supernatural revelation could be supplemented by Greek insights into natural revelation. The historical confluence of the New Testament and right reason is an event of great importance because it highlights "the intrinsic necessity of a *rapprochement* [reconciling] between Biblical faith and Greek inquiry."[37]

Let us now consider a few concrete examples of why it is so important to be rational in our faith and faithful in our reasoning if we desire to know who God is and what God wants. That is, why we must reject the blind faith of *fideism* and the blind reason of *rationalism* in order to arrive at the fullness of truth.

Fideism

When a religion is not in accord with right reason, any belief or behavior can be justified by simply claiming that God has commanded it. Any thought or action perceived to be "God's will" is valid even when it is contradictory, unjust, or outright ugly. Modern examples of faith which does not respect the true, the good, and the beautiful are Christian extremists such as the Ku Klux Klan, and Islamic extremists such as the Taliban or Al Qaeda. In both cases, there is blindness to the objective moral law regarding the inherent dignity of the human person. In other

---

35   Pope Benedict XVI, *Faith, Reason, and the University: A Lecture Presented at the University of Regensburg*, September 12, 2006 (emphasis in original).
36   Pope John Paul II, *Fides et Ratio*, #77.
37   Pope Benedict XVI, *Faith, Reason, and the University: A Lecture Presented at the University of Regensburg*, September 12, 2006 (emphasis in original).

words, the problems of fideism stem from interpretations of God's will which contradict or simply reject right reason.

As a case in point, the underlying thinking error for Muslim extremists is that God can command us to act contrary to right reason, contrary to the human nature which He created, because His "transcendence and otherness are so exalted that our reason, our sense of the true and good, are no longer an authentic mirror of God."[38] They believe God is a capricious master who demands blind obedience from his servants. In an attempt to assign Him more power, they believe God can contradict Himself as He sees fit because He is all-powerful and does whatever He wants.

A being who cannot contradict Himself is not less powerful, however, because *contra-diction* (speaking against) is not a power but an anti-power. Meaningful communication is powerful because it communicates something, reveals something; but when communication is contradictory it is devoid of meaning and reveals nothing, it is an absence of power. God's omnipotence is not at all diminished by the inability to exercise impotence.[39]

Non-contradiction is a requirement for creating words that are legible and intelligible to human nature. Like the words contained in God's first book, the words of God's second book would be unknowable if they violated the principle of non-contradiction. For example, "Do whatever He tells you" cannot mean "Don't do whatever He tells you"; "Be fruitful" cannot mean "Don't be fruitful", etc.[40]

For non-Catholic Christians, human nature has fallen so far and is so corrupt that it is no-longer equipped to know God, morality, and the spiritual soul. Our ability to read creation was not only damaged by sin but destroyed, leaving us to see "by faith alone" (*sola fide*).[41] Ironically, the belief that we are completely blind without faith leads to the blindness of fideism. Instead of seeing our nature as *depraved*, Catholics believe our spiritual gifts have only been *deprived* of the fullness they once had.

---

38   Ibid.

39   This should serve to answer the silly question, "Can God create a rock so heavy that he can't lift it?"

40   John 2:5; Genesis 1:28

41   *Sola fide* was one of the battle cries of the Protestant reformation and the phrase "by faith alone" does indeed appear in the Bible, just not in the way Martin Luther would have liked: "See how a person is justified by works and *not by faith alone.*" (James 2:24) emphasis mine

Nevertheless, Catholics are also accused of exercising blind faith by allegedly believing in doctrines that violate the principle of non-contradiction. For example, how can we believe that God is both one and three at the same time and in the same sense? While recognizing the limitations of human knowledge, the Catholic answer is that we cannot and we do not. Rather, in one sense we believe that there is only one true God, and in another sense (but at the same time) we believe that this one God is a family of three persons, Father, Son, and Holy Spirit: in one sense a unity, and in another sense a tri-unity. God is both one and three at the same time but not in the same sense. This is analogous to how *being* and the *transcendentals of being* are both one and three; or how water remains unified as H20 even though it can be solid, liquid, or gas.

Catholicism rejects fideism and holds that faith should be compatible with right reason. The other extreme, rationalism, denies that faith can lead us to any knowledge whatsoever. But is it reasonable to believe that reason is all we need when reason alone cannot resolve questions concerning the existence of evil, the meaning of life, or what happens after death? And isn't the belief that only reason can arrive at objective truth more like an act of faith than an application of reason?

Rationalism

The skeptical current of philosophy from Descartes through Kant (17th-19th centuries) had the double effect of casting doubt upon the objectivity of metaphysical reasoning (which arrives at first principles) while exalting scientific reasoning as the sole source of knowledge. The metaphysical principles implicit in the scientific pursuit of knowledge were put on trial, and the guardian of all reasoning, supernatural revelation, was held in contempt. We will clarify the difference between scientific and metaphysical reasoning in the following chapter, but for now let us simply introduce the relationship that supernatural knowledge has with these two types of natural knowledge.

When supernatural knowledge is marginalized or rejected, natural knowledge can easily go astray. Just as a cattle drive needs cowboys to keep the herd moving in the right direction (even though they are free to graze along the trail) scientific and metaphysical thought need the Catholic faith. Without it, they will inevitably try to cross a river where there is no ford and be swept away, or wander into a box canyon where all progress ceases. In our fallen condition, whenever natural reason is severed from supernatural faith the resulting stampede is anything but rational. A modern example is the attempt by some scholars to study God's supernatural book with natural means alone, that is, to apply scientific reasoning to the "book of faith" without the assistance of faith.

Historical Critical Method (Historical Criticism)

Being raised a Catholic I learned the story of Jesus in a typical fashion. My mom faithfully brought my brother and me to CCD classes and to serve as altar boys, my grandma taught me how to pray the rosary, and at Sunday mass I listened to readings from scripture and daydreamed through stained glass windows. I also learned the Bible was special. Being raised an American, however, gave me the impression that the Bible, not the Church, was the real place to find God's will. And so it was that during my freshman year of college (after simultaneously losing three of my passions in life), I began reading the scriptures on my own for the first time. The physical pain of injuries that prevented me from running track and playing the piano, and the emotional pain of losing my high school sweetheart, turned me toward God like never before. I read the Gospel of Matthew straight through, I read the letters of James, Peter, and Paul . . . and I fell deeply in love with The Messiah.

Naturally, the more you love someone the more you want to know about them, so after I transferred to the University of Colorado I enrolled in a class called *Jesus and the New Testament.* What I discovered, however, was not the person Jesus Christ, but the doubt and suspicion that plagued biblical scholarship in the twentieth century. My professor focused only on the pre-history of the text, not how it stood in its final form. Every book of the bible was dissected in order to uncover the ulterior motives behind the alleged warring factions of the early Church. Any miracle was discredited with pseudo-science or portrayed as an outright lie by someone trying to establish credibility for their view. We also speculated about the conspiracies behind variations in writing style; phrases that had not been previously used were considered proof that there were many authors not just one. Matthew didn't write the *Gospel of Matthew,* John didn't write the *Gospel of John,* and the early Church was locked in such a dramatic power struggle for the allegiance of Jesus' followers that they crafted stories of His resurrection and His establishment of a Church with a pope and bishops. The historical critical scholars we studied held that many of Jesus' words were never really spoken by Him and many of

67

the events described never really happened. The New Testament was mostly a power-play, a manipulation, a pious fraud.

As the semester wore on, I became somewhat disillusioned with Scripture and "higher" education, for where I had once found illumination I was now burdened by many unresolved difficulties. The great Jesus, whom I had come to love so much, became harder and harder to find in the dry and sterile environment of modern biblical scholarship. My friend Bud, who was also enrolled in the class, was perplexed as well; and because best friends are not always the best influence on each other at that age, we began to play the latest video games instead of attending the lectures.

Years later, I discovered three disturbing things about these modern "experts" of the bible: (1) for all their research, the "reason alone" scholars had not come to a consensus on even one passage of Scripture but had only stacked theory upon theory with no objectivity in sight; (2) no saint in history had ever emphasized this method as a means to becoming Christ-like; and (3) the sudden popularity of the method could be traced to Protestant German scholars in the 1870's who sought to discredit the idea that Matthew was the real author of the *Gospel of Matthew*. But why, I wondered, would these scholars want to prove that someone besides the apostle Matthew had written that gospel?

The rise of the historical critical method was to some extent a reaction to the Catholic Church's clarification in 1870 on the special role of Peter and his successors, the popes. When the pope and bishops of the world convened for the First Vatican Council, one of the ancient doctrines of the Church that was under attack was papal infallibility. A clear definition of the authority given to Peter by Jesus was produced, but the only Scripture verse cited was from Matthew's gospel: "And I tell you, you are Peter and on this rock I will build my Church, and the powers of death shall not prevail against it. I will give you the keys of the kingdom of heaven".[42] If Protestant scholars could prove that someone besides Matthew had written the *Gospel of Matthew*, and just used his name, then the words of Jesus when He changed Simon's name to Rock (which is translated Peter) could be called into question. After all, if the writer of the *Gospel of Matthew* was not Matthew the apostle, then it was probably someone who was not an eye-witness and was just trying to manufacture credibility for the followers of Peter to use against

---

42   Matthew 16:18-19

the followers of John or Paul. In other words, since the *Gospel of Matthew* is the only gospel to record Jesus explicitly establishing His Church on Peter, if it was written by a non eye-witness with an agenda to keep Peter in power, it raised doubts as to whether Jesus ever spoke those words.

As it turned out, this supposed conspiracy within the early Church brought to light the anti-Catholic bias of 19th century Germany more than it shed light on historical truth. And it was these ulterior motives of Protestant historical critical scholars (and the many dissenting Catholic scholars who followed in their steps), which helped me realize that becoming a master at *Donkey Kong Jr.* just may have been time well spent.

Historical Science vs. Historical Criticism

Because of its potential to be used against Catholic doctrine by Protestants and dissenting Catholics alike, Pope Leo XIII prophetically warned of the dangers of historical criticism in 1893:

> It will make the enemies of religion much more bold and confident in attacking and mangling the sacred books; . . . it will only give rise to disagreement and dissension, those sure notes of error, which the critics in question so plentifully exhibit in their own persons; and seeing that most of them are tainted with false philosophy and rationalism, it must lead to the elimination from the sacred writings of all prophecy and miracles, and of everything else that is outside the natural order.[43]

By focusing only on human authorship, hidden agendas, power struggles, and natural explanations for miracles, the historical critical method approaches the bible like it's just another historical document, and from the jaundiced perspective of rationalism. The pope was not saying that historical science isn't valid, but that historical criticism is an irrational method when it compromises the role of faith and is poisoned by doubt, suspicion, and anti-supernatural bias. As John Paul the Great noted, the method must be "freed from its philosophical presuppositions" in order to be faithful and fruitful.[44]

---

43 Pope Leo XIII, *Providentissimus Deus,* I.D.2a.
44 Pope John Paul II, *Address on Interpretation of the Bible in the Church,* 13.

When the *Catechism of the Catholic Church* was published in 1994, it was criticized by some for not quoting the work of historical critical scholars, but only scholars who were saints. The general editor of the *Catechism*, Cardinal Shonborn of Vienna, responded with the wisdom of the ages: "Who reads and understands scripture better than the saints? There testimony is vital for our understanding of the faith because they ... are living commentaries on the Gospel."[45] So how *do* these living words interpret the Word? Simply put, with reason *and* faith.

By recognizing both human authorship *and* divine authorship, the saints do not just analyze the human element of the text, but remain open to all that God wanted to say. They approach the Bible theologically to discover its divine meaning, not just scientifically to dissect its human influence. Because Scripture is supernatural revelation, reason alone is incapable of unveiling the full meaning. As Benedict XVI noted: "The scientific study of the sacred texts is important but is not sufficient in itself because it would respect only the human dimension."[46] Without faith, reason remains tethered to the human dimension and becomes prone to doubt when confronted with difficulties: "only faith's hermeneutic is sufficient ... because it alone has a vision of unity which is wide enough to accommodate the apparent contradictions."[47]

Biblical Contradictions?

The Bible is often criticized as violating the principle of non-contradiction on account of its apparent contradictions. Men of faith like St. Augustine, however, teach that once it had been granted that God has co-authored the sacred page, its inerrancy is so necessary that even if we come upon something which seems to be contradictory, we should have the faith to believe that God does not contradict Himself and the humility to admit that our understanding may be deficient.[48]

Imagine, for example, trying to understand how we receive the gift of the Holy Spirit by reading the *Acts of the Apostles* without faith. Initially, we find Peter addressing the multitudes at Pentecost (ten days after Jesus

---

45   Christoph Cardinal Shonborn, *Introduction to the Catechism of the Catholic Church*, 54.
46   Pope Benedict XVI, *Address to the Pontifical Biblical Commission*, April 23, 2009.
47   Joseph Cardinal Ratzinger, *Behold the Pierced One*, 7.1.
48   St. Augustine, *Epistolae*, (Letters), LXXXII. 1.

ascended into heaven and only moments after the Holy Spirit descended upon the apostles with wind and fire): "Repent and be baptized, every one of you, in the name of Jesus Christ so that your sins may be forgiven; and you will receive the gift of the Holy Spirit."[49]   Later, we find Peter laying hands on believers so "that they might receive the Holy Spirit (for as yet the Spirit had not come upon any of them; they had only been baptized in the name of the Lord Jesus.)"[50] So which is it? Does a person receive the Holy Spirit at baptism or not? It can't be both at the same time and in the same sense, so how can these two passages be reconciled?

The early Church, informed by faith, saw that in one sense we receive the Holy Spirit in baptism for the forgiveness of sins, and in another sense we do not receive the fullness of the gifts of the Holy Spirit until they are stirred within us "through the laying on of the apostles' hands".[51] When an apostle or a successor of an apostle, a bishop, lays hands on a person, it is known as the sacrament of confirmation. This sacrament strengthens the gifts of the Spirit that were received at baptism. So while it is true that in one sense we receive the Holy Spirit when we are baptized, in another sense the Holy Spirit is not fully activated or fully "received" until we are confirmed.

Another example can be found in the gospels, where Matthew recalls an event as Jesus was *leaving* Jericho, while Luke describes the same event as He was *entering* Jericho. Clearly it can't be both at the same time and in the same sense, so how can the two passages be reconciled? This apparent contradiction was not solved until the middle of the twentieth century when archeologists unearthed an older Jericho only a mile from the newer Jericho, which was being built at the time of Jesus' public ministry. Thus, it could be true that Jesus was both leaving Jericho and entering Jericho, depending on how the author chose to describe the event.

St. Augustine is not teaching us to bury our heads in the sand, but to admit that since we can't always see how all the pieces fit together we should trust that God's revelation is non-contradictory. Within a world of human error and ignorance, we are called to be confident that "there can never be a true divergence between faith and reason, since

49   Acts of the Apostles 2:38
50   Acts of the Apostles 8:15-16
51   Acts of the Apostles 8:18

71

the same God who reveals the mysteries and bestows the gift of faith has also placed in the human spirit the light of reason. This God could not deny himself, nor could the truth ever contradict the truth".[52] Beyond all objections and difficulties, therefore, God remains a being "who can neither deceive nor be deceived."[53]

---

[52] First Vatican Council, *Dogmatic Constitution on the Catholic Faith, (Dei Filius),* IV.
[53] Ibid. III.

CHAPTER 9

Scientific and Metaphysical Reasoning

Since the age of the so-called Enlightenment, there has been so much confusion about the relationships between science, metaphysics, and faith that many now disregard first principles and religion, believing that objectivity is found in science alone. But this is neither necessary nor even plausible if we are thinking clearly.

First of all, let us explore the relationship between scientific and metaphysical reasoning – two types of natural knowledge that are complementary not competitive. To think that: (a) a Creator exists; (b) a Creator has endowed us with reason, freedom, and creativity; and (c) a Creator has infused the universe with principles of non-contradiction, finality, and causality, is to arrive at objective truth by way of metaphysical reasoning. Such reasoning about the *non-physical laws* of the physical universe is the domain of metaphysics, whereas reasoning about the *physical laws* of the physical universe (i.e. how things work and interact) is the domain of the science. The scientist looks at physical causes, the metaphysician at non-physical causes lying beneath those physical causes. In other words, the scientist looks at a creature and asks, "What physical causes make this creature act and react the way it does? What physical laws does it follow?" Whereas the metaphysician looks at a creature and asks, "What non-physical cause made this creature exist in the first place? What non-physical laws does it follow? What brought me into existence? What causes me to want to know? Why do I want to be fair and expect others to be fair to me? Why do I want to carve, construct, experiment, and invent? Where does my drive to make things better come from? What gifts or powers do I possess that allow me to ask and answer such questions?

In addition to asking different questions, a further distinction can be made between these two modes of inquiry. Consider that the scientific study of creation would not be possible if: (a) creatures were contradictory and therefore unidentifiable; (b) creatures were without finality or causality and therefore had no predictable laws or effects; and (c) we did not have the necessary spiritual powers to ponder a question, pursue a solution, and design an experiment. Thus, the scientist depends on first principles in the pursuit of knowledge, whereas the metaphysician does not depend on scientific method.

The Big Bang Theory

Since scientific study is limited to physical things, whenever scientists speculate about the ultimate origins of the physical universe they have trespassed into the non-physical domain of metaphysics. The non-physical, uncaused cause of the physical universe is simply beyond the scope of scientific discovery:

> Scientific proofs in the modern sense of the word are valid only for things perceptible to the senses, since it is only on such things that scientific instruments of investigation can be used. To desire a scientific proof of God would be equivalent to lowering God to the level of the beings of our world, and would therefore be mistaken methodologically in regard to what God is. Science must recognize its limits and its inability to reach the existence of God. It can neither affirm nor deny his existence.[54]

When scientific reasoning postulates the Big Bang theory of how the universe developed, metaphysical reasoning would simply insist on the

---

54   Pope John Paul II, *General Audience,* July 10, 1985. (A modern example of a scientist being a poor philosopher is Stephen Hawking, the physically challenged physicist who claims that, "Because there is such a law as gravity, the Universe can and will create itself from nothing").

logical necessity of an omnipotent cause, a Big Banger. Only metaphysical reasoning can address the issue of where the stuff that "exploded" came from to begin with. Even if it was a super-heated primordial atom, which predated the four forces of nature (i.e. electromagnetic, gravitational, weak nuclear, and strong nuclear), it must have been brought into being by God. Who else could have caused this first physical something to exist? Who else could have heated it up and charged it with combustibility? And finally (for the purposes of our next discussion), who else could have directed it to explode in an orderly progression of four forces, interrelated elements, and adaptable life forms, as opposed to chaotic disarray? In other words, who else could have set creation on course and then kept it on course toward the finality of order? [55]

Evolution

The theory of evolution was built upon Charles Darwin's observation of pigeon breeders who could develop birds of a desired color and size within a few generations by simply selecting those with the desired characteristics for reproduction. A more familiar example is dog breeding. If the desired characteristics are a blunt nose and stocky legs, the new breed might be an English bulldog. If a large head and big bones are selected, a St. Bernard might be the result. When Darwin observed variations in the size and shape of finch beaks during his exploration of the Galapagos Islands, He speculated that the human process of selecting characteristics for breeding is an artificial application of the selection process which happens in nature.

Whenever a living organism produces offspring there are slight variations in the characteristics of those offspring (such as sharper teeth, a curved beak, or webbed toes) which are better adapted for survival. As the offspring's environment undergoes change (such as drought, flooding, overpopulation, or disease), those with advantageous traits are "selected" by nature to have a better chance of survival, and are thus more likely to reproduce and pass on their genes. In brief, Darwin proposed that the mechanism behind differences within a species is random gene mutations acted upon by fluctuating environmental conditions as each creature struggles to survive.

---

55   See *Appendix B* for Pope Benedict's summary of evolutionary processes and contingent being.

Let us carefully distinguish, however, between *macro* evolution and the *micro* evolution we have just defined. Micro evolution refers to the adaptations and changes that occur *within* a species. Where Darwin's scientific observations ceased and his theoretical speculations began, however, was with *macro* evolution. He believed that if small differences in characteristics were acted upon by natural selection enough times, the result would be an entirely new species. He also believed that if his theory was correct the transformation from one species to the next would be become manifest as fossils were unearthed. The problem is the fossil record has not shown small incremental changes but great leaps which modern science has given fancy names like "punctuated equilibrium". All too often, atheistic scientists have struggled to account for the missing links, irresponsibly promoting new theories as indisputable fact without acknowledging the discrepancies; and without acknowledging when they are exploring questions that are not scientific. This does not make any new theory false, just an exercise in bad science.

The latest research for explaining the physical origins of species comes from the field of DNA. Certain codes within our genes, which determine specific characteristics and stages of development, have been identified and found to be shared among many living things. Different sequences of those genetic codes are found in different species. What is important for our discussion, however, is not the scientific validity of the latest phylogenic tree, but the metaphysical principles which evolutionary theory assumes.[56]

According to evolutionists, random gene mutations, the struggle to survive and reproduce, and environmental conditions, all have a role in shaping physical life-forms. A contradiction arises, however, whenever they assert these processes are without guidance or direction, that is, without finality. First, if random gene mutations are generally very small, what is the cause of this consistency? What reason do we have to believe that slight mutations are part of a blind process? Why shouldn't we see them as part of an orderly plan, that is, as a consistent mechanism of adaptability? Second, if individual living things struggle to survive and reproduce, what is the cause of these consistent urges? Where does that inner dynamism we call "the law of the jungle" come from? And third, if environmental conditions are continually fluctuating, though not so

---

56 A phylogenic tree illustrates lines of descent and evolutionary development.

drastically as to prevent things from moving forward and diversifying, what is the cause of this constant yet relatively benign flux?

Since all living beings have been directed toward the goal of adaptation, survival, and reproduction, and environments have been directed to undulate within a relative stability, even if science eventually proved that this is the process by which new species have emerged, it would not affect what metaphysics has already proved: namely, that creation has been inscribed with a general law which gives consistency and direction to the specific laws of mutation, perpetuation, and fluctuation. This fundamental law, which has been written by God within everything that lives, is nothing less than the principle of finality:

> The evolution of living beings, of which science seeks
> to determine the stages and to discern the mechanism,
> presents an internal finality.... This finality, which directs
> beings in a direction for which they are not responsible
> or in charge, obliges one to suppose a Mind which is its
> inventor, its creator."[57]

In other words, because genes randomly but consistently mutate, species consistently strive to perpetuate, and environments consistently fluctuate, they prove the metaphysical truth that there is a Director behind the evolution process: a creative intelligence who designed things to be oriented toward a goal. As St. Thomas proposed over 750 years ago, since "nature works for a determinate end under the direction of a higher agent", it can be traced back to a Creator.[58]

The fact that God has caused primeval matter to exist then diversify and has inscribed adaptive processes through which individual species may have emerged, demonstrates that His creative hand "extends to all being, not only as to constituent principles of species, but also as to the individualizing principles."[59] So even if evolution is someday definitively proven on the macro level, it would simply represent God's means of making new creatures.

In Darwin's time, the prevailing assumption was that living creatures were stable and had not changed since the moment of creation. The

---

57   Pope John Paul II, *General Audience,* July 10, 1985.
58   St. Thomas Aquinas, *Summa Theologica,* I. 2.3. ad 2.
59   Ibid. I. 22. 2.

theories of micro and macro evolution challenged that idea and caused an unnecessary hostility toward science among Christians duped by fideism, as well as an unfounded exuberance among atheists duped by rationalism: both camps displayed an ignorance of first principles. As we've said, regardless of what scientific theory is proposed about how the diversity of creatures emerged, metaphysical reason would simply insist on the realities of non-contradiction, finality, and causality, the reality of the non-physical human soul, and the "reality which is the first cause and final end of all things, a reality 'that everyone calls God'"[60]

The Ultimate Missing Link

The development of the human body through time is a matter for scientific reason which is currently being studied. The powers of the human soul, however, constitute what John Paul II called an "ontological leap"[61] whereby the human species possesses spiritual abilities altogether unique in the animal kingdom. And whereas the existence and powers of the soul is a certainty of metaphysical reason, we need supernatural revelation to affirm that God directly creates the spiritual soul and infuses it into the physical body:

> . . . from the viewpoint of the doctrine of the faith, there are no difficulties in explaining the origin of man in regard to the body by the theory of evolution. But it must be added that a hypothesis proposes only a probability, not a scientific certainty. However, the doctrine of the faith invariably affirms that man's spiritual soul is created directly by God. According the hypothesis mentioned, it is possible that the human body, following the order impressed by the Creator on the energies of life, could have been gradually prepared in the forms of antecedent living beings. However, the human soul, on which man's humanity definitively depends, cannot emerge from matter since the soul is of a spiritual nature.[62]

---

60   *Catechism of the Catholic Church*, #34, (St. Thomas Aquinas, *Summa Theologica*, I.2.3.)
61   Pope John Paul II, *Message to the Pontifical Academy of Sciences*, 6. (October 22, 1996)
62   Pope John Paul II, *General Audience*, April 16, 1986.

Note that the Church is not saying that any of the several theories of macro-evolution are false or even that they are incompatible with Catholic doctrine, but it is saying that we should recognize what is still only theoretical and be aware when science wanders into metaphysics or supernatural revelation.

There is perhaps no better example in American history of the failure to distinguish between scientific and metaphysical thinking, or to recognize the limits of either faith or reason, than the Scopes "Monkey Trial" of 1925. The trial pitted an atheist lawyer, Clarence Darrow, against a fundamentalist Christian, William Jennings Bryan over the issue of whether evolution should be taught in schools. On the one hand, Darrow took the position of *blind science* by ignoring metaphysics and saying there is no God and man is just a highly evolved animal with no spiritual soul. He embraced the errors of rationalism, which stem from a "science alone" view, by not acknowledging that we learn of the Creator and our spiritual gifts from reading nature metaphysically. On the other hand, Bryan took the position of *blind faith* by ignoring science and insisting that the Bible should always be interpreted literally. He embraced the errors of fideism, which stem from a "bible alone" view, by not acknowledging that we learn the timeline of the physical world and the human person from studying nature scientifically. This popular trial had the effect of polarizing the American psyche into one or the other of these two extremes.

Fideism fails to acknowledge that the chronological progression of how individual species emerged and the human body developed are within the domain of science. We must remember that the first chapter of the Book of Genesis is not a science text but a theology text. The six "days" of creation could have literally been six 24 hour periods since God is all-powerful, but we are in no way bound by such an interpretation. If a 24 hour day is one full rotation of the earth as it revolves around the sun, consider what is implied by the sun not being created until the 4th "day". Since the first three "days" have light but no sun, our reading of Genesis should not focus on geological or biological timelines, but on the theological meaning known only through faith. Scientific reasoning, metaphysical reasoning, and faith all contribute to the quest for truth, but each in its proper domain.

Many who espouse the theory of evolution also believe that the conditions for the Big Bang were the result of blind chance and were without any direction or order. They would suggest that the order and design of the universe is simply a cosmic accident. But who would consider it an accident if a deck of cards left by an open window were later found on the floor spelling out the words "Have a nice day!"? Would anyone not immediately recognize that someone with intelligence had willfully arranged them that way? Is it even a reasonable application of reason to suggest that if the wind blew the cards off the window sill, even billions of times, they could be found in such meaningful order? Of course not, but this is precisely what some atheistic scientists want us to believe.

But why is it so difficult for those who see order and design in human creations to see it in divine creations? None of us look at a guitar, a bicycle, or a cave drawing and think that it just happened by chance. Although it's possible that something like a cave drawing happened by chance (perhaps by a tornado passing the mouth of the cave and splattering pigments from uprooted plants to look like four legged animals with antlers), it's so improbable that it's not rational. In fact, it's beyond irrational; it's absurd, no matter how many billions of tornadoes have passed by. Precisely because a cave drawing bears the *human* stamp of intelligence, willfulness, and creativity, we intuit that it cannot be the result of blind chance. When it comes to the *divine* stamp of intelligence, willfulness, and creativity, then, what prevents us from being equally as certain?

The Speed of Eternity

One of the problems is that God writes really small words like the cell, bigger words like canyons, as well as unfathomable words found among the galaxies – all at an eternal pace. Compared to our way of creating, God's creations seem to "take an eternity". Let us remember, however, that a billion years or a billionth of a second are irrelevant to a discussion of a Being who has always been. For the Creator, there is no passage of time; every astronomical, geological, and biological event is within the same timeless instant of creativity, which transcends concepts of before, during, and after. A chisel strike from God can cause a rock slide upon a mountain and may seem to be random, because His next strike may not be for days or even decades. Viewed apart from the whole mountain, or limited to the span of a human life, a rock slide may seem as chaotic as a sculptor's first strike upon a piece of marble.

When we were twenty years old, Bud and I received the first part of a lecture on this subject. Two miles up the Boulder Creek drainage of the Gore Range in northern Colorado lays Boulder Lake. While in high school, we had camped there with our other dimwitted friends, but now were poised to get the "upper lake" as we called it, which was an additional six miles and right at timberline (about 11,000 feet). We were still developing our backcountry system and our young bodies could still be abused with such "maximalist" items as axes, full-sized binoculars, and canned goods. We managed to lose the trail after about three miles, so the remaining five was a steep, unrelenting bushwhack. Eventually, we crested the rim of the upper lake and found it nestled among a 13,000 ft. cirque. Fatigued yet exhilarated, we whooped and yelled . . . then dropped to our knees in gratitude. A few seconds later we thought we heard a fighter jet from the Air Force Academy passing overhead and the moment was lost. It was regained when we realized that our jubilant praise had instead triggered a rock slide on the peak behind the lake. We were completely awe-struck. A chunk of granite the size of a buffalo was bounding along a cascade of smaller boulders and finally came to rest near the inlet where we would set camp later that night. The other rocks had spread in an alluvial fan which leveled the brush and temporarily choked the creek. Twenty-five years later Bud and I returned to the slide on a day hike where we received the second part of the lecture. We were amazed at how what was once a destructive torrent of granite was now a delicate talus slope framed with alders, punctuated with columbines, and homesteaded by pikas.[63]

Our creations may have less diversity in size and font than God's, but they do express a distinctively human touch. No rock slide has ever produced a pyramid, no tornado a cave painting, no earthquake or tsunami a sand castle. It's easier to recognize a creator behind things made by human hands, that is, with pre-existing matter, because it is more familiar. But it should not be hard to also recognize that the geological and meteorological phenomena which shaped the earth simply represent God's chosen means of sculpting. When God wanted to place a boulder half the size of a school bus in the middle of a forest in Yellowstone, for example, He took granite from Beartooth Plateau

---

63   A pika is a small rabbit-like creature which lives within talus and skree slopes near timberline.

fifty miles away and moved it there with a glacier.[64] Glacial advance and retreat, plate tectonics, volcanic activity, and erosion, are merely the tools of the Creator's trade.

In sum, the remarkable stability of the time in which human life has flourished is unprecedented in the geological history of earth. We may be between ice ages in a prolonged period of ideal climactic conditions, but it is an error to think that it was all just an accident, a meaningless blip. Instead we should acknowledge God's goodness for designing a beautiful environment in which His family would thrive. Every scientific theory which holds that natural processes are accidental, random, or blind, contradicts itself and demonstrates that some scientists are just poor philosophers. To insist that creation has intelligent design, intentional direction, and an artistic cause is just sound metaphysical thinking. First, it is implausible that individual creatures, from meteors to mollusks, have not been given an *identity* as certain types of things which are then able to be investigated scientifically. Second, it is implausible to suggest that laws of nature, environmental fluctuations, and genetic variations are truly random, without rhyme or reason, and then posit that living things are aimed directly at the *finality* of adaptation, survival, and reproduction. Both animate and inanimate things are "studyable" and verifiable for scientists precisely because they have been given rhyme and reason. And third, it is implausible to suggest that the physical universe spontaneously emerged out of nothing. As we have seen, there must be a non-material, all-powerful, uncaused *causality* which initiated and sustains its existence. Even if the physical source of all living organisms (including the human body) is eventually traced to a single primordial cell, and the physical source of the universe traced to a single primordial atom, it would not in the least affect the primordial certitudes of right reason.

Love is Not Blind

The tendency to reject right reason, however, is nothing new. Pope Benedict XVI is particularly aware of the age-old phenomena of blindly asserting that everything is blind and denying the existence of the Creator:

> I find the words of this fourth-century Father [St. Basil the Great] surprisingly up to date when he says that some

---

64 A rock of this kind is known as a *glacial erratic*. This particular boulder can be seen along North Rim Drive.

people, "deceived by the atheism they bore within them, imagined that the universe lacked guidance and order, at the mercy, as it were, of chance". How many these "some people" are today! Deceived by atheism they consider and seek to prove that it is scientific to think that all things lack guidance and order as though they were at the mercy of chance. [65]

Since many will never study metaphysics and its relation to science (and because we cannot figure out what went wrong on our own), God's second book revives right reason then reveals that we have not been abandoned – there is hope for us and the rest of the universe – for God is more than Creator, He is our loving Lord:

> The Lord through Sacred Scripture reawakens our reason which has fallen asleep and tells us: in the beginning was the creative Word. In the beginning the creative Word – this Word that created all things, that created this intelligent design which is the cosmos – is also Love.[66]

Love is not reducible to material causes. It cannot be adequately explained by pheromones, endorphins, or psychology because, as we have continually reiterated, it transcends the domain of science. Science can never account for the love and beauty which have been breathed into the physical world and the human person, precisely *for* the human person. We can't do a lab experiment on the transcendent desire to fly off into a sunset or to embrace someone forever, including God. Rather, our hearts are simply captivated and converse in the universal language of loving and being loved.

But why, one might ask, does there have to be a Creator who expresses love through the things of the universe? Why can't creatures love with there own voice? Why can't we just say that "unguided evolution" speaks? Because creatures are words, and words don't just form themselves; they are signs intentionally written by an author to express something meaningful.

---

65   Pope Benedict XVI, *General Audience,* November 9, 2005.
66   Ibid.

CHAPTER 10

Meaning

The words of creation are signs, and signs are *significant* precisely because of there power to *signify* something. If there is no reason for creation, if it's all just the result of blind chance, if an accident gave rise to the universe rather than an all-powerful artist who designed things as meaningful words, then our desire to find meaning in life is truly just a projection of our own fear and anxiety – a human invention, a cosmic joke. If it all just happened to happen, beauty is a mockery of human longing and the best we can logically say when holding a newborn baby or standing before Bridal Veil Falls in Yosemite National Park is, "That's so random" or "That's so meaningless." If creatures are just random artifacts of chaos, with no *significance*, then we are left to echo the words of despair found in Shakespeare's *Macbeth*:

> Life's but a walking shadow, a poor player
> That struts and frets his hour upon the stage
> And then is heard no more: it is a tale
> Told by an idiot, full of sound and fury,
> Signifying nothing.[67]

Yet who is content with a meaningless outlook on life? Who in there right mind looks upon their first-born child or the Grand Canyon and remains uninspired? Beauty can inspire us and speak to us because

---

67   William Shakespeare, *Macbeth*, V.5.

there is an intelligent and beneficent artist behind it. Whenever we say, "That's so cool!" or "That's so awesome!" we are presuming that creatures have been given the intent to convey meaning – a meaning which stirs within us wonder and awe.

Only the blind believe in blind chance.

Our Common Quest

If our yearning for truth, goodness, and beauty is to be fulfilled, things must be meaningful; and human history attests to the fact that this desire is universal:

> . . . a cursory glance at ancient history shows clearly how in different parts of the world, with their different cultures, there arise at the same time the fundamental questions which pervade human life: *Who am I? Where have I come from and where am I going? Why is there evil? What is there after this life?* These are the questions which we find in the sacred writings of Israel, as also in the Veda and the Avesta; we find them in the writings of Confucius and Lao-Tze, and in the preaching of Tirthankara and Buddha; they appear in the poetry of Homer and in the tragedies of Euripides and Sophocles, as they do in the philosophical writings of Plato and Aristotle. They are questions which have their common source in the quest for meaning which has always compelled the human heart.[68]

Our great "quest for meaning" cannot be satisfied by scientific reasoning because, as we've said, the *signi*ficance of a word is not a scientific question. Scientific reasoning probes physical matters, not non-physical matters; and whereas metaphysical reasoning does probe non-physical matters, it is limited. Only supernatural revelation can fully disclose the meaning of the physical world and the human person, only eyes of faith can see the answers to life's biggest questions.

---

68   Pope John Paul II, *Fides et Ratio*, #1, (emphasis in original).

Why Did God Create?

Among these big questions is the ultimate meaning of creation. Supernatural revelation goes beyond science to answer *why* God created the physical world and the human person. It is not concerned with "knowing when and how the universe arose physically, or when man appeared, but rather of discovering the meaning of such an origin."[69] If the main theme of creation is that God exists and is speaking to us, the reason He decided to write that song was that He loves us.

Love by nature is fruitful. Love wants to give, to share, to overflow in acts of generosity. And when you yourself are the ultimate gift (as is the case with God), to share yourself is the most rational, benevolent, and loving thing you can do. God is no egomaniac who needs everyone to love Him. Rather, God is a Trinitarian family who needs nothing from His creatures to have the fullness of love, but freely willed to communicate that love *precisely out of love.*

In the physical world, God's love is expressed through the glorious transcendentals of being: "God created the world to show forth and communicate His glory. That His creatures should share in His truth, goodness, and beauty – this is the glory for which God created them."[70] In diverse and immeasurable ways, each individual creature mirrors an aspect of the Creator's glory: "There is one glory of the sun, and another glory of the moon, and another glory of the stars; indeed, star differs from star in glory."[71] Still, even the totality of creatures in the physical world is but an infinitesimal manifestation of the infinite glory of God.

In the human person, God's love is expressed through our unique power to resound His glorious transcendentals: first, by communicating *truth*, as He has done in words of creation; second, by freely extending *goodness* to others, as He has done in giving us benevolent laws; and third, by creating *beauty* through gifts of self, as He has done in His masterpieces of nature and newborns.

When God decided to bring the physical world into being, it was as a personal gift for man and woman. They alone had been endowed with the ability to read and respond to His words. They alone could know He loved them and love Him in return. Creating such a magnificent cosmos is glorious in itself, but God went further when He created us

---

69   *Catechism of the Catholic Church*, #284
70   Ibid., #319
71   1Corinthians 15:41

to enter into communion with that glory. Perhaps the great second century theologian, Saint Irenaeus, summarized it best when he wrote: "The glory of God is man fully alive."[72] When man is fully in touch with being, fully immersed in God's books, then and only then is he fully alive, fully in love. Then he is a greater manifestation of the glory of God than the sum of all other creatures.

The Stimulus of Science

Scientific thinking cannot yield the meaning of a text in scripture any more than a text in nature, but advances in science and technology can stimulate new insights. When biblical science studies a supernatural word in the Bible it seeks to know how that word developed and functions within the sentence or book as a whole. Similarly, when natural science studies a word in creation, it seeks to know how that creature developed and functions within the ecosystem or universe as a whole. Natural science can enrich our understanding of words within the entire "canon of nature" just as biblical science helps us discern the context of words within the entire canon of scripture.

Some words of creation remain hidden until scientific research and technology grant us access. For instance, a veterinarian friend of mine in Jackson Hole has seven daughters. When the seventh was on the way, he volunteered to teach a confirmation class about the inherent value of unborn life. Over the course of the school year, he and his wife would periodically show their unborn child on an ultrasound monitor. The unequivocal meaning of this particular word of creation, "I am a person!" confronted the students in the form of little hands and feet . . . and a tiny beating heart.[73]

The more we understand the etymology of a word, the richer our understanding of its theological meaning (provided we are led by faith). As John Paul II noted, faith serves the information gathered by science in order to "place it within the ultimate order of things, in which everything acquires true meaning."[74] Certainly, pre-natal technology has

---

72   St. Irenaeus, *Adversus Haeresis (Against the Heresies)*, 4.20.7.
73   It is worth noting that the latest Gallup poll (May 2009) indicates that 51% of Americans identify themselves as pro-life. It is believed that one of the reasons for pro-lifers becoming a majority again is the profound clarity, both visually and morally, which ultrasound technology provides.
74   Pope John Paul II, *Fides et Ratio*, #20

enriched our understanding of how we develop and of what it means to be a human person.

It should come as no surprise that the deeper we probe into atomic substructures or peer in the far reaches of space the more we encounter mystery and beauty. Why? Because that's who God is: an artist who inspires awe and wonder. Unfortunately, the invention of the microscope and telescope turned many scientists toward rationalism instead of the truly rational approach of faith seeking understanding (*fides quarens intellectum*). The discoveries of science should always lead to a deeper appreciation of God's goodness and a more profound gratefulness for our gift of reasoning:

> Scientific studies . . . have splendidly enriched our knowledge of the age and dimensions of the cosmos, the development of life forms, and the appearance of man. These studies invite us to even greater admiration for the greatness of the Creator, prompting us to give him thanks for all his works and for the understanding and wisdom he gives to scholars and researchers."[75]

Unfortunately, many misguided souls persist in pitting the Catholic faith against scientific reasoning.

Galileo

It is a neglected historical fact that science owes a large debt to the Catholic world-view. Without the Church's insistence that faith serves to galvanize and guard the principles of right reason, the systematic study of the universe would not have flourished as it did. In general, the explosion of science in Western civilization was due to the belief that universe was consistent and non-contradictory, that creatures were not gods but just that, creatures, and that we had been given the necessary powers of inquiry. Catholic pioneers in science include the Augustinian monk Gregor Mendel, who is considered the father of genetics, Bishop Nicholas Steno, who is known as the father of stratigraphy,[76] and the

---

75   *Catechism of the Catholic Church*, #283
76   The geological study of the distribution, deposition, and age of rock strata.

Jesuit priest Georges Lemaitre, who worked out the expanding "primeval atom" of the Big Bang theory.

Ironically, the Catholic Church is often criticized for allegedly being anti-science. The evidence which is presented invariably involves the errors made by Church officials in criticizing Galileo's hypothesis that the earth revolves around the sun. Since this event is cited as "exhibit A" out of 2,000 years of Church history, however, it serves more to prove that the Church is *pro*-science, because no modern examples can be cited. Nonetheless, given that it has become such a popular slur, let us summarize the incident without prejudice.

In 1543 the astronomer Nicholas Copernicus, theorized that the earth revolved around the sun, not vice versa, as was the common belief at that time. His theory was not yet proven and celestial phenomena could still be explained by the theory that the sun revolved around the earth. Years later, Galileo Galilei adopted Copernicus' theory but still could not provide the evidence to prove it. Since this heliocentric model had not been proven and would disturb the common man's view of the world, theologians within the Vatican over reacted and wrongly condemned the view as false. They then commanded Galileo to cease from teaching it and placed him under house arrest on charges of heresy.[77] These members of the Vatican did not include the pope and had no apostolic authority to make an infallible pronouncement on the subject. Even so, they were guilty of being imprudent and impulsive, and eventually were proven to be flat-out wrong. This was a huge blunder on the part of the Vatican committee because it left the impression that the Church was not part of the scientific revolution. The Catholic Church has apologized repeatedly for this error because no matter how well intentioned the Church officials were, they had failed to distinguish between matters of faith and matters of scientific reason. On the other hand, we should remember that the heliocentric model was only a theory at the time, and the committee who rejected it was genuinely concerned for the spiritual welfare of the people.

The Church learned a valuable lesson from this incident and became less fearful that the study of nature would ever contradict the revelation of super-nature. As Galileo himself declared, God does not speak one

---

77   Heresy is defined by the obstinate belief in something that is irreconcilable with the Catholic faith. Contrary to popular opinion, Galileo was never condemned as a heretic.

word in scripture and then a contradictory word in creation; they are a two-volume set:

> Sacred Scripture and the natural world proceed equally from the divine Word, the first as dictated by the Holy Spirit, the second as a very faithful executor of the commands of God.[78]

The words of God's first and second book originate from the same source and therefore have a profound complementarity. With the supernatural knowledge gained through faith, we can understand the meaning of God's natural words; and with the natural knowledge gained through reason, we can deepen our understanding of God's supernatural words.[79]

Moreover, if we believe that the words of nature and scripture both have God as their Author, we should expect their theological meaning to be interpreted in similar ways, and be taught using similar methods.

---

78   Galileo Galilei, *Letter to Father Benedetto Castelli*, December 21, 1613.
79   As we've seen, we could never understand that the one true God is three divine persons through the scientific study of water, but since the Trinity has been supernaturally revealed, reason helps those with faith penetrate the mystery by showing how something can be one and three without violating the principle of non-contradiction.

CHAPTER 11

The Divine Pedagogy

Now that we have lost our original innocence, God's primary teaching method, or pedagogy, is to accommodate His speech to our special needs. God's first book was written by Himself, whereas the second was co-authored with various human writers so "that we may come to know the ineffable loving-kindness of God and see for ourselves how far He has gone in adapting His language with thoughtful concern for our nature."[80] By using human words to reveal what is no longer easy for us to understand from the words of creation, God has shown that *accommodation* or "coming down to our level" is His way of adapting His lessons to our fallen nature.

Divine Accommodation

Every good parent and teacher knows how to accommodate their speech to the capacity of a child; we speak simply and with dramatic gestures to a toddler and adapt our vocabulary as the child grows and learns. If the child has dyslexia, we employ techniques that help overcome that disability. Whenever we adjust our language to make our teaching more effective, we are merely imitating the divine pedagogy.

In addition to modifying His language, God has accommodated himself to our nature by employing one of the most universal teaching tools – drawing an analogy. A good teacher can demonstrate similarities and differences between things which are familiar and things which are not so familiar, resulting in a new understanding. And what is more

---

80   St. John Chrysostom, as quoted in *Dei Verbum*, #13

familiar to us than natural things? As soon as a child can speak, he echoes the human words spoken to him that refer to God's words of creation: mommy, daddy, puppy, baby, flower, moon, etc. Through the gift of intellect, the child learns more and more about those things and is able to abstract the essence by seeing how things are analogous: in some ways the same and in some ways different. Likewise, God's pedagogy is to begin with our knowledge of what is natural, physical, and temporal in order to reveal what is supernatural, spiritual, and eternal. As Paul explains to the Corinthians, "it is not the spiritual which is first, but the physical, and then the spiritual."[81]

When Jesus gave the Sermon on the Mount, He taught his disciples spiritual things by referring to physical things. The following is a list of those physical things from the most influential speech ever given: children, salt, light, head, hair, face, eye, tooth, hand, cheek, sun, rain, oil, moth, rust, food, birds, lilies, grass, dogs, pearls, swine, stone, fish, snake, sheep, wolves, grapes, thorns, figs, thistles, trees, fruit, rock, wind, sand.[82] By drawing skillful analogies with creatures, "Jesus teaches us to see the Father's hand in the beauty of the lilies of the field, the birds of the air, the starry night, fields ripe for the harvest, the faces of children, and the needs of the poor and humble."[83]

In order to understand scripture on a deeper level, St. Augustine recommended that three things be studied: (1) the original languages of the Bible, that is, Hebrew and Greek; (2) the symbolism of numbers, like seven being the number of perfection; and (3) creatures, so as to better understand the analogies made in scripture:

> Ignorance of things, too, renders figurative expressions obscure, as when we do not know the nature of the animals, or minerals, or plants, which are frequently referred to in Scripture by way of comparison. The fact so well known about the serpent, for example, . . . that the serpent gets rid of its old skin by squeezing itself through a narrow hole, and thus acquires new strength . . . appropriately fits in with the direction to imitate the

---

81 1 Corinthians 15:46
82 Cf. Matthew 5:1-7:29
83 Pope John Paul II, *World Youth Day: Address for the Vigil of the Assumption of Mary*, August 14, 1993; Cherry Creek State Park, Colorado.

wisdom of the serpent, and to put off the old man, as the apostle says, that we may put on the new; and to put it off, too, by coming through a narrow place, according to the saying of our Lord, "Enter through the narrow gate!" As, then, knowledge of the nature of the serpent throws light upon many metaphors which Scripture is accustomed to draw from that animal, so ignorance of other animals, which are no less frequently mentioned by way of comparison, is a very great drawback to the reader.[84]

The degree of knowledge we have of the creature being referred to in scripture is to some extent the degree we are able to see similarity and dissimilarity. The more knowledge we have of a little lamb, for example, the more insights we might have into the innocence, gentleness, and vulnerability of Jesus when John the Baptist calls Him "the Lamb of God".[85]

Divine Inspiration

Unlike any other text, ancient or contemporary, the bible has been co-authored by God and various human writers. God did not merely dictate to them what he wanted written, however, nor did he just approve what they wrote; rather, He "inspired" (literally "breathed into") them so that they wrote only what He wanted while at the same time respecting their freedom and talents as writers, storytellers, editors, and poets.

Divine inspiration not only ensures that Scripture is without error or contradiction, but also gives each word a sacramentality: a supernatural power whereby the literal truth of a word can have three spiritual truths "embedded" within it.[86]

The Spiritual Sense – A Threefold Analogy

The *literal sense* is the historical truth conveyed by a word of Scripture. For example, the literal sense of the word "temple" is the physical

---

84   St. Augustine, *On Christian Doctrine*, II.16.
85   John 1:29 (Cf. St. Paul's reference to Jesus being the new Passover lamb in 1Corinthians 5:7)
86   The comparison here is with words that have been "embedded" on a computer screen: where a definition, explanation, or deeper meaning has been attached to the highlighted word.

structure built in Jerusalem, but the physical temple is itself a word which conveys three spiritual truths: the allegorical, the moral, and the anagogical. This threefold analogy, known as the *spiritual sense*, reveals the divine meaning of the physical structure of the temple which the literal sense signifies. We can understand the spiritual sense of scriptural words from the analogies drawn in scripture itself. First, the *allegorical sense* provides an analogy of our faith in the risen Christ; and so the temple is a sign of Jesus' body: "Destroy this temple and in three days I will raise it up."[87] Second, the *moral sense* provides an analogy of how we should live in charity; and so the temple is a sign of our own bodies: "Do you not know that you are God's temple?"[88] And third, the *anagogical sense* provides an analogy of what we should hope for; and so the temple is a sign of heaven: "Then God's temple in heaven was opened . . ."[89]

To summarize, when a word written in Scripture is a sign of a physical reality, the physical reality which that word designates can itself be a sign that reveals spiritual realities. As St. Thomas explains, "The author of Sacred Scripture is God, in whose power it is to accommodate not only words for expressing things (as man is able to do) but also the things themselves."[90] Since the words of the Bible are fully human as well as fully divine, to read Scripture fluently we must "distinguish between two senses of scripture, the literal and the spiritual; the latter being subdivided into the allegorical, moral and anagogical senses."[91]

This same method of interpretation should be applied when reading the words of creation. And again, we need look no further than scripture to find these analogies being made. For example, Jesus and John the Baptist allude to the spiritual sense of a tree: *allegorically* we are shown to be dependent on Jesus in bearing good fruit, just as branches are to a trunk or vine: "Every branch of mine that bears no fruit, He[the Father] takes away. . . for apart from me you can do nothing."[92]; m*orally*, we are shown how we must be fruitful if we are to avoid the fires of hell: "every

---

87   John 2:19
88   1Corinthians 3:16
89   Revelation 11:19
90   St. Thomas Aquinas. *Summa Theologica*, I.1.10.
91   *Catechism of the Catholic Church*, #115. (Scripture, in a certain sense, is like the union of God and man in Christ. Just as divine nature becomes one with human nature in the person of Jesus, so God's Word becomes one with human words in Scripture – both are fully divine and fully human.)
92   John 15:2,5

tree that does not bear good fruit is cut down and thrown into the fire."[93]; and *anagogically*, we are shown how heaven is where we can hope to build our homes: "The kingdom of heaven is like a mustard seed that . . . becomes a tree, so that the birds of the air come and make nests in its branches." [94]

Perhaps no one in the history of the Church has been able to express the spiritual sense of creation like the great Franciscan scholar and mystic, St. Bonaventure:

> Therefore the first meaning is the literal. After that, because things themselves have a sense, there are three other meanings. For God manifests himself in every creature in a threefold manner; . . . and every creature represents God, who is Trinity, and shows the way to Him. And since the way to God is through faith, hope, and love, every creature is a suggestion of what we should believe, expect, and do . . . the allegorical concerning what we should believe, the anagogical concerning what we should expect, and the moral concerning what we should do.[95]

This interpretive method is foundational to the faithful exegesis of scripture and creation, but due to our fallen nature it is no longer easy for us. Now we must diligently cultivate our ability to read God's words. Fortunately, however, since both of God's books require an ability to see how His signs can signify more than ordinary signs, the more literate we become in reading one book the more literate we may become in reading the other.

* * *

In sum, all the words of creation communicate the one word of God that encompasses all others, they all resound that one overture of being: "I Am . . . and I am speaking with you." God is the source of all being, of all that is true and good and beautiful. He is a loving God who has endowed us with the spiritual ability to think with our intellect,

---

93   Matthew 3:10
94   Matthew 13:31-32
95   St. Bonaventure, *Collations on the Six Days*, XIII. 11. (cf. CCC #115-118)

choose with our will, and create with our heart. These gifts call us to seek truth, practice goodness, and emulate beauty. By means of the transcendentals, which are interwoven into the very fabric of that all-encompassing overture, we can arrive at objective truth about God's existence and attributes, the soul's existence and attributes, and the basic laws which are infused into reality: non-contradiction, finality, and causality. Though each transcendental is to some extent superimposed on the others, non contradiction is implicit in truth, finality is implicit in goodness, and causality is implicit in beauty. God's first revelation still sings of this "implicit philosophy", but evil blurs those general messages as well as the particular messages found only in particular creatures. Now we must wear the prescription lenses of a second revelation in order to restore our sight.

The Bible reveals things that are simply beyond human reason (like that God is a Trinitarian family), but it also includes things which are within reason's grasp. As He begins His second book, God subtly reiterates the principles of right reason which can still be known naturally through a metaphysical reading of His first. This is because our ability to reason has only been hindered, not annihilated.

Scientific reasoning about scripture or creation can discover how words or creatures work, interact, and develop – which can stimulate new insights – but the disclosure of what scripture or creation means must be guided by faith. Since reading scripture helps us read creation (both by providing clarity to general first principles and by revealing the meaning of specific creatures), and reading creation (either metaphysically or scientifically) helps us read scripture, there should be no tension between God's first and second book.

The initiation and development of the universe and its life forms is within the domain of science, but from a metaphysical point of view is only a study of the chosen mediums of the Great Artist. Right reason rejects the idea that something can spontaneously emerge from nothing without a cause, or that order can spontaneously emerge from chaos without receiving guidance.

Among the most common errors in the modern world are to read the book of nature scientifically but without right reason (like the atheistic scientist or the skeptic), to read the book of super-nature without faith (like the unfaithful biblical scholar), or to read the book of faith with faith but without right reason (like the fideist Christian).

God's first book can be read without the help of Scripture, but the truths revealed in His second book cast light on His first, and the insights gained from His first book facilitate a deeper understanding of His second:

> Not only can there be no conflict between faith and reason; but they also support each other, since right reason demonstrates the foundations of faith and, illumined by its light, pursues the understanding of divine things, while faith frees and protects reason from errors and provides it with manifold insights.[96]

The God who wrote the words of creation is the same God who wrote the words of the Bible. He writes in a language that adjusts to the level of the reader, teaching us supernatural things by way of analogy with natural things, and impregnating words with spiritual senses: layers of meaning that speak of faith, hope, and charity.

Let us now turn to reading some particular words of God's first book with the aid of God's second book, under the guidance of those who read both so well – the saints.

---

96   First Vatican Council, *Dei Filius*, IV.

Part III

A Reading from the Physical World

* * *

Prologue

Whether we are learning perseverance from the ant, or the wisdom of building for the benefit of others from the beaver, we are reading from a book which is as old as time itself. Every creature in God's first book was intended to have meaning for us, and though creation's words can be read by those who do not know God's second book, invariably their comprehension will be limited and contain some degree of error. Without faith, it's as if they are reading an abridged edition containing poor grammar and countless typos. God's second book adjusts our vision to values of moral light and hues of divine color which unveil otherwise hidden meanings.

The fullness of truth about creation is reserved for those who know God intimately, those who are fluent in both of His books. Therefore, to help us discern the theological symbolism of creatures we will rely mainly on the saints and shepherds of the Catholic Church while allowing for personal and scientific insight. Also, the chapters of Part III will be arranged according to the realms and respective rulers of the six days of creation which we discussed in Chapter 7.

CHAPTER 12

Day and Night

I read a wonderful story recently where a philosophy professor from Notre Dame and some colleagues were having dinner. Some were atheists and some theists. One of the atheists asked one of the theists how he would state his case for the existence of God to a non-believer. The philosopher responded simply, "Come and look at my garden." The atheist, dumbfounded that the reply was not more sophisticated, then asked what response he would give if someone were to look at the garden and still find no evidence of God. The philosopher again responded simply: "Look closer."[1]

For most of us it's easy to see there is a God when we look at creation, but for some many difficulties obscure the matter. Perhaps the greatest of these is the problem of evil – a difficulty which can be summarized as follows:

> If God created everything in the universe (and evil is in the universe), then how can we call God all-powerful and good? Either He is not all-powerful because He cannot eliminate evil (even though He wants to), or if He is all-powerful, He is not good because He created it.

---

1   Tom Morris, Ph.D. *Philosophy for Dummies*, VII. 19.

The Problem of Evil

A difficulty is only an inability to see how two or more things can be reconciled: in this case, a good and all-powerful God, and evil. A doubt, however, is an assertion that two or more things cannot be reconciled; like the assertion that God is not good and all-powerful (or does not exist at all) because there is evil. It is appropriate, then, that the first words spoken by God in Scripture, "Let there be light!" help us avoid doubt by showing how evil can exist in a universe created by an omnipotent and loving God.

Light and Darkness

The relationship between light and darkness offers a solution to the difficulty presented by the problem of evil. We will first look at what is resolved by comparing *physical* light and darkness, and then what is resolved by comparing *spiritual* light and darkness.

Physical light is a creature.[2] It has *being* in the form of photons and electromagnetic waves. Darkness, however, does not have being, it is just a term we use to refer to low levels or the absence of light. Similarly, if God has "fashioned all things that they might have being"[3] (and all being is good), then evil is not something which God created but just a term we use to refer to low levels or the absence of good. As St. Thomas explained, all creatures are good in that they have being, but insofar as there is a defect in what they were made to be evil is present as a privation: "No being can be spoken of as evil, formally as being, but only so far as it lacks being. Thus a man is said to be evil, because he lacks some virtue; and an eye is said to be evil, because it lacks the power to see well."[4]

If God did not create evil (since it does not have being), then how did this privation or *lack of what ought to be there* enter the universe? Ironically, through the only creatures with the capacity to love.

Freedom Put to the Test

As we've seen, free-will is a prerequisite of love; and the only two types of creatures which have been given that gift are angels and humans.

---

2   Here we refer to visible light as opposed to invisible light, i.e. infrared or ultraviolet.
3   Wisdom 1:14
4   St. Thomas Aquinas, *SummaTheologica*, I.5.3. ad 2. (Notice how St. Thomas uses an excerpt from both the human person and the physical world to make his argument.)

The free choice to trust God and lay down one's life in His service is an expression of love precisely because it is not involuntary and robotic, but voluntary and heartfelt. Conversely, the free choice *not* to trust God is a turning away from love and service which constitutes "an abuse of the freedom that God gives to created persons so that they are capable of loving him and loving one another."[5]

Angels are spiritual beings created outside the physical universe. They are eternal creatures made at the same "time", if you will, that temporal creatures were made: "from the beginning of time, [God] made simultaneously out of nothing both orders of creatures, the spiritual and the corporeal, that is, the angelic and the earthly."[6]

When God spoke light into being, it revealed how all the angels were created good as pure *spiritual* light: "And God said, 'Let there be light'; and there was light. And God saw that the light was good."[7] At the moment of their creation, however, every angel's freedom was put to the test. They had to choose between reciprocating God's love and trusting Him, or leaving His love unrequited and trusting themselves . . . and because they exist outside of time and space, their decision was eternal.

Fallen Angels

All sin is a lack of trust. Whenever a free and intelligent being turns away from the Light they are claiming to have more knowledge of themselves than the one who created them: in effect saying, "I will decide what is good or evil for me, not you, God." This seems silly and unreasonable at first glance, but the gift of freedom carries with it the burden of being susceptible to the irrational self-assertion known as pride.

Various saints have speculated about how the angels were put to the test. One view is that when God asked if they would trust that He knew what was best for them (even if it meant serving men and women) two responses echoed throughout heaven – one of trust, the other of distrust. The first response was led by an angel who shouted "Micha 'el?" (Who is like God?) and was then named Michael according to his testimony. The second response was led by the angel Lucifer, who growled, "I will be my own God! I will not trust! I will not serve!" In Genesis, the phrase

---

5   *Catechism of the Catholic Church*, #387
6   *Fourth Lateran Council*, IV (1215 A.D.), cf. CCC #327.
7   Genesis 1:3-4a

which follows God's acknowledgment of light being good reads, "And God separated the light from the darkness."[8] This indicates that those who would not trust had become darkness by permanently extinguishing the spiritual light they were created to be:

> . . . once we understand the creation of the first light to refer to the creation of the angels, then we should take the distinction between the good and bad angels as the meaning for the words: 'God separated the light from the darkness' (Genesis 1:4).[9]

Those angels who turned away from the light could not remain in heaven because "God is light and in him there is no darkness at all."[10] By rejecting God and His light, the bad angels freely became dark spirits who were no longer spiritual light, but the absence of that light: "The devil and the other demons were indeed created naturally good by God, but they became evil by their own doing."[11]

Spiritual light and darkness (i.e. *spiritual* day and night) are angelic realms we must distinguish as good and evil respectively; but temporal light and darkness (i.e. *temporal* day and night) are realms which God made on earth and are therefore good. Genesis makes this distinction when God created the sun, moon, and stars on day four "to rule over the day and over the night, and to separate the light from the darkness". His pleasure with the realms of *temporal* light and darkness is confirmed by the phrase, "And God saw that it was good."[12] Notice also that of the six days of creation, only the first day does not conclude with the refrain, "And God saw that it was good." This is so there would be no confusion that spiritual darkness was not something He created, but became separated from spiritual light by an absence of trust . . . . . . and by a declaration of war on those who did trust:

---

8   Genesis 1:4b
9   St. Augustine, *City of God*, XI.19. (cf. St. Thomas Aquinas, *Summa Theologica.* I.67.4.4. "we must understand the production of light to signify the formation of spiritual creatures")
10   1 John 1:5.
11   *Fourth Lateran Council*, I. (1215 A.D.) cf. CCC #391
12   Genesis 1:18

And war broke out in heaven; Michael and his angels fought against the dragon. The dragon and his angels fought back, but they were defeated, and there was no longer any place for them in heaven. The great dragon was thrown down, that ancient serpent, who is called the Devil and Satan, the deceiver of the whole world – he was thrown down to the earth, and his angels were thrown down with him.[13]

The Tree of Trust

When God commanded Adam and Eve not to eat from the tree of the knowledge of good and evil, it was a test similar to the one given the angels. The ancient serpent had chosen once and for all to be his own god, deciding for himself what he thought was good and what he thought was evil. Once he and his army of demons had been cast out of heaven, their main objective became to tempt man and woman with that same allurement of self-determination: "you will be like God, knowing good and evil."[14]

The tree of the knowledge of good and evil could also be called the tree of "naming" good and evil; just as Adam's "naming" of creatures was "knowledge" of creatures. Adam and Eve could choose either to trust in God, or to trust in themselves apart from God in order to name things good or evil as they saw fit. We are faced with the same decision. Respecting the forbidden fruit represents our willingness to acknowledge that our Creator knows what is objectively good and objectively evil for us:

> The tree of the knowledge of good and evil symbolically evokes the insurmountable limits that man, being a creature, must freely recognize and respect with trust. Man is dependent on his creator and subject to the laws of creation [laws of nature] and to the moral norms that govern the use of his freedom [natural law].[15]

---

13   Revelation 12:7-9
14   Genesis 3:5
15   *Catechism of the Catholic Church*, #396.

But why, then, are so many contradictory actions and beliefs professed to be sincere acts of trust in God? Why do so many become confused about what is good and what is evil? And why do some believe that there are no objective moral norms to begin with? Quite simply, because the Devil is a masterful liar.

Lucifer, "The Light Bearer"

The nature of a persuasive lie is believability. When the devil and other demons seek to deceive us, it is not with pitchfork in hand or by any other means of intimidation, but by appearing to be good angels who are trying to enlighten us: "Even Satan disguises himself as an angel of light. So it is not strange if his ministers also disguise themselves as ministers of righteousness."[16]

We are often deceived as to what is truly light versus what only appears to be light. The enemy presents things to us that are true, or good, or beautiful, and then distorts them. One way he does this is by promoting good things like food and sleep to the point they become bad things like gluttony and laziness. The Devil can turn almost anything into too much of a good thing . . . even prayer.

When I was an undergrad, there was a movement among the student body to become whole-heartedly devoted to Jesus through Mary. We had been inspired by Pope John Paul II's papal motto *Totus Tuus* and by his repeated admonitions to recite 5 decades of the rosary daily.[17] We were further encouraged by perhaps the finest Mariology professor in the English-speaking world. Time after time, however, I would see a student embrace the call to pray the rosary and then give it up because they had not matured enough to balance the rigors of intellectual formation with those of spiritual formation. The Devil's tactics followed a pattern. First, encourage the over-zealous student to pray the rosary. Second, draw there attention to the fact that John Paul II prayed all 20 decades everyday even though he had one of the busiest schedules of any man on earth. Third, suggest to them that if they really loved Jesus and Mary then they would also pray all 20 decades (after all, how could they say they were busier than the pope?). And finally, when the young soul

---

16   2 Corinthians11:14-15
17   "Totally Yours": the art of living which John Paul II learned from St Louis Maire de Montfort's book, *True Devotion to Mary*.

became despondent after biting off more than he or she could chew, the devil would whisper words of confusion:

> It is a mark of the evil spirit to take on the appearance of an angel of light. He begins by whispering thoughts that are suited to a devout soul and ends by suggesting his own. For example, he will suggest holy and pious thoughts that are wholly in conformity with the sanctity of the soul. Afterwards, he will endeavor little by little to end by drawing the soul into his hidden snares and evil designs.[18]

Furthermore, Satan will often begin by affirming that freedom or love is good, but then redefine those objective realities according to his own plan, which, of course, rejects God's plan of true freedom and true love.

True freedom is the ability to do what is objectively good for oneself and others, whereas what Satan proposes is the false freedom of doing whatever you want, whenever you want. This is the very definition of license. When JPII visited American youth in St. Louis, he made this critical distinction:

> True freedom is a wonderful gift from God, and it has been a cherished part of your country's history. But when freedom is separated from truth, individuals lose their moral direction and the very fabric of society begins to unravel. Freedom is not the ability to do anything we want, whenever we want. Rather, freedom is the ability to live responsibly the truth of our relationship with God and with one another. Remember what Jesus said: "you will know the truth and the truth will set you free." [19]

It is fitting that these words were spoken in St. Louis, Missouri, because historically it was the point of departure for all who pursued happiness on the frontier. Seven hundred miles to the west, the high

---

18 St. Ignatius of Loyola, *Spiritual Exercises, "Rules for Discernment of Spirits"*, II. 4.
19 Pope John Paul II, *Message to Young People in St. Louis, Missouri,* January 26, 1999.

plains of Colorado run right up against 20,000 square miles of brutally rugged mountains. From an eastern vantage, the Front Range of the Rockies looks like an impenetrable wall, making it is easy to see why wagon trains went north along the Oregon Trail or south along the Santa Fe Trail. The whole point is that no pioneers ever left St. Louis thinking they were less free or slaves just because they had a guide. Certainly they were "free" to go in any direction they desired, but without following a trail that avoided gorges, deserts, and marshes, they would not safely arrive at their destination. Rather, safe arrival meant staying on a trail that had a correct bearing, and had food and water along the way.

Even today, a traveler from the east who is driving their car to California is not less free just because he stays on roads that head west and obeys the rules. One who drives too fast around sharp curves or on icy roads is not free to arrive safely at their destination. If such a person crashed and happen to survive but then said, "Well at least I was being free", it would only show that they are confused about freedom. Free-will is the ability to choose, freedom is the ability to choose what is good and true, and leads to fulfillment.

Perhaps the most tragic example of free-will gone wrong is the so-called "free love" movement of the late sixties. What that generation was pursuing was peace, love, and of course, freedom. But since these things were pursued in a way which did not trust God's law, they led instead to conflict, hatred, and ironically, the slavery of sex and drugs, "for people are slaves to whatever masters them"[20]. Let us be clear, however, that sex is good, in fact, a great good; but only when it is between a man and a woman who have become one in marriage and are open to life. Drugs also are good, but only when they are used to heal or relieve pain, not to escape from reality or idolize pleasure. The Apostle Paul makes this distinction when he repeatedly condemns drunkenness, which is the *abuse* of the drug alcohol, but recommends that his friend Timothy *use* it properly: "have a little wine for the sake of your stomach and your frequent illnesses."[21]

We are frequently deceived by something that is light in itself, but is offered to us in a way which renders it only an apparent light, a charade or simulation of light. Those who enter that false light "by choosing

---

20   2 Peter 2:19
21   1 Timothy 5:23

the evil of sin which presents itself under the appearances of good"[22] and then refuse to return to the true light, falsely claim to have been enlightened by darkness:

> Woe to those who call evil good, and good evil, who change darkness into light and light into darkness. . . as dry grass shrivels in the flame, even so their root shall become rotten and their blossom scatter like dust. For they have spurned the law of the Lord.[23]

The "law of the Lord" is meant to set us free from the confusion of deciding for ourselves what is right and wrong. Instead of imposing on our freedom, obedience to the law of the Lord actually prevents us from stumbling into the darkness of slavery. It is the "law of freedom".[24] For example, the law of the Lord warns us that if we refuse to forgive and cling to hatred, bitterness will slowly poison our lives and become our dark master. As St. John teaches, "Whoever says, 'I am in the light' while hating a brother or sister, is still in the darkness."[25] The law of freedom also teaches us to distinguish true love from false love.

True love is to will the *true* good of another; to desire what is objectively good for the beloved, not just apparently good.[26] If we do not bring what is truly good into another's life, we have not truly loved them. We may desire to love them, but if what is offered is not objectively good then it is not true love, just the intention to love. Consider the example of letting one's 14 year-old daughter go out alone on a date. The intention of the parent may be to love her and help her feel loved, but this situation is such a grave occasion of sin that what she may experience is only the pseudo-love of her boyfriend, and the pseudo-love of her parent for not willing her objective good. Consider also the example of a woman who advises her friend to get an abortion so she can maintain a certain lifestyle or be free from the child's father. The woman has desired to bring good into her friend's life, but in reality

---

22   Pope John Paul II, *Homily in Gdansk, Poland*; June 5, 1999.
23   Isaiah 5:20,24
24   James 1:25
25   1 John 2:9
26   This applies equally to *storge* (love between parents, children, and extended family), *philia* (love between friends), *eros* (romantic love), or *agape* (self-sacrificing love)

has brought evil. Her friend will be traumatized by killing her own child, and no matter how insignificant it seems at the time, she will eventually suffer great spiritual disorder.[27] The desire to *truly* love another is why it is so important to know the objective truth about who God is and what God wants. We'll discuss how this truth can be known with certainty in the following section on the moon, but for now it is enough to see that His laws are meant to lead us toward true light, true love, and true happiness.

* * *

When someone objects to God having allowed evil to enter the world, perhaps it would be constructive to respond, "How would *you* have done it? Paint me a picture of how you would make a creature who was free to love without being free to hate or disobey?

The issues surrounding the existence of evil arise from our thinking that we understand more about God than we do. If we are not attentive to His transcendence and our creaturely limitations, then we will more than likely not be humble enough to trust. God did not create the evils of death, suffering, and disorder; rather, "everything created by God is good".[28] But within the sanctuary of the human heart, where we should have been inspired to create gifts of trust and light, we were duped into darkness under the illusion of light:

> Man, tempted by the devil, let his trust in his Creator die in his heart and, abusing his freedom, disobeyed God's command. This is what man's first sin consisted of. All subsequent sin would be disobedience toward God and lack of trust in his goodness.[29]

The Devil's whole purpose in tempting us is to confuse, distract, distort – anything to dissuade us from God's law and persuade us that it is good to be our own god: "When he lies, he speaks according to his own nature, for he is a liar and the father of lies."[30] Trust is always a step

---

27 Thirty-five years of legalized abortion in America has demonstrated the inescapable spiritual consequences of murdering one's own child.
28 1 Timothy 4:4
29 *Catechism of the Catholic Church*, #397
30 John 8:44

toward fruitfulness and freedom; sin always a step toward sterility and slavery. Sin is a dimming of the light, and human beings usher darkness into the world by accepting less than the fullness of light that God offers.

The trust of Jesus, however, reversed the distrust of Adam. Jesus remained equal to the Father and the Holy Spirit, retaining His *divine nature* as the second person of the Trinity while He assumed a *human nature* and became man. In His humanity, then, He refused the false light of deciding what is good and evil apart from God, for He "did not regard equality with God something to be grasped at."[31] Jesus restored the light and healed us, but the scars of original sin remain. We have indeed been armed with the hope of eternal life, but must still contend with the inner conflict of our fallen human nature during this life: "Man therefore is divided in himself. As a result, the whole life of men, both individual and social, shows itself to be a struggle, and a dramatic one, between good and evil, between light and darkness."[32]

"Man's life on earth is warfare."[33]

---

31   Philippians 2:6
32   Vatican II, *Gaudium et Spes (Joy and Hope)*, #13.
33   Job 7:1

CHAPTER 13

The Sun, Moon, and Stars

With some creatures, like the garden slug, the spiritual sense is difficult to read; but to see the spiritual sense of light we need to look no further than scripture. *Allegorically* Jesus said, "I am the light of the world. Whoever follows me will not walk in darkness but will have the light of life."[34] *Morally* Jesus said, "You are the light of the world . . . let your light shine before others so that they may see your good works and give glory to your Father in heaven."[35] And *anagogically* John said, heaven "has no need of sun or moon to shine on it, for the glory of God is its light."[36] Indeed, since God *is* light, it should come as no surprise that the creatures which give us light are rich in theological meaning.

The Sun

When Copernicus speculated that the earth revolved around the sun, it was seen as a threat to the consciences of Catholics because it was opposed to the worldview of the earth being at the center of God's plan. But the heliocentric model makes better sense theologically. God does not exist to revolve around man. His existence and power is not dependent upon mankind any more than the sun needs the earth in order to radiate light. On the contrary, the earth needs the sun to be a planet of life.

---

34   John 8:12
35   Matthew 5:14-16; cf. John 3:20-21
36   Revelation 21:23

As we've said, it is an error to think that we know everything about God and it is an error to think that we can know nothing about God. Like the sun, God is both distant and near, both blinding and soothing: "No one can look on the light when it is bright in the skies"[37] ; and conversely, "Light is sweet and it is pleasant for the eyes to see the sun."[38]

Sunlight is indeed sweet and pleasant and warm. For rich and poor, saints and sinners, believers and non-believers, the graces of God are as diffusive and personal as rays from the sun:

> Like the sunshine, which permeates all the atmosphere, spreading over land and sea, and yet is enjoyed by each person as though it were for him alone, so the Spirit pours forth his grace in full measure, sufficient for all, and yet is present as though exclusively to everyone . . . "[39]

God is not a cold, indifferent force. He is a personal God. He is so personal that He sent His only Son to be our personal friend and redeemer.[40]

Like the Son of God, the sun in the sky is our source of life-giving light on earth. So when Jesus took Peter, James, and John on a hike up a high mountain, it was appropriate that as He was transfigured before them "his face shone like the sun".[41] But even though Jesus does not need us in order to be radiantly happy within His Trinitarian family, even though He does not exist in order to orbit our little blue planet, out of love for us He gave us a moon that does.

The Moon

The moon does not have any light of its own but receives all its luminous power from that one light of the world, the sun. Thus, early Christians saw the moon as a symbol of the Catholic Church: "The Church has no other light than Christ's; according to a favorite image of the Church Fathers, the Church is like the moon, all its light reflected

---

37 Job 37:21
38 Ecclesiastes 11:7
39 St. Basil the Great, *Office of Readings*, Seventh Tuesday of Easter.
40 Cf. Luke 12:4 ; John 15:13-15
41 Matthew 17:2

from the sun."[42] As one might expect, the four characteristics or "marks" of the Church (one, holy, catholic, and apostolic) are echoed within that lunar word.

One

The only planet where human beings exist has only one sun and only one moon. The opening scene of the Star Wars trilogy, however, shows two suns setting on the horizon of Luke Skywalker's planet. This is a depiction of creation which is inconsistent with Scripture, a *fictional* science rather than a *faithful* science.[43] If God is omnipotent, omniscient, and omnipresent, how could there be another God? God #2 would have to have some quality or power that God #1 (who was supposed to have everything) didn't have. Either there is only one God or we should change our definition of what "God" means.

Furthermore, other planets have several moons but the Creator has ordained that only one moon reflect the fullness of light upon planet earth. Similarly, there is only one Church with the power to emanate the fullness of light upon us. That is not to say other Christian communities and other religions do not possess various elements of light, but rather that *all* the light God wanted to share with mankind regarding faith and morals has been entrusted to the Catholic Church. In other words, the fullness of truth *subsists* as a unified whole within the Catholic Church, even though many rays of sanctification and truth are found in other faith communities and religions.

Holy

At various times and in various places, the Catholic Church has failed to shine the light of Christ on the nations. Catholic clergy, religious, and laity have been hypocrites, liars, warmongers, adulterers, murderers, slanderers, pedophiles, pimps, sodomites, misers, and gluttons – just to name a few. But none of these shortcomings and crimes invalidates the mission or authority given to the Church by Jesus. The abuse of a God-

---

42   *Catechism of the Catholic Church*, #748 ("Church Fathers" refers to the scholarly saints of the first few centuries of Catholicism.)
43   Science fiction portrays a universe which does not really exist. Likewise, any philosophy which denies first principles also portrays a universe which does not really exist. Much of the philosophy of the last three centuries should be placed in this category of "metaphysical fiction".

given authority does not in any way invalidate the proper use of that authority.

An ancient Latin maxim states that abuse does not remove proper use *(abusus non tollit usum)*. Some argue that Catholicism is not the true Church of Jesus because of mistakes that were made regarding The Crusades, The Inquisition, The Protestant Reformation, or most recently, the American sexual abuse scandal. But if we took that line of reasoning to its logical conclusion, no authority or privilege on earth would be valid. How could anyone consider it reasonable to conclude that motherhood is invalid just because some mothers have abused there children by locking them in a closet or using them as sex slaves? Or that democracy is inherently evil because it can pass laws in support of slavery or the genocide of Native Americans and the unborn? Or that building an orphanage is wrong because someone had embezzled donations?

Like her symbol the moon, the Catholic Church waxes and wanes through history. At times she seems to be overshadowed or even eclipsed by the cares and anxieties of the world. The Church recognizes within herself this tension between being entrusted with the full revelation of God's will and the imperfect administration of His will by some of her members. Alongside the heroic example of her saints and her pure transmission of the Gospel, there exists the scandal of individual and corporate sin. The Catholic Church teaches that she herself is a light shining in the darkness of human weakness and distrust which is "at once holy and always in need of purification".[44]

Prior to the Protestant Reformation, for instance, some Catholics were abusing the privilege of being ordained a bishop by purchasing that apostolic office for financial gain, then not even living within their own diocese to shepherd their sheep. Others were misrepresenting the Church's teaching on indulgences. When Martin Luther protested Catholicism in 1517, it was partially because he mistakenly believed these abuses of individual Catholics invalidated authentic Catholic teaching and practice.

While the Church was waning in Europe, however, it was waxing in the Americas. Six million left the Church in the Old World to join various sects of Protestantism as eight million joined in the New. But here we find yet another example of how important it is to distinguish between abuse and legitimate use. *Abusus non tollit usum!*

---

44 Vatican II, *Lumen Gentium (The Light of the Nations)*, #8.

When I was in high school, we were taught that Cortez and the armies of Spain forced Catholicism upon the inhabitants of Mexico, the Aztecs, and later upon the indigenous peoples of the Southwest. It is true that there were instances of abuse where villages were forced to convert or suffer the consequences, but these were the exception not the norm. Instead, we should see God's intervention into one of the most satanic cultures in history, which, in spite of their agricultural and astronomical insights, thought it good to sacrifice innocent men, women, and children to the Humming Bird Wizard or the sun god. It was at this point of injustice in history that she who had conceived the fullness of light, but was not herself the light, intervened. The Blessed Virgin Mary appeared to St. Juan Diego in 1531 and performed a miracle. In less than twenty years, eight million people were converted and baptized at the hands of Franciscan missionaries because Our Lady of Guadalupe showed them the light of Christ and His Church, not because they were coerced.

Catholic

Catholic literally means universal, and there are few things more universal than the moon – it is a light for the nations. The earth's gravity holds the moon in orbit just as man's grave need of salvation keeps the Church tethered to earth. Conversely, the moon's gravity pulls on the earth just as the Church draws the hearts of men toward God. Even when she waxes and wanes, or doesn't seem to reflect any light whatsoever, the power of the Church presides over the earth, making the tides of salvation continually ebb and flow. Once again, the Catholic Church has no power which she has not received. She exists only to transmit the power of Christ's light.

Apostolic

But how are we to know what is Christ's light as opposed to the deceptive light of Lucifer? Consider the following example from Scripture:

> Be sure of this, that no fornicator or impure person, or one who is greedy, (that is, an idolater), has any inheritance in the kingdom of Christ and of God. Let no one deceive you with empty words, for because of these things the wrath of God comes on those who are

> disobedient. Therefore do not be associated with them.
> For once you were darkness, but now in the Lord you are
> light. Live as children of light – for the fruit of the light
> is found in all that is good and right and true . . .[45]

It is clear that fornication (pre-marital sex) is a turning away from the light, but what precisely makes someone "impure" or an "idolater"? Who is to say? Who has the authority to determine what this scripture passage means? When "inheritance in the kingdom" is at stake, it certainly seems worth making sure one's interpretation is correct.

If we simply think about it for a moment, the common statement "Well that might be true for you but it's not true for me", is ludicrous when applied to faith and morals, because it assumes that God can simultaneously approve and disapprove of a belief or action. As we saw in Part I, the principle of non-contradiction requires that something cannot both be true and not be true at the same time and in the same sense.

Another appealing statement, "Christianity really comes down to love of God and neighbor", also does not sufficiently take into account the principle of non-contradiction. For while it is true that the commandments can be summed up as love of God and neighbor, when we try to determine what that means specifically, we find it not so simple. For example, Catholics believe that Jesus is really present in the Eucharist – body, blood, soul, and divinity – under the appearances of bread and wine. On the other hand, most Protestants do not believe He is really present, but that the bread and wine are merely symbolic. Again, it must be stressed that according to the principle non-contradiction that we all assume, Jesus cannot be both present and not present in the Eucharist. When He spoke the words "my flesh is true food and my blood is true drink"[46], or at the Last Supper, "this is my body . . . this is my blood"[47], He could not also mean "my flesh is *not* true food and my blood is *not* true drink", or "this is *not* my body. . . this is *not* my blood". The difficulty we are confronted with, then, has tremendous implications: Should adoration of the Eucharist be encouraged, since it would be sacrilege not to worship God when He is truly present? Or should this practice

---

45   Ephesians 5:5-11
46   John 6:55
47   Matthew 26:26-27

be condemned, since it would be idolatry to worship mere bread when He is not truly present? Which is the love of God? It can't be both. Along the same lines is the question of abortion. Is it an act of authentic freedom which should be promoted? Or is it an act of murder which should be opposed? Which is the love of neighbor? Again, it can't be both. So the question remains: how do we know who God is and what God wants?

The Sacred Magisterium of the Catholic Church claims to have been given the power to know just that. The term *Magisterium* refers to the light Peter and the Apostles received from Jesus to teach the truth infallibly regarding faith and morals. Accordingly, the twelve moons per year we call months (derived from "moonths"), correspond to the twelve Apostles.

Jesus was very clear about His mission on earth: "For this I was born, and for this I came into the world, to testify to the truth. Everyone who belongs to the truth listens to my voice."[48] He was also very clear about the role of the twelve Apostles in the implementation of that mission: "Whoever listens to you listens to me, and whoever rejects you rejects me".[49] When Jesus changed Simon's name to Peter (which means Rock), He was establishing him as the leader of His Church: "And I tell you, you are Peter [Rock] and upon this rock I will build my Church, and the gates of Hell will not prevail against it. I will give you the keys of the Kingdom of Heaven".[50] He then added, "whatever you bind on earth will be bound in heaven, and whatever you loose on earth will be loosed in heaven."[51] Jesus later used the same words to impart that extraordinary power upon Peter and the other Apostles as a group: "Whatever you bind on earth will be bound in heaven, and whatever you loose on earth will be loosed in heaven."[52] Furthermore, Jesus told the Apostles at the Last Supper that He had many more things to tell them which they would not yet be able to understand, so He made them a promise: "the Holy Spirit, who the Father will send in my name, will teach you everything" and "will guide you into all truth."[53] Then, just

---

48   John 18:37
49   Luke 10:16
50   Matthew 16:18-19a (Note how we say that wood has become petrified when it has "rockified")
51   Matthew 16:19b
52   Matthew 18:18
53   John 14:26; John 16:12-13

before He ascended into heaven, He gave them the great commission to evangelize and teach:

> Go therefore make disciples of all the nations, baptizing them in the name of the Father and of the Son and of the Holy Spirit, and teaching them to obey all that I have commanded you. And remember, I am with you always, until the end of the age.[54]

We could reasonably expect that what Jesus intended by this commissioning would be put into practice over the past two-thousand years. Thus, since the time of Christ, the Church has implemented that the successor of Peter, or the successor of Peter along with the successors of the Apostles, can teach infallibly on matters of faith and morals. Perhaps the following examples, which span the history of Christianity, will help us clarify how important it is to have some God-given authority to determine what scripture means.

After the death and resurrection of Jesus, the Apostles were confronted with whether or not someone was "impure" if they had not been circumcised according to the God's covenant with Abraham, which He later reaffirmed with Moses.[55] After all, teaching that circumcision was necessary for salvation had biblical grounds:

> Every male among you shall be circumcised . . . If a male is uncircumcised, that is, if the flesh of his foreskin has not been cut away, such a one shall be cut off from his people; he has broken my covenant.[56]

The scriptures are clear about the necessity of circumcision for the Israelites of the Old Covenant, but what about Gentiles who had embraced Jesus and the New Covenant? Who could say with certainty whether or not this command applied to them? As one might imagine, not every adult male was thrilled with the prospect if it wasn't absolutely necessary. When opposing views could not be reconciled, Peter had

---

54   Matthew 28:19-20
55   Genesis 17:9-14; Leviticus 12:3
56   Genesis 17:10,14

settled the matter at the first ecumenical council, the Council of Jerusalem:

> After there had been much debate, Peter rose and said to them, "Brethren, you know that in the early days God made a choice among you, that by my mouth the Gentiles should hear the word of the gospel . . . we believe that *we shall be saved through the grace of the Lord Jesus,* just as they will.[57]

Later, many eighth century Christians questioned whether creating statues, paintings, and mosaics constituted "idolatry", again on biblical grounds: "You shall not carve idols for yourselves in the shape of anything in the sky above or on the earth below".[58] When the Second Council of Nicaea convened in 787 A.D., the bishops declared that while Scripture forbid the making of graven images to be worshipped (as the next verse suggests: "you shall not bow down to them or worship them."[59]) it did not forbid images from being venerated as reminders of loved ones and heroes of the faith.

In our own day, even something as explicitly forbidden in the Bible as homosexual sex has been accepted among many Protestant interpreters. The whole point is that if there is not an infallible mechanism to interpret the Bible, it can and will be misinterpreted in any number of ways.

Each time that the Apostolic Church has gathered, it has settled matters which have been called into question by a misinterpretation of scripture. Whenever a teaching becomes distorted, the Holy Spirit prompts the Apostolic Church to exercise its God-given teaching authority to clarify God's will. Since the Council of Jerusalem, there have been twenty-two other councils of bishops, the most recent being Vatican II from 1962-1965.

The vast majority of Protestants believe that Scripture alone is the source of knowing God's will. They are "protesters" of the claim that the Catholic Church has the fullness of truth in faith and morals, and do not believe that the first pope and first bishops were given any special power to know and teach God's will. In short, Jesus did not establish His Church on Peter and the Apostles (and all the subsequent popes and bishops as their successors), but simply guided some of them in writing

---

57   Acts of the Apostles 15:7,11 (emphasis mine)
58   Exodus 20:4
59   Exodus 20:5

the New Testament which now has the fullness of truth. Let us now examine the rational and scriptural validity of this belief.

One of the most common ploys of the Devil is to misinterpret scripture in an effort to mislead us of who God is and what God wants. When Jesus went into the wilderness to pray and fast, Satan tempted Him with quotes from scripture.[60] All Christians agree that "scripture is inspired by God and is useful for teaching"[61], but if Satan has the audacity to tempt Jesus with scripture, that is, to tempt the Word with the Word, why wouldn't we expect the same?

Since the Protestant reformers rejected the Catholic Church's authoritative interpretation of Scripture, more than 30,000 Christian denominations have emerged which contradict each other on many issues yet all claim to interpret Scripture correctly. The problem which presents itself is that if God is truly a good and loving Father, He would provide His children with a way to sift through contradictory interpretations and know His will with certainty. He would not leave us with just the Bible.

For many Christians, the belief that Jesus is the Son of God and that we are specially loved by Him is the truth that the Devil begins with. The belief that Jesus has revealed the true meaning of the Bible to us alone, regardless if any Christian in history would share our view, is the lie. Without a sacred Magisterium to interpret the Bible infallibly, we have no way of knowing for sure what it means. For that matter, we have no way of knowing which early Christian writings were truly written under the inspiration of the Holy Spirit and truly belong in the New Testament.

First century Catholics had written many books about Jesus and His teachings, but only some were co-authored by the Holy Spirit. Consider, for example, the so-called gospels of Peter and Thomas (which were not really written by Peter or Thomas but were nevertheless widely distributed). Who had the authority to determine that they were not inspired and, therefore, did not belong in the New Testament? In the fourth century, the Magisterium of the Catholic Church (under the promised guidance of that same Holy Spirit) infallibly recognized which books were truly inspired, infallibly declared them to be the inerrant

---

60   Cf. Matthew 4:1-11
61   1 Timothy 3:16

Word of God, and infallibly compiled them into what we now know as the New Testament canon.[62]

Furthermore, Scripture itself teaches that not everything Jesus said and did is recorded in Scripture. As St. John states at the end of his Gospel, "there are also many other things that Jesus did; if every one of them were written down, I suppose that the world itself could not contain the books that would be written."[63] Some of these "other things that Jesus did" have been preserved in the Sacred Tradition of the Church. Especially during the forty days between His resurrection from the dead and ascension into heaven, the Apostles were enlightened by the resurrected Jesus as to how to celebrate the Sacraments (especially the mass), and how to interpret scripture. They then handed down what they had learned to their successors. As the Gospel spread, the men who were ordained as new bishops inherited the commission to preach, teach, and sanctify in God's name, according to God's plan. Thus, we see St. Paul exhorting the new church at Thessalonica to "stand firm and hold fast to the traditions that you were taught by us either by word of mouth [Sacred Tradition] or by letter [Sacred Scripture]."[64]

One final point: if scripture alone (not Scripture, Tradition, and the Magisterium) teaches us the truth about who God is and what God wants, why isn't that teaching found in Scripture? Why would St. Paul write instead that the Church is "the pillar and foundation of truth"?[65]

Certainly one can learn many things about Jesus and become devoted to Him by reading Sacred Scripture, but unless it is complemented by Sacred Tradition and the authoritative guidance of the Magisterium, it will inevitably lead to an interpretation which God did not intend. St. Peter warns us to avoid this temptation: "First of all you must understand this, that no prophecy of scripture is a matter of one's own interpretation."[66]

---

62   Infallibility refers to the authority given to the pope, as well as the pope and bishops in communion with him, to be free from error in matters of faith and morals. It must be distinguished from impeccability, which means free from sin, because every pope and bishop has sinned to some degree.

63   John 21:25

64   2 Thessalonians 2:15 (It should be noted that some Protestant translations of this New Testament verse, most notably the popular New International Version (NIV), avoid the correct translation of the Greek word for tradition (*paradosis*) and instead insert the word "teaching", which in Greek would be *didache*, not *paradosis*.

65   1 Timothy 3:15

66   2 Peter 1:20

The Bible was never intended to be a book which could stand alone and provide all the answers.

In addition to Bud Page, I have been blessed with another life-long friend and backcountry brother, Steve Herrmann. He was raised in the Baptist tradition but was always inspired by the Catholic saints. Over the years, he was again and again confronted with the dilemma of contradictory interpretations of the Bible; and one particular scene from the Acts of the Apostles seemed to hound him. As Philip traveled down "a wilderness road", he overheard an Ethiopian man reading from the Scriptures. When Philip approached and asked if the man understood what he was reading, the man humbly replied: "How can I unless someone guides me?"[67] After the passage was explained to him, the man asked Philip to baptize him then and there.

When Herm eventually converted to Catholicism, I had the honor of being his sponsor, and when it came time to select a confirmation name He chose Philip to symbolize his new found humility before the sacred page, and his new found appreciation of Church authority. He had exposed the Deceiver's ploy of first agreeing that we are special to God, then leading us to believe that we have been specially chosen to know what the Bible really means.

Those who believe that Church authority has been abused are correct, but not when it comes to its infallible authority *to protect the faith* (ad tuendam fidem). They would do well to consider the light which that authority has shined on the world. Without the authority of the Catholic Church, there would be no way to establish which books and letters were inspired and truly belonged in the canon of the New Testament and which were not. Without the authority of the Catholic Church, Christians would not have annual celebrations. The Church established the shifting date of Easter to be the first Sunday following the first full moon after the vernal equinox (March 20/21); and the Church established Christmas as a set date near the winter solstice to symbolize the increasing light of each day now that God's Son has dwelt among us. In addition to these feast days which celebrate the highlights in the story of salvation, the Church sets annual feast days to honor her stars – the angels and saints.

---

67   Acts of the Apostles 8:31

The Stars

The Catholic Church has always seen stars as symbols of those who have an appointed place in eternity, of those free and intelligent beings who chose to trust. The angels made one eternal choice in heaven, whereas the saints made many temporal choices on earth, choosing to trust day after day. For both, the wisdom of trusting in God has eternal repercussions, for "the wise shall shine brightly like the splendor of the firmament, and those who lead the many to justice shall be like the stars forever."[68]

Before the invention of the Global Positioning System (GPS), anyone who sailed upon the sea would navigate according to the fixed position of the stars. Likewise, anyone who attempts to set a course for eternal life can use the angels and saints as sure points of reference, because they are joyful servants who stand ready to do God's will: "[T]he stars at their posts shine and rejoice; when He calls them they answer, 'Here we are!' shining with joy for their Maker."[69] On the other hand, anyone who neglects to reference the angels and saints has set a course for eternal death by adopting the slogan of sinful pride: "I will raise my throne above the stars of God . . . I will make myself like the Most High!"[70]

There is also a grave difference between reading the stars as symbols of readiness to do God's will and reading them as signs of predestination. Astrology is a misreading of the stars because it is trespasses into the domain of God, who is the Lord of time and history, and to a certain extent it denies that we are free to create good or evil lives with our choices.

The Rainbow

We've seen how the one source of natural light for the world, the sun, is a symbol of the one source of supernatural light for the world, the Son. What is striking, however, is the correspondence between how natural light and supernatural light are refracted.

During the Protestant reformation, the Church's teaching on the number of sacraments was called into question. Some reformers

---

68   Daniel 12:3; cf. Judges 5:20; Job 38:7
69   Baruch 3:34-35. (Also, in Philippians 2:15 we are called to live as children of God, who "shine like the stars in the sky among a twisted generation.")
70   Isaiah 14:14

believed that Baptism was the only sacrament, others Baptism and the Eucharist, still others that sacraments were irrelevant. To respond to these objections, and to prevent the divine plan from veering off course, the Holy Spirit called upon the successor of Peter, the pope, and the successors of the Apostles, the bishops, to gather at the Council of Trent in 1545. There the Magisterium defined that Jesus had instituted seven sacraments to impart His light: Baptism, Penance, Eucharist, Confirmation, Matrimony, Holy Orders, and Anointing of the Sick. Over a century later, Sir Isaac Newton reaffirmed that teaching with a scientific discovery. In 1666 he found that the light of the sun is refracted into the seven colors of the rainbow: red, orange, yellow, green, blue, indigo, and violet. This is a prime example of how the discoveries of science will always vindicate and complement the truths of the Catholic faith. We have learned so much about creation scientifically since the early Church Fathers, we should be able to perceive more provided we first have "eyes to see, or ears to hear."[71] Every authentic scientific discovery should lead us to greater theological insights, but also to greater humility before the mysteries of creation; for no matter how advanced modern science may seem, many discoveries "greater than these lie hidden and we have seen but few of his works."[72]

During the first summer of writing this book, I was buying supplies in a general store in West Yellowstone, Montana, when I noticed two nuns in sky blue habits. They were Marian Sisters who had driven a bus from Spokane with eleven other sisters. We all spoke for a time about God and beauty and their new CD – and Sister Therese and I had an all too brief conversation about rainbows. Like any encounter with holiness, I left the sisters renewed and more open to the sacred. In retrospect, they had prepared a place in my heart for what I was about to be shown.

About an hour later I arrived back at camp and immediately noticed that two large geysers were beginning to fume. The closer of the two, Castle geyser, was only a quarter mile away. I knew that its eruptions lasted up to an hour, so I tried to approach without the anxiety that I was going to miss something. After I had settled in, the steam began to swirl furiously as it exited the vent, causing a few children to cry out, "It looks like a tornado!" Without further warning, the boiling subterranean water gushed and pulsated 50 feet high, forming a small cloud, which

71   Deuteronomy 29:4
72   Sirach 43:32

began to drift gently north just as the sun was setting. The large drops of thermal water beat a rhythm upon the earth, while a fine mist from the cooling steam fell from the cloud. What only seconds ago was a scalding hydrant had been transformed in the high mountain air into a refreshing shower. Then, as if on cue, a poignant theophany of the seven sacraments appeared. A rainbow slowly emerged from the vent, went up into the cloud, and continued to arc, passing only a few feet in front of me before completing the circle where it began at the fountain head. At first I was incredulous, and like a child I physically tried to step into the rainbow's circle – naturally, it eluded me. When I spiritually tried to step in, however, I was supernaturally embraced. Thanking God for the sacraments seemed involuntary at that moment, and when I returned to an awareness of my surroundings I noticed that a man had joined me on the path. He was standing before the cloud not 30 feet away, and with eyes closed had lifted his face to greet the geyser rain. In what bordered on hallucination, the circular rainbow seemed to pass right through his heart. It entered his left shoulder and exited above his right hip, and yet was unbroken. I then began to ponder how the water of baptism restores grace to the soul, initiating us into God's family so that we might receive his other sacramental gifts. So just as the seven colors of the rainbow are introduced by light shining through vaporous water borne on the wind, the seven sacraments of the Church are introduced by Light shining through baptismal water, in which we are born in the Spirit.

* * *

The earth has one radiant source, the Son of God, who imparts that radiance to His one, holy, catholic, and apostolic Church. The Church exercises a celestial gravitation on the human heart, separating light from darkness, true good from apparent good, under the guidance of a twelve-fold authority which is assisted by those angels and saints who shine from the highest heavens. And just as the sun's natural light is refracted into seven colors, the Son's supernatural light is refracted into seven sacraments, which the Church then communicates to the nations, fulfilling the spiritual needs of God's covenant family.

129

CHAPTER 14

The Sea

Since seventy percent of our planet is covered by water, it's clear that it plays a major part in the story of creation and salvation. When God decided to institute the sacrament of Baptism, for example, it is not as though He then looked around for something that was a symbol of purity, cleansing, and restoration; rather, from the beginning He created water with this spiritual sense in mind. It is also no accident that when one is being baptized, either by pouring of water or immersion, this sign of how God is both one and three coincides with the Trinitarian formula, "I baptize you in the name of the Father, and of the Son, and of the Holy Spirit."

Adults are typically baptized into the Catholic Church at mass the night before Easter. Because we celebrate all three sacraments of initiation (baptism, confirmation, and first communion) at the Easter vigil mass, it holds pride of place in the realm of liturgy (like Cheyenne Frontier Days is "The Daddy of 'em All" in the world of rodeo). And just before the *Rite of Baptism*, there is a prayer to bless the water which is worth quoting at length, for it unfolds the meaning of water in God's plan:

> Father, you give us grace though sacramental signs, which tell us of the wonders of your unseen power.
>
> In baptism we use your gift of water, which you have made a rich symbol of the grace you give us in this sacrament.

At the very dawn of creation your Spirit breathed on the waters, making them the wellspring of all holiness.

The waters of the great flood you made a sign of the waters of baptism that make an end of sin and a new beginning of goodness.

Through the waters of the Red Sea you led Israel out of slavery to be an image of God's holy people, set free from sin by baptism.

In the waters of the Jordan your Son was baptized by John and anointed with the Spirit.

Your Son willed that water and blood should flow from his side as he hung upon the cross.

After his resurrection he told his disciples: "Go out and teach all nations, baptizing them in the name of the Father, and of the Son, and of the Holy Spirit."

Father, look now with love upon your Church and unseal for it the fountain of baptism.

By the power of the Holy Spirit give to this water the grace of your Son, so that in the sacrament of baptism all those whom you have created in your likeness may be cleansed from sin and rise to a new birth of innocence by water and the Holy Spirit.[73]

We now that our bodies can be cleansed with water and need it to survive, but how do we know it can cleanse our souls and give us "a new birth of innocence"? The answer to that question is inseparable from the question of who Jesus of Nazareth was and is.

Who is Jesus?

The identity of Jesus can be linked to His relationship with the sea. In the Old Testament, only God had power over the sea so when the Apostles feared that their boat might sink on the Sea of Galilee and Jesus calmed the storm, they asked each other: "What sort of man is this, that even the winds and the sea obey him?"[74] That's the real question: what sort of man is Jesus? Is He a man who is also God, infusing sanctifying grace into the water and words of baptism, or is He just a man?

---

73 Easter Vigil Mass, *Celebration of Baptism: "Blessing of the Water"*.
74 Matthew 8:27 (Cf. Job 26:12; Psalm 89:9; 107:29)

I turned 44 years old in the summer of 2008 and my annual retreat was to a place in Yellowstone called Heart Lake. Roughly the size of the Sea of Galilee, it is the largest backcountry lake in the lower 48. I was working on two portions of this book at the time (sea and sky) so I brought rough drafts to reflect on. I offered up the nine-mile hike for all who suffer from addictions by not stopping or drinking water, and periodically repeating the prayer taught to the children at Fatima: "Jesus, this sacrifice is for love of you, for the conversion of poor sinners, and in reparation for the sins committed against the Immaculate Heart of Mary." When I arrived at camp, I leveled a spot on a small beach near Beaver creek inlet and set my tent. The view of Mt. Sheridan was astounding, and the lake teemed with life: cormorants, grebes, pelicans, and mergansers were all happily fishing. As I unpacked my gear and hung my food, I noticed some thunderclouds developing across the lake, but something about them didn't seem right – unusual shades of gray and green. The Lord then raised His voice from the clouds, and I began to count the seconds between flashes of lightning and audible thunder to measure their progress. Then the birds left. I secured the tent, and situated myself so that I could kneel down and peer through a small opening below the tent awning. The squall came straight at me. It was no more than a mile wide, not even spanning the width of the lake, but when the storm front hit it lifted me and the tent, ripping the stakes from the ground. I didn't want a ride in a tent-kite, so I laid down to brace the floor and called on the name of the Lord: "Jesus. Mercy. Jesus, you are everything." Again I was lifted. I sat up and bent down the pole which supported the awning so that the wind could not generate as much lift. Just then hail began to froth the surface of the lake, and as I watched storm the rush forward, I imagined the twelve Apostles fearing for their lives on the Sea of Galilee:

> A windstorm arose on the sea, so great that the boat was being swamped by the waves; but he [Jesus] was asleep. And they went and woke him up, saying, "Lord, save us! We are perishing!" And he said to them "Why are you afraid, you of little faith?" Then he got up and rebuked the winds and the sea; and there was a dead calm.[75]

---

75 Matthew 8:24-26

Truly, if a man had calmed Heart Lake that day, I would worship him as God. It was all over in less than ten minutes. Exhausted, I collapsed on my sleeping pad and opened my bible. My eyes fell on Psalm 50: "Our God comes and does not keep silence, before him is a devouring fire, and a mighty tempest all around him."[76] I drifted off to sleep and was awakened at first light by the warning slap of a beaver's tail in its pond, the splash of a startled grizzly charging through the creek, and the mourning prayer of a loon.

Frequently, Jesus is called a great prophet, or teacher, or moral leader, but this presents a problem – He claimed to be God: "The Father and I are one."[77] We are then confronted with three options: (1) He was lying and knew it, and therefore was not a morally good person; (2) He was lying and did not know it, and therefore was delusional; or (3) He was telling the truth. What is important to see here is that if one denies Jesus was the God-man, the alternatives are He was a con-man or a crazy-man. As C.S. Lewis put it, we must decide if He is a liar, lunatic, or Lord, "but let us not come with any patronizing nonsense about His being a great human teacher. He has not left that open to us. He did not intend to."[78]

Perhaps it is easier to frame the question by imagining oneself in the boat with the Apostles, not only during the storm but later, when they were again on the sea and Jesus was on the shore. We either believe that Jesus has power over the sea and can walk on water or we don't. It's that simple. If we do believe, we can join our voice with those in the boat, a symbol of the Church: "And those in the boat worshiped Him, saying, "Truly you are the Son of God."[79]

Waves

When I was a boy, I often fished for eels in the tide-pools near my dad's house on The Big Island: where all winter long the cliffs are pummeled by ground shaking waves. These big waves demand respect, so Dad gradually introduced me to places where I could get in and out of the water safely. When I was a teenager, I began to explore the coastline

---

76   Psalms 50:3
77   John 10:30
78   C.S. Lewis, *Mere Christianity*, II. 3.
79   Matthew 14:33

on my own and found a naturally formed seat in the rock at the mouth of a sea cave. As the sea surged the cave became choked with water, causing it to cough a fine mist, which, since the sun was right, acted as a temporary screen for God to project a small rainbow. The next swell would draw the water out in a deafening cascade only to swallow it up and choke the cave again. Between big sets, the water fizzled to a calm, exposing all the coral and reef fish of the little cove. And my soul was drawn to contemplation. Over the years, this phenomenon has proved a compelling witness to anyone who sits there and settles; so at some point I began to call it *the sacred space.* I still do.

On many shores of the Hawaiian Islands, the voice of the Lord can be heard thundering through big waves.[80] Our littleness before such authority (which by design fades into summer), as well as our littleness before such expanse, should prompt a humble thought: "His is the plan that calms the deep and plants the islands in the sea."[81]

On any shore, however, the immensity of the sea captivates us – then invites us to be still. When St. Therese of Lisieux visited the ocean as little girl, she experienced this pattern of becoming awestruck, then contemplative:

> Never will I forget the impression the sea made upon me; I couldn't take my eyes off it since its majesty, the roaring of its waves, everything spoke to my soul of God's grandeur and power. . . In the evening, at that moment when the sun seems to bathe itself in the immensity of the waves, leaving a luminous trail behind, I went and sat down. . . . I contemplated this luminous trail for a long time. It was to me the image of God's grace shedding its light . . . [and] I made the resolution never to wander far away from the glance of Jesus in order to travel peacefully toward the eternal shore.[82]

Note how His power had opened her heart to the transcendent, allowing her to settle and become more receptive to His word.

---

80 Cf. Psalm 93:3; 96:11; 98:7
81 Sirach 43:23
82 St. Therese of Lisieux, *Story of a Soul,* 48.

Rain

For a man of the 8th century B.C., the prophet Amos had remarkable insight into weather systems as God "calls for the waters of the sea, and pours them out on the surface of the earth."[83] God draws waters from the ocean and carries them on the wind to their appointed destination, just as He draws graces from the unfathomable "treasury of the Church" and carries them in the Spirit to the hearts of the faithful.[84] Though not always as we will, but as He wills:

> Water comes down from heaven . . . and although it is always the same in itself, it produces many different effects, one in the palm tree, another in the vine, and so on throughout the whole of creation. . . . In the same way the Holy Spirit, whose nature is always the same, simple and indivisible, apportions grace to each man as he wills.[85]

As St. Paul explains, not everyone has been given the gift of teaching, or leading, or counseling, or healing, but each person is watered with grace according to the plan of God: "there are varieties of gifts, but the same Spirit."[86] Like the waters that fall from the sky, the gifts of grace come in a variety of forms so that we may serve Him in a variety of ways.

Answers to prayer also come in various ways. If what we pray for is good for us, He might give us what we want directly or delay the gift until the proper season; if what we pray for is not good for us, He will give us a better gift than the one we asked for, either right away or later. A person who prays for things which would not be good for them is like a man dying of thirst who prays for sand instead of water, or a child who begs not to be given a shot of penicillin when they have an infection. A good parent does what is best, and Jesus invites us to gain this perspective when we pray: "If you then, who are wicked, know to give good gifts to your children, how much more will the Father in heaven give the Holy Spirit to those who ask him?"[87]

---

83   Amos 5:8
84   The *treasury of the church* is the sum of all graces, that is, the merits of Jesus on the cross, as well as those of Mary and the Saints.
85   St. Cyril of Jerusalem, *Office of Readings,* Seventh Monday of Easter.
86   1 Corinthians 12:4
87   Luke 11:13

God responds to our prayers by pouring out the Holy Spirit for our good. No matter how confusing the answer, it is best to realize that God knows how to best quench our thirst. Surrender to divine providence is accomplished by receiving His water as a gift, just as the earth does. One of our favorite backcountry antiphons to rain addresses this posture of trust: "From your dwelling you water the hills; earth drinks its fill of your gift."[88]

But what about those times of apparent silence when it seems that no one is listening?

Snow and Ice

When God seems to delay giving an answer to prayer or does not dispel the confusion, it is crucial that we persevere with patience and trust. He has answered, but often our hearts are not ready to be watered and some time must go by for us to see the big picture. Waters which have already been sent from heaven, yet are suspended in the form of snow and ice, can give us a fresh outlook on God's apparent silence, especially when we seem to undergo meaningless suffering. Consider the following examples from the high country.

In central Wyoming, along the northern slope of the Wind River Range, the water content of glaciers and snow fields is released by sun and wind. The lengthening days and warm Chinook breezes symbolize the release of graces after a winter of darkness and trial, the answers to prayers made known in due season by Son and Spirit: "The Lord sends a command to earth, his word runs swiftly. Thus snow is spread. . . . Again he sends his word and they melt; the wind is unleashed and the waters flow."[89]

In central Colorado, there is a peak with a glacier in the shape of a cross. The first known artistic rendering of the Mount of the Holy Cross was in 1875 by Thomas Moran.[90] A few years ago, my cousin's wife was hiking up to the top of this peak with a friend when she became ill just below the summit. She decided to rest by the trail while her friend went on to the summit and then returned to meet her on the way back down. No trace of her was ever found. She and my cousin Ben had

---

88   Psalm 104:13
89   Psalm 17:16,18
90   Moran is the same artist whose pastels had given Congress a visual account of why preserving Yellowstone in 1872 was a good idea.

four children ranging in age from 2-15 years old. And while it is at first an unbearable thought that a good and loving Father would allow such a thing to happen, this glacier in the shape of a cross is a sign of God's unwavering trustworthiness and a call to faith:

> The fact that God permits physical and even moral evil is a mystery that God illuminates by his Son Jesus Christ who died and rose to vanquish evil. Faith gives us the certainty that God would not permit an evil if he did not cause a good to come from that very evil, by ways we shall fully know only in eternal life.[91]

With the eyes of faith, we gain the confidence that His will is always best for us, even if that means allowing physical and moral evil to affect our lives. Sometimes the graces of God are reserved on peaks; other times they are imperceptible, watering our roots from below like aquifers. Graces are not always sent according to our timetable or in a way that we can readily perceive . . . but He always sends them:

> For just as from the heavens the rain and the snow come down and do not return there until they have watered the earth, making it fertile and fruitful, giving seed to him who sows and bread to him who eats, so shall my word be that goes out from my mouth; it shall not return to me empty, but it shall accomplish my will, achieving the end for which I sent it.[92]

Conversely, *without the eyes of faith*, we are prone to rely too much on our own perspective, on our limited view of how God should do things. I have often fallen into this error myself; but consider how arrogant it is to think that we would be better at being God than He is. Such thoughts are undercurrents of the age-old temptation to be our own lord and king. To align our own will to His, confident that he will never give us more than we are able to bear, that is the challenge.[93]

---

91   *Catechism of the Catholic Church*, #324
92   Isaiah 55:10-11
93   1 Corinthians 10:13

The Great River

As the longest free flowing river in the lower 48, the Yellowstone is truly a "great river", but another river of the West already bears that name. From the skies above New Mexico, the *Rio Grande* (Great River) resembles the Jordan River in Israel. Flanked by arid arroyos, canyons, and mesas, the wooded river bottom cuts through the middle of the state like a long green vein, and eventually spills into the Gulf of California where its waters are gathered up and placed back up in the mountains. This cycle of the Great River's life-giving waters is similar to the cycle of God's grace.

Since St. John was the only apostle standing at the foot of the cross to witness blood and water flowing from Jesus' side, it is fitting that he is the only gospel writer to record Jesus citing a prophecy from Isaiah which referred to Him. This prophecy compares His Most Sacred Heart – the source and summit of all graces – to a river of life: "Out of his heart shall flow rivers of living water."[94] Analogously, the headwaters of the *Rio Grande* flow from alpine summits in the St. John and Blood of Christ mountains. These graces from the Heart of Christ flow down to water the trees in the valley below, answering their prayers and becoming gifts that go out "from the Great River to the ends of the earth", by way of the sea.[95]

---

94   John 7:38
95   Psalm 72:8; (The *San Juan* and *Sangre de Cristo* mountain ranges are the two sources of the *Rio Grande*.)

CHAPTER 15

Fish

We can read God's grace not only from the waters of the Sea, but also from what is contained in those waters. In a variety of fonts, the fish of the earth's rivers, lakes, and oceans signify gift. Some are pleasing to look at, like the spectacular little jewels we call reef fish (the Moorish idol and yellowtail coris are my favorites); some are pleasing to look at and good to eat, like *ono*; and some are pleasing to look at, good to eat, and fun to catch, like *ahi* (yellow-fin tuna) and rainbow trout. In each instance, fish speak of God's gratuitous disposition toward us, for they are gifts freely given.

Salmon

Annual salmon migrations suggest self donation, the determination to lay down one's life so that others may live, but they also suggest God's faithfulness for all who rely on them for sustenance. Those who complain that God doesn't answer or doesn't seem to care are frequently the same people who make little effort to learn His language and discover His will. In a word, they do not put themselves in a position to get a response.

At Katmai National Park in southwest Alaska, grizzlies gather at Brooks Falls as salmon head upstream to spawn. Because the falls span the breadth of the river, bears position themselves along the brink to catch the leaping fish. What is striking is the patience and confidence the bears seem to have as they wait. Eventually, a salmon will jump within reach. The gift is then received with jaws and unwrapped with claws. The point is, the bears actively put themselves in a position to receive the gift. They weren't asleep under a tree expecting God to grant them a fish, but made an effort to seek the occasion of gift (albeit by instinct alone). In an animal sense, they petitioned God and trusted Him to respond.

If God so faithfully answers the prayers of bears, how much more diligently should His sons and daughters seek the occasion to be answered:

> Ask and it will be given to you; seek and you will find; knock and the door will be opened to you. For everyone who asks, receives; and whoever seeks, finds; and the one who knocks, the door will be opened. Which one of you would hand his son a stone when he asks for a loaf of bread, or a snake when he asks for a fish?[96]

Fish so clearly signify gift that Jesus uses them as an analogue to answered prayers.

Admittedly, asking God for something is easy compared to being in a situation to receive His answer, but prayer entails both asking for fish and receiving them, both knocking on doors and opening doors.

Jesus tells us that He stands at the door and knocks, yet if we simply yell "Come in!" without ever getting out of bed or off the couch to unlock the door, He will not enter: "Behold, I stand at the door and knock. If anyone hears my voice and *opens the door*, then I will enter his house and dine with him".[97] The grace we seek in prayer is a free gift that we must willingly open the door of our hearts to receive. Opening doors and going fishing signify how we do our part, that is, how we become actively receptive.

Trout

Anyone who is serious about knowing God's will, should create circumstances in which to catch a response. My brother Scott is one of the great fly-fishermen of the northern Colorado Rockies. He is not the kind that ties his own flies or is outfitted with the latest gear (we both still use the fishing vests we received in middle school), but his uncanny ability to catch lunker trout has earned him the nickname, "The Fishin' Magician". As we were growing up, he had learned the simple truth

---

96   Matthew 7:7-11
97   Revelation 3:20 (emphasis mine)

that you can't catch a fish without your line in the water. Just as the indispensable condition for catching fish is to learn to fish then go fishing, the indispensable condition for catching a response from God is to learn to pray then go praying.

Prayer requires casting into a somewhat hidden realm where we can't always see what's going on below the surface. Like fish, answers to prayer are gifts that can strike at any moment. We must persevere like the woman in the parable, who kept knocking and was eventually answered by the judge; or like the Apostles, who obeyed Jesus' command even though they had caught nothing all night: "Put out into the deep and let down your nets for a catch."[98]

In addition to being persistent in casting, becoming a good fisherman includes learning how to read the water to locate where the fish live. Casting into class 5 rapids will rarely yield a trout. Thus, the second indispensable condition for catching a response from God is to learn to read then go reading. As St. Isidore teaches in his *Book of Maxims*, "When we pray, we talk to God; when we read, God talks to us."[99] God writes to us primarily through the physical world, the human person (especially saints), Sacred Tradition, and Sacred Scripture. Spiritual directors, faithful friends, devout family members, and other holy books are further examples of good places to find fish. The point is, to be successful at fishing we must learn to read where the gifts are.

Sharks and Barracudas

In the late seventies, my dad took my brother and me to visit relatives in Florida. He outfitted the two of us with inflatable rafts, masks, and fins . . . and then turned us loose. One day, my brother Scott was snorkeling some distance from shore while Dad and I stood waist deep near the break. A man next to us suddenly yelled in bewilderment, "That boy just threw 30 fish way up in the air!" As we looked up, a school of fish was panicking all around my brother and his little raft. He had his face down and was pointed out to sea. Slowly, he turned around . . . then sped toward land creating an impressive wake. Before we could blink it seemed he was standing on the beach, out of breath and pale. He told us how he was looking at a large school of fish, when suddenly

98   Luke 5:4
99   St. Isidore, *Book of Maxims*, Office of Readings, April 4; cf. St. Ambrose, *On the Duties of the Clergy*, I.20.88.

they vanished and a large barracuda swam beneath him – which was about the time Dad and I looked up to behold the human jet ski.

Barracudas and sharks are words that speak of danger. Compare the look of a barracuda or shark, which seems fixed on death or bad intent, to the "smile" of a dolphin. No creature is inherently evil, for God created all things to be good, but some are reminders that during our pilgrimage on earth we are surrounded by creatures that might harm us: physical creatures that might harm our bodies (like snakes and viruses); and spiritual creatures that might harm our souls (like fallen angels and immoral persons). Vigilance in protecting our bodies, then, should translate into vigilance in protecting our souls.

In case of a chance encounter, we should know the habits of our enemies, but we should never seek them out and engage them in places where they have the upper hand. Using drugs to induce mind-altering states, being isolated with someone of the opposite sex you are attracted to, or surrendering your mind to New Age guru, is like swimming in shark infested waters. Demons and the followers of false light reign in those places, yet unlike sharks and barracudas, they do so with a seductive smile.

Angler Fish

Some fish are reminders of demonic threat, whereas others are signs of demonic seduction. Angler fish, for example, entice unwary prey by wiggling a *bioluminescent* lure in front of their jaws. What appears to be a good to an unsuspecting fish is really an evil, a false light. Similarly, evil is presented to us as an attractive light. This is especially true when something "just feels right", but cannot stand to reason or the teachings of the Church: like when the powerful feelings of an "awakening" lead one into a self-help cult or individualized belief system; or the powerful feelings of ecstasy during sex between unmarried persons mask the exigencies of commitment and parenthood. In a myriad of circumstances, we can be duped by the intensity or guile of false light; thus, angler fish are gifts, words of warning to be on guard.

144

CHAPTER 16

Sky

The most common reading from the physical world is taken from the sky. Throughout each day God speaks to us with the colors of sunrise and sunset, and with weather systems which move freely over all the earth:

> The heavens proclaim the glory of God and the skies show forth the work of his hands. Day unto day takes up the story, night unto night makes known the message. No speech, no word, no voice is heard yet their voice goes out through all the earth and their words to the ends of the universe. [100]

No matter where we are or who we are, no matter what our differences, the story of the sky is a familiar starting point for agreeable conversation and extending basic human kindness. For tourist and native alike, talking about the weather is a universal ice-breaker, a first step toward building community and engaging one another as a brother or sister. As a shared experience it is also a great equalizer – the sun doesn't shine brighter on the rich, nor does hail fall harder on the poor. We are all writing our own stories – some good and some evil – but the sky reminds us that we are all living within the one story of the one Author. And it is a children's story.

Seasons

In a temperate zone, weather conditions bring such dramatic changes in temperature, foliage, and wildlife that they display the

---

100 Psalm 19:3-5.

dispositions we call seasons. Over the course of a year, each of the four seasons has basic characteristics which can be seen to correspond to the four human temperaments: phlegmatic, sanguine, choleric, and melancholic.

A temperament is a tendency to act or react in certain ways. It is the raw material which education, environment, and free choices build upon in the formation of personality. Understanding temperaments is indispensable for appreciating one's own mode of operating as well as the *m.o.* of one's neighbor.[101] As a teenager, I became aware that no one in my family dealt with things quite the same way I did; we all seemed to have different tendencies, some good and some bad. It would have been less confusing to know that the reason my dad, mom, brother and I acted or reacted differently (to some degree) was because we each had a different temperament. Let us now expound the strengths and weaknesses of these innate constitutions with a reading from the four seasons.

Winter

The phlegmatic temperament is blessed with patience, peacefulness, and sensitivity. Phlegmatics are calm and dependable. They struggle, however, with putting too much value on leisure and too little on productivity. Because of this they are prone to becoming sedentary, putting tasks off until tomorrow which should be done today. The outlook of a phlegmatic is like winter in that the days are short but getting longer. Their glass is half-empty but filling up, that is, semi-optimistic. They tend to think that since there is plenty of cold weather ahead, its best not to get too excited or too anxious – better to sit by the fire and relax, than to go out and chop wood.

Winter is the season of the peacemaker.

Spring

The sanguine temperament is blessed with optimism, spontaneity, and passion. Sanguines are the life of the party and enjoy variety. They struggle, however, with being too easily distracted and don't take the time to think things through. Because of this they are prone to

---

101 From the Latin *modus operandi* (mode of operating, or way of doing things).

be consumed by the present, and neglect future consequences. The outlook of a sanguine is like spring in that the days are long and getting longer. Their glass is half-full and filling up, that is, optimistic. They tend to think that since there are sunny warm days are ahead, its best not to worry – better to embrace every exciting opportunity and seize the pleasures of the day.

Spring is the season of the enthusiast.

Summer

The choleric temperament is blessed with decisiveness, perseverance, and productivity. Cholerics are confident and magnanimous. They struggle, however, with putting too much value on getting the job done and too little on how others are being treated. Because of this they are prone to becoming frenetic, doing today what should be left for tomorrow, and becoming more focused on activity than leisure. The outlook of a choleric is like summer in that the days are long but getting shorter. Their glass is half-full but emptying, that is, semi-pessimistic. They tend to think that since summer will soon be over its best not to sit and visit too long – better to "make hay while the sun shines" and provide for the harvest.

Summer is the season of the achiever.

Fall

The melancholic temperament is blessed with introspection, compassion, and contemplation. Melancholics are principled and thorough. They struggle, however, with being too focused on possible difficulties and spending too much time thinking things through. Because of this they are burdened by indecision, anxiety about the future, and not appreciating the present. The outlook of the melancholic is like fall in that the days are short and getter shorter. Their glass is half-empty and emptying, that is, pessimistic. They tend to think that since summer was less than fulfilling and a long winter lies ahead, it's best not to spend too much time chasing ephemeral pleasures or working too hard – better to see that we all fade and fall like leaves, and ponder what is ultimately meaningful.

147

Melancholics are given to pause, to reflect deeply upon all which God has given. All the faces, the places, and the graces of the past can haunt them simply because they have indeed passed. Their acute awareness of this life's transitory nature is both a blessing and curse. For them, autumn's palette is painfully sublime, so glorious yet so fleeting, so beautiful it hurts . . . like a requiem for summer's light and landscapes, and for "soft June days forever done".[102]

Fall is the season of the poet.

Though usually one pattern of behavior is dominant, the strengths and weaknesses of the four temperaments can be found in any person in varying degrees. Like the four seasons, they are not mutually exclusive. Finally, it should be noted that these reflections are not meant to be used as an evaluation tool (other books certainly do that well), but simply as an introduction to the distinct yet complementary nature of the climates of personality.

Clouds

Forty days after He rose from the dead, Jesus was with the Apostles when "a cloud took him from their sight".[103] Two angels then appeared to reassure them: "This Jesus who has been taken up from you into heaven will return in the same way as you have seen him going into heaven."[104] For His ascension as well as His second coming, where He will judge the living and the dead, clouds have the privilege of giving Jesus a ride.

Clouds also have the privilege of being a preferred vehicle for God's many tones of color. Consider how He could have chosen to send out "words to the ends of the universe" in black and white, but instead chose to add colors in order to flood our hearts with joy. When the sky is dull gray for days on end, God is just cleaning His brushes, perhaps allowing us to deepen our appreciation when He decides to paint again.

In the scriptures, clouds are symbols of the Holy Spirit and the presence of God. We read in the Old Testament that God "called to Moses out of the cloud" on Mt. Sinai, and in the New Testament that God spoke from a cloud when Jesus was transfigured as well as when

---

102 George Parsons Lathrop (1851-1898), *The Child's Wish Granted.*
103 Acts 1:9
104 Acts 1:11

148

He was being baptized by John.[105] But what does His voice sound like? Many passages in the bible provide a clear answer. For example, when Jesus asked the Father to glorify His name before raising Lazarus from the dead, "a voice came from heaven, 'I have glorified it and will glorify it again.' The crowd heard it and said it was thunder."[106]

Thunder and Lightning

In addition to crashing waves, the scriptures also refer to thunder and lightning as the voice of the Lord: "The voice of the Lord flashes forth flames of fire. The voice of the Lord shakes the wilderness."; "the Lord thundered from heaven, and made His voice heard"; "Moses would speak and God would answer him in thunder." [107] There is nothing like a big thunderstorm (or a big set of waves) to humble us and return us to a sense of awe and wonder. It is one of the ways God gets our attention.

This was never clearer than when Bud and I were on retreat in the Thoroughfare at a Yellowstone site called Mountain Creek. In that particular area, the great fires of 1988 had left most of the lodgepole pines dead but still standing. As the roots had rotted, the trees became increasingly unstable and, with no other options, Bud and I were forced to pitch our tent among these "widow makers". Shortly after we went to sleep, a storm moved in that lasted four hours. The wind, thunder, and lightning were so violent that it toppled dozens of trees, some not twenty yards from our tent. God's voice echoed up and down the long valley and we became very small . . . and very, very, attentive. Our fear led to prayer, which by God's grace was transformed into trust. Grizzlies had become the least of our concerns. Our friendship at that moment intensified, and in a state of such openness to all that is – including the sobering reality of death – prayer and honesty came easy. We prayed the rosary and talked of how we appreciated each other's friendship, and of the many other blessings of God.

And just as we had established an antiphon to respond to wind ("ruah"), during those long midnight hours our response to thunder and lightning became a simple affirmation, again born of reverence: "The voice of the Lord."

---

105 Exodus 24:16
106 John 12:28-29
107 Psalm 29:7-8; Sirach 46:17; Exodus 19:19

CHAPTER 17

Birds

More than any other type of creature, birds are words of levity. Whether they are whistling a tune, ascending to the heights, or just bouncing through branches, birds are reminders of not letting ourselves become weighed down by sorrow, frustration, anxiety, or fear.

Songbirds

Many songbirds are accomplished soloists, and when performing outside a tent or bedroom window they express the joy of being alive. However, in forests where species are abundant and diverse, the sound of their various melodies can seem dissonant, disharmonious. Whether performed in tropical forests like on the slopes of Mauna Kea or the vast river bottoms in Jackson Hole, these avian orchestras require periods of attentive silence before one can hear themes resolve or detect patterns of syncopation. What initially sounds like a cacophony, through stillness becomes an uplifting symphony. Songbirds speak of how delightful life is, whereas other birds speak of how we long to be free from life's burdens.

Eagles

About twenty years ago, I lived in a cabin right on the west bank of the Snake River. Frequently during the winter I would sit in the snow, listen to the water, and pray. Occasionally some diving ducks would speed by, but without exception those afternoons of brief riparian leisure would be blessed by the stately passing of a bald eagle. The great symbol of our nation, an eagle bears an expression which is noble and purposeful. It is a universal word of the freedom we all aspire to. For that matter, all birds that soar or glide carry our hopes of liberation with them. In late spring of that same year I traveled to Kauai to thaw out. One morning I took a trip to Kilauea Point National Wildlife Refuge and was captivated by the flight of the Frigate Birds and Blue Footed Boobies which nested there. Observing their winged bodies suspended between heaven and earth led me to reflect on the human condition of being physical body and spiritual soul. We are tethered to earth by our bodies, but our souls long for wings which will raise us above the frustrations and limitations of this world. Soaring and gliding can inspire us to lighten our load, that is, to defy the gravity and burdens of this life with the hope that we will one day be "flying like an eagle toward heaven."[108]

Songbirds are signs of joy, eagles are signs of hope, and other birds are signs which Jesus himself encouraged us to read specifically as words of trust.

"Consider the ravens"

Because of their tendency to feed on carrion, ravens have often been seen as harbingers of death, bad omens. But Jesus sees an alternative definition. He reads them as daily reminders to not worry so much, to "lighten up" as it were:

> Consider the ravens: they neither sow nor reap, they have neither storehouse nor barn, and yet God feeds them. Of how much more value are you than the birds! And which of you by worrying can add a single hour to the span of his life? If then you are not able to do as small a thing as that, why are you anxious about the rest?[109]

Ever since high school I have loved Latin and ornithology, and somewhere along the line I learned that the word for raven, *corvus*, was related to the word *corvid*, which designates the family of ravens, crows, magpies, and jays. From that moment on, the words of Jesus in the Latin Vulgate, "Considerate corvos!" expanded to include all the corvids. It took a while to develop ears to hear, but now I am reminded not to worry everyday. Often I don't even look up because I know who has spoken.

---

108 Proverbs 23:5
109 Luke 12:24-26

Sometimes it's a common voice like a crow or magpie, other times it's a special voice like a pinyon jay. In each instance, the meaning is the same: "Do not worry. Do not be afraid. Look how He takes care of us!" And why shouldn't we trust Him? After all, He is a Father who "covers the heavens with clouds, provides rain for the earth, makes grass sprout on the mountains; who gives animals their food and ravens what they cry for."[110]

Ravens build "neither storehouse nor barn", so Jesus warns us not to be like "those who store up treasures for themselves but are not rich toward God."[111] But He is not saying we should never prepare for the future – don't squirrels harvest pine nuts then stash reserves to survive the winter? Certainly they do, but note also that squirrels are not anxiously looking past the upcoming winter, storing up capital so that spring and summer can be spent in pursuit of disordered pleasures.[112] Like the ravens, the squirrels security is in having a Father who can be trusted even after a poor harvest. Joseph of Arimathea and Zacchaeus are good examples of men who have wealth but have not neglected their soul, who are rich yet are detached from their riches for the sake of the gospel.[113] And Susanna and Joanna are good examples of women who provide for the Church out of their means.[114]

Doves

The dove is singled out in the animal kingdom as the preferred symbol of the Holy Spirit. As St. Luke reveals, "the Holy Spirit descended upon him in bodily form, as a dove."[115] This is to teach us that the Spirit is gentle and humble in the pursuit of souls, which complements the symbol of the Spirit as fire:

> For the dove symbolizes simplicity, and the fire, intense dedication. Thus the dove and the fire, taken together, have a special significance: whoever is filled with the Spirit becomes so dedicated to this gentle simplicity that

110 Psalm 147:8-9
111 Luke 12:21
112 Cf. Matthew 27:57; 6:19-21,24; Luke 19:1-8
113 Luke 8:3
114 Luke 12:19
115 Luke 3:22

he is also aflame with the zeal of righteousness against
the faults of sinners.[116]

The simplicity of the dove also prevents us from becoming too
complicated or calculating in our wisdom. As Jesus said, "Be wise as serpents
and simple as doves."[117] Regarding this imperative, Pope St. Gregory the
Great noted: "In this command he has deliberately joined the two ideas
together: the serpent's cunning complements the dove's simplicity, and
the dove's simplicity moderates the serpent's cunning."[118] The wise man
should never let himself become manipulative or disingenuous. Being
clever is one thing, being deceptively clever or scheming is quite another.
A dove is an occasion to reflect on whether our application of wisdom
has been weighed down with the fear of making the wrong political or
social maneuver, or has been chained by intellectual pride. Wisdom
sometimes requires that we calculate the risks and rewards of complex
situations, discerning when to reveal and when to conceal, for example,
but it also requires that we are always honest, fair, and simply Christ like.

* * *

We all struggle with becoming burdened by sorrows, frustrations,
and anxieties. Birds are meant to help us alleviate the fear that this life
is all there is, that we might not have enough food to eat and clothes to
wear, or that God's will might not be done unless we resort to conniving.
Once again Jesus points to a light little bird to show us we have nothing
to worry about: "Are not two sparrows sold for a small coin? Yet not one
of them falls to the ground without your Father's knowledge. Even all
the hairs of your head are counted. So do not be afraid; you are worth
more than many sparrows."[119] God wants us to know that He will take
care of things – both the heavy loads of the present and the uncertainties
of the future – so He advises us to find solace in His lighthearted words
on the wing: "Look at the birds in the sky."[120]

---

116 Pope St. Gregory the Great, *Office of Readings*, Eighth Sunday in Ordinary Time.
117 Matthew 10:16
118 Pope St. Gregory the Great, *Office of Readings*, Eighth Sunday in Ordinary Time.
119 Matthew 10:31-32
120 Matthew 6:26

CHAPTER 18

Land

One of the greatest gifts my mom and stepdad Paul ever gave me was a ten day pilgrimage to the Holy Land. The impact of that trip was immediate. All of my meditations on the mysteries of the rosary and other scenes from the Gospels were transformed because the Holy Land provided new backdrops and stage-sets for the drama of salvation. The land itself, known as the fifth gospel, allowed me to hear a fuller sense of Jesus' words and deeds as they gathered texture, color, and fragrance.

The Fifth Gospel

Part of our pilgrimage was spent in the region of Galilee, where I was able to read the Sermon on the Mount on the mount itself and meditate on fish sipping insects from the surface as I stood on the shore near Peter's home. These experiences spoke volumes; but there was one moment in particular when the fifth gospel raised its voice with exceptional clarity. We were in a boat on the Sea of Galilee, and one of my professor's little boys was sitting on my lap leaning over the gunwale, scanning the water for fish (or anything else which might satisfy his curiosity). As we passed by a pristine canyon, I began to imagine how it would be a good place for a retreat and wondered if backpacking was permitted. Suddenly, I was overwhelmed by the thought that Jesus and the Apostles may have camped there and built a fire on one of the many occasions they withdrew into the wilderness to pray – then our tour guide announced its name over the loudspeaker: The Valley of Doves.

Rock

In the region of Caesarea Philippi, there is a large rock outcropping. It is believed that against this backdrop Jesus asked Simon who he thought Jesus was. When Simon responded, "You are the Messiah, the Son of the living God", Jesus said to him, "And I tell you, you are Peter [Rock], and on this rock I will build my church". [121] From then on Simon was called Rock, a name which up to that point had been reserved for God alone. At least 27 times in the Old Testament God is called the Rock. In Psalm 18, for instance, it is forcefully put as a rhetorical question: "Who but our God is the Rock?"[122] Clearly, Jesus wanted to convey the idea that His Church would be built upon a permanent and stable foundation. And what is more stable than rock?

The photograph of *Chapel on the Rock* on the back cover depicts how a stable edifice depends on a stable foundation – and the New Testament bears witness to the fact that the early Church believed that foundation to be Peter.[123] First, Rock heads the meeting to find a new bishop to replace Judas, Rock preaches to the Jews and calls them to be baptized when the Church was born at Pentecost, Rock excommunicates the first heretic, Rock receives the revelation that the Gentiles too were to be saved, Rock leads the first council of bishops, and, whenever the Apostles are named, Rock heads the list.[124] Second, Jesus is the one shepherd of the one flock and yet He says to Peter, "Feed my lambs" and "Tend my sheep".[125] And third, St. Paul repeatedly refers to Simon as Rock, yet he also writes that "the rock was Christ."[126] So the Lord is our Shepherd and Peter is our shepherd. Jesus is the Rock and Peter is the Rock.

My Dad has always said that the one thing which impressed him most about the Catholic Church (which one of the reasons he converted while in the Marine Corps) was that it could trace its history all the way back to Peter and the Apostles. Pope Benedict XVI is the 265th successor of Peter and every other bishop of the Church can trace his roots back to one of the Apostles. If you think about it, it's just a matter of common

---

121 Matthew 16:16,18
122 Psalm 18:32 (cf. Psalm 89:27; 95:1; 1Samuel 2:2 ; Deuteronomy 32:3-4)
123 The *Chapel on the Rock* is located just outside of Rocky Mountain National Park at the St. Malo retreat center.
124 Acts 1:15-26; 2:14-40; 8:18-23; 10:46-48; 15:6-12
125 John 10:14-16; 21:15-17
126 Cf. Galatians; 1Corinthians 10:4

sense. Since Jesus wanted to establish a Church that would endure to the end of time and be free from error regarding who He is and what He wants, it would need a hierarchy and a God-given authority right from the start. But Jesus never said that it was a matter of common sense; He more specifically stated that it was a matter of wisdom:

> Everyone who hears these words of mine and does them will be like a wise man who built his house upon the rock; and the rain fell, and the floods came, and the winds blew and beat upon that house, but it did not fall, because it had been founded on the rock. And everyone who hears these words of mine and does not do them will be like a foolish man who built his house upon the sand; and the rain fell, and the floods came, and the winds blew and beat against that house, and it fell; and great was its fall.[127]

Most Protestants believe that Jesus did not intend to build His Church on Peter but on Peter's profession of faith. So which is it, Peter or his profession? Here again we have come upon the error of thinking that something must be *either/or* versus *both/and* – Jesus builds His Church on *both* Peter *and* his profession.

Sandstone

Nevertheless, it is not as if those Christians who reject papal authority have absolutely no wisdom and have built their house on sand, because they at least share Peter's profession that Jesus is "the Messiah, the Son of the living God." Their foundation is more like sandstone, part rock and part sand, and historically this has been proven to be true. Wind and rain have not washed away Protestantism in a sudden flood; rather, the erosion has been slow and steady. Consider how the Anglican/ Episcopalian community, which closely resembled Catholicism at first, has slowly deteriorated over the past 500 years. They claim to have apostolic succession, but ever since King Henry VIII rejected the Pope as shepherd of the Church on earth they have seen a gradual wearing away of their original beliefs and practices – the most recent being allowing active homosexuals to become bishops. In June 2003, the Episcopal hierarchy ordained their first openly gay bishop. In June of 2008, that

---

127 Matthew 7:24-27

same bishop was "married" to his male companion. And in October of 2009, that bishop came to speak to Episcopalians in Jackson Hole, leading them astray by eroding the teaching of the Apostles. Would the same community consider ordaining a bishop who was openly adulterous or polygamous? Time will tell.

Nevertheless, our first pope warned against becoming too rigid or too pliable with the image of a Church built of "living stones".[128] Modern architectural science has found that for a building to be stable under stresses from storms and earthquakes, it has to have a little give, a little flexibility, but never so much as to affect the integrity of the structure. In order to absorb the jolts and rumblings which seek to demolish papal authority and faith in the Messiah, the Church follows an ancient maxim: In essential matters, unity; in non-essential matters, freedom; and in all matters, charity. (*In necessariis, unitas; in dubiis, libertas; in omnibus, caritas.*)

Mountains

Anyone who has visited or resided in Jackson Hole knows how everything seems to revolve around a particular granite peak: The Grand Teton. Towering above the other Tetons, "The Grand" is visible from almost anywhere in the valley. For visitor and resident alike, every gaze is eventually drawn to it as a sure point of reference. For the Catholic, this corresponds to the call of living in constant reference to the one true God and the one true Church of The Rock.

From a certain vantage point, known as *The Cathedral Group*, the Tetons take on the features of Gothic architecture. As the park's first Ranger Naturalist put it:

> The Gothic note . . . is seen in the profiles of the countless firs and spruces congregated like worshippers on the lower slopes; it reappears higher in the converging lines of spire rising beyond spire; it attains supreme expression in the figures of the peaks themselves that, towering above all else, with pointed summits direct one's vision and thoughts yet higher.[129]

---

128   1 Peter 2:5
129   Fritiof Fryxell, *The Tetons – Interpretations of a Mountain Landscape*, 1938.

Perhaps nowhere in the Rockies is there such a majestic symbol of the reverence owed to God; or for that matter, of what the prophet Isaiah had in mind when he described the eternal dwelling of God, the mountain where peace and justice shall reign:

> In the days to come, the mountain of the Lord's house shall be established as the highest mountain, and raised up above the hills. All nations shall stream to it, many peoples shall come and say: "Come, let us climb the Lord's mountain . . . that he may teach us his ways and we may walk in his paths."[130]

The Scriptures often portray God as residing on a holy mountain where those who seek His will can find it.[131] Whenever we hike up a mountain with an open heart, it is as if we are moving closer to heaven so that "he may teach us his ways and we may walk in his paths." Along with the fresh air and inspiring surroundings of mountain trails, we encounter the ways of extreme justice (especially extreme gravity). Mountains have hard ways. Every misstep has a consequence, every error in judgment a penalty. The perseverance required to ascend a peak is similar to the perseverance required in the spiritual life; and no matter how often we fall or become discouraged we are called get up and step up, to "tirelessly climb toward the summit of the mountain of holiness."[132]

Jesus often went up into the mountains to pray, and for many the high country speaks more powerfully than any other environment.[133] Few descend into caves to speak with God but countless ascend mountains. Why? Because that is the trajectory of the human heart – upward – and mountains are places of privileged encounter.[134]

Being up on a mountain lifts the heart and mind, offering panoramic vistas. There we may gain fresh insights, greater clarity, and a broader view of things: a perspective closer to God's. As with all things which might bring us closer to God, however, there are many temptations. Mountains are places of great light . . . and great false light.

---

130 Isaiah 2:2-3
131 Cf. Psalm 43:3; 3:4, Hebrews 12:22
132 John Paul II, *General Audience,* July 16, 2000.
133 (Cf. Matthew 14:23, Mark 6:45-46, Luke 6:12; 9:28, John 6:14-15)
134 There is nothing wrong with "spelunking"; caves are just different words than mountains.

As Jesus was transfigured on a high mountain, Peter, James, and John saw him speaking with Moses and Elijah. One particular story of the prophet Elijah is a cautionary tale of what is perhaps the greatest temptation of high mountain retreats – idolatry.

When Queen Jezebel and her false prophets had deceived the people into worshipping Baal, the god of fertility, Elijah challenged them on the summit of Mt. Carmel. Since there can only be one true God (in this case either Baal or the God of Abraham, Isaac, and Jacob), everyone agreed that the true God should be able to light a fire as a sign that prayers were heard. So wood was gathered and the false priests implored their false god all morning. Then Elijah taunted them to pray louder:

> Cry aloud! Surely he is a god; either he is meditating, or he has wandered away, or he is on a journey, or perhaps he is asleep and must be awakened. Then they cried aloud and, as was their custom, they cut themselves with swords and lances until the blood gushed over them. As midday passed, they raved on . . . but there was not a sound: no one answered, and no one was listening.[135]

Elijah then soaked the wood with water three times and called upon the name of the Lord . . . then the one true God consumed everything with fire. Long ago, Bud and I had learned just how natural it was to call upon God from a mountaintop.

The San Juan range of southern Colorado is dominated by Uncompahgre Peak. At 14,300 feet, it soars above the landscape and is truly a holy mountain. The summit is not clear of snow until late summer, so we decided to make our ascent at the end of August. Most people who climb the mountain leave their base camp before dark and return by noon in order to avoid the afternoon thunderstorms. But since we are always seeking to avoid the distraction of crowds (which on this occasion was just one other group of hikers), Bud and I began late in the morning. Our hike was at first uneventful and serene. Pikas cheeped from talus slopes and alpine wildflowers flashed their array of brief yet brilliant colors; but then, when we were about 200 feet from the summit, a storm billowed up a short distance away . . . and began rushing toward us. Like frightened marmots, we scurried over the rocks until

---

135 1Kings 18:27-29

we found a small ledge to hide under. As the storm clouds enveloped the peak, the voice of the Lord exploded, and just as we had done in the Thoroughfare, we became very small . . . and very, very, attentive. Instinctively, we felt unworthy to address God directly and began crying out a litany of saints whose powerful intercession had made them close friends: St. Francis! St. Therese! St. Joseph! Pray for us! The deafening thunderclaps were neither above us nor below us, we were inside the tempest. A half-hour later the storm had passed (as had even the smallest impulse of vanity or pride). Restored by humility and brimming with confidence that our prayers had been heard, we took the summit and talked of God for hours.

For some, unfortunately, the insidious temptation to worship something other than the true Creator is especially powerful in places that are spiritually powerful. Precisely because the high country speaks of spiritual things, those deceived by false light flock there to call upon false gods of nature, or to idolize the self under the guise of personal achievement or "spiritual" experience. On the contrary, the reason for climbing a mountain should never be for the glory of self, but to expand our physical, intellectual, and spiritual gifts for the glory of God.

Lava

Liquid rock seems like an oxymoron, a contradiction in terms; but from the Kilauea crater high upon the slopes Hawaii Volcanoes National Park, rock flows like a river into the ocean. We can't witness the creation of new sky or new sea, but we can witness the creation of new land. Here God shapes the newest real estate on earth with lava in one hand and waves in the other. The current rate is thirty-two acres per year.

Typically, those who stand before such primordial power are reduced to silence or a dumbfounded repetition of their favorite adjective: amazing, cool, awesome, unbelievable, unreal, etc. Native Hawaiians saw this power and sacredness in lava and called it Madame Pele, the goddess of creation, for it appeared to them that the earth was giving birth to new earth. Indeed, as Pope Benedict XVI has reminded us, even in scripture "the mother's life-giving womb is compared to the depths of the earth."[136]

The dramatic change in temperature as molten lava meets crashing waves, causes some lava to explode into tiny pieces, forming sand.

---

136 Pope Benedict XVI, *General Audience*, December 28, 2005. (cf. Psalm 139:15)

I once stood on a beach that was less than one day old. It was so charged with creative energy that the sand seemed to pulsate with life. Both the lava flows and the new beaches seemed to be alive, just as rivers and crashing waves are called "living waters" in Scripture. At that moment, I became more understanding of how many native religions had become confused, failing to distinguish between the Creator and the Creator's infusion of power within His works.

The various creatures of the universe vibrate with truth, goodness, and beauty, with the power of having been brought into being. In the words of Pope John Paul the Great, He is "a personal God, who is infinitely good, wise, powerful and eternal, who transcends the world and at the same time is present in the depths of his creatures."[137] However, when the Holy Father said God "is present in the depths of his creatures" he was not implying that God is the universe taken as a whole, as pantheism believes, but only that He sustains creation as the Uncaused Cause of all that has being. The pope went on to clarify: "We must not confuse the Creator with his creation."[138] To say that the Creator *is* creation is like saying Michelangelo *is* the ceiling of The Sistine Chapel. Rather, God surpasses every display of power in the universe. He is greater and more glorious than lightning or lava, as the Book of Wisdom makes clear:

> If through delight in the beauty of these things men assumed them to be gods, let them know how much better than these is their Lord, for the Author of Beauty created them. And if men were amazed at their power and working, let them perceive from them how much more powerful is the one who formed them.[139]

Lava is a creature, not a god. Praying to a creature, or to the collective physical universe, is as meaningless as praying to the words or pages of a book.

Since the 1960's, many Native Americans have embraced the civil rights movement as well as the American Indian Movement (which is a return to polytheism and mythology). However, if the leader of the

---

137 Pope John Paul II, *World Youth Day: Vigil of the Assumption of Mary*, August 14, 1993; Cherry Creek State Park, Colorado.
138 Ibid.
139 Wisdom 13:1-4 (Polytheism is the belief in a plurality of gods).

civil rights movement were alive today, he would challenge the religious beliefs of AIM with right reason. As Dr. King explained, when one's faith becomes incompatible with reason it is the duty of those who are thinking clearly to demonstrate the inherent contradictions within that belief system, just "as Socrates felt it was necessary to create a tension in the mind so that individuals could rise from the bondage of myths and half truths to the unfettered realm of creative analysis and objective appraisal."[140] Whether in ancient Greece, ancient Israel, or modern America, liberation from mythology begins with reason creating a "tension in the mind", so that one might re-evaluate their ideas objectively.

Assigning a divine power to a creature is an illusion of light. Demons darken our lives by such ideas because they are children of The Liar. And what is it that liars do? They lie. In tempting souls, these masters of deception often begin by agreeing that God is like the sun, then suggest that God *is* the sun; or that the earth is like our mother, then suggest that the earth *is* our mother. The desire to commune with the greatness and beauty found in the natural world is a natural impulse, but if nature leads one away from nature's maker – the source of that greatness and beauty – it has become a ruse.

"Rich Soil"

For all the years I've lived in the pristine valley of the Snake River, my most intimate *daily* connection with creation was during the four years I lived in the ravaged valley of the Ohio River. This was for at least two reasons: (1) I was immersed in the study of theology as I earned my undergraduate and graduate degrees; and (2) I made hiking trails through the woods to get to and from school because I had no car.

Periodically during the fall and winter, I would notice how miniature stalagmites of ice would emerge from the earth. These frozen little spires lifted the matted debris and leaf litter up to four inches high in order to create little crevasses for seeds to be sown. I reflected on how the triune conditions of water – liquid, ice, and steam – cooperated in the production of fertile soil. Melting snow and rain saturated the earth, expanding ice tilled it, and humidity allowed bacteria to break down the debris into compost. I reflected further on how we might cooperate

---

140 Martin Luther King Jr., *Letter from a Birmingham Jail*, April 16, 1963.

with the Trinity in making our hearts into good soil, and turned to Jesus' parable of the sower for clarity:

> A sower went out to sow his seed. And as he sowed, some seed fell on the path and was trampled, and the birds of the sky ate it up. Some seed fell on rocky ground, and when it grew, it withered for lack of moisture. Some seed fell among thorns, and the thorns grew with it and choked it. And some fell on good soil, and when it grew, it produced fruit a hundredfold. . . .This is the meaning of the parable: The seed is the word of God. Those on the path are the ones who have heard, but the devil comes and takes away the word from their hearts that they may not believe and be saved. Those on rocky ground are the ones who, when they hear, receive the word with joy, but they have no root; they believe only for a time and fall away in time of trial. As for the seed that fell among thorns, they are the ones who have heard, but as they go along, they are choked by the anxieties and riches and pleasures of life, and they fail to produce mature fruit. But as for the seed that fell on *rich soil*, they are the ones who, when they have heard the word, embrace it with a generous and good heart, and bear fruit through perseverance.[141]

One aspect of being a person of "rich soil" is humility. In fact, St. Augustine believes it is more than one aspect:

> If you should ask me the ways of God, I would tell you that the first is humility, the second is humility, and the third is still humility. Not that there are no other instructions to give, but if humility does not precede all that we do, our efforts are fruitless.[142]

The word humility is derived from the Latin word *humilitas* (close to the ground), which is derived from the Latin word *humus* (soil).

---

141 Luke 8:5-8, 11-15 (emphasis mine)
142 St. Augustine, *Letter 118*, III.

Remarkably, when a woman caught in adultery was brought before Jesus, He simply "bent down and wrote with his finger on the ground."[143] By doing this, He was reminding the woman's accusers to be humble, to recall that they are dust, to not think of themselves as better than others – for we are all sinners. But since they could not read His actions, He spoke to them audibly: "Let the one among you who is without sin be the first to throw a stone at her."[144] Then, as if to reiterate what he had been saying all along, "once again he bent down and wrote on the ground."[145]

Learning to have a "generous and good heart" involves learning to be humble, and learning to be humble involves learning to endure the suffocating weeds and humiliating trials which come from believing in God's word. As Mother Teresa teaches us, "We learn humility through accepting humiliation cheerfully. We have been created for greater things; why stoop down to things that will spoil the beauty of our hearts?"[146] Humiliation, when accepted in God's will, is like Miracle-Gro for the soul.

Consequently, our ability to "bear fruit with perseverance" depends largely upon our willingness to build upon the ideas and lifestyles of those who have gone before us. As John Paul II wrote in his last book, to cultivate "the rich humus of tradition" means to have "an openness toward the future and at the same time an affectionate respect for the past . . . a past that endures in human hearts in the form of ancient words, ancient signs, memories, and customs inherited from previous generations."[147] To be a person of rich soil who produces fruit a hundredfold, is to be a person who does not exalt their own opinion, but is humble enough to work hard at understanding the insights of the past, especially regarding God's books. Humility and perseverance are essential when reading the Bible, and equally so when reading creation: "Our human understanding, which shares in the light of the divine intellect, can understand what God tells us by means of his creation, though not without great effort and only in a spirit of humility".[148]

---

143 John 8:6
144 John 8:7
145 John 8:8
146 Mother Teresa, *from a letter to her religious sisters dated August 4, 1962.*
147 Pope John Paul II, *Rise, Let Us Be On Our Way*, 180. s
148 *Catechism of the Catholic Church*, #299.

As we mentioned in the *Preface,* the hallmark of Catholic catechesis is to situate any personal insights within the objective teaching of the Church. The idea is to point away from oneself to someone who is worth listening to: a saint, pope, council, or co-author of Scripture. Our role is to present that objective truth in such a way that it might resonate within a particular culture or historical situation. The Latin phrase *non novo sed nove* (not new things, but a new way) captures the essence of this teaching method, the pedagogy of remaining close to the ground.

CHAPTER 19

Vegetation

Trees

Trees play a central role in the story of creation. In most parts of the world, they are primary resources for shelter, fuel, food, and furnishings. Thus, they are signs of God's providence. The word "providence" literally means "seeing on behalf of"; and one only needs to pass through any of the great lodgepole pine forests of the Rockies to observe a prime example. By creating such long straight trunks for teepees and cabins, God is seeing on our behalf; He is *providing* for us.

Trees also play a central role in the story of salvation. Just as a tree was instrumental in our fall from grace (i.e. the tree of the knowledge of good and evil in the Garden of Eden), a tree was instrumental in our redemption. As the scriptures tell us, the people had Jesus killed "by hanging him on a tree", then "took him down from the tree and placed him in a tomb."[149] Many saints have seen how it was fitting for the tree of the cross to counteract the tree of betrayal:

> The fruit of this tree is not death but life, not darkness
> but light. This tree does not cast us out of paradise but
> opens the way for our return. . . . This was the tree upon
> which the Lord, like a brave warrior wounded in hands,

---

149 Acts 5:30; Acts 13:29 (Additionally, the "tree of life" is found on each side of the river of life in heaven to provide food and medicine.)

feet, and side, healed the wounds of sin that the evil serpent had inflicted on our nature. A tree once caused our death, but now a tree brings life.[150]

Consequently, the tree of the cross is powerful symbol of how to live well. When Jesus was asked what commandment was the greatest, He first said, "You shall love the Lord your God with all your heart", then added, "You shall love your neighbor as yourself."[151] The love of God represents the vertical dimension of Christian life and the love of neighbor the horizontal. Like a tree, these two loves must grow in harmony. Our vertical relationship with God is what anchors and supports our horizontal relationships. Our love of neighbor cannot grow beyond our love of God because branches can only spread as far as the strength of the trunk will allow. If love of God is weak, love of neighbor collapses. A toothpick cannot support a 2x4. On the other hand, when love of God is strong it redounds to an authentic love of neighbor, including one's enemies. This type of love is deeply rooted in the humility of laying down one's life for others and blossoming in due season. In general, then, trees speak of God's providing for us as well as our duty to provide for others.

"Learn a lesson from the fig tree"[152]

There are over one thousand different types of fig trees in the world, but one in particular, the *sycamore fig*, feeds a greater variety of wildlife than any other tree on earth. In a single season, a mature tree can produce 100,000 figs which benefit over one hundred species of birds and multitudes of other creatures. However, this "being for others" in providing shade, shelter, and food is the role of a mature tree, not an adolescent tree. Adolescents are mostly self-centered, but this is not entirely a bad thing. To become a man or woman means to be able to offer oneself as a gift; and since no one gives what they don't have to begin with, it is appropriate to spend some time finding oneself. That is, to be somewhat absorbed in discovering and developing one's gifts for the service of neighbor and the glory of God.

Perhaps the greatest youth minister in American history, Father Michael Scanlan, often advised new students at Franciscan University

---

150 St. Theodore the Studite, *Office of Readings*, Second Friday of Easter.
151 Matthew 22:37,39
152 Matthew 24:32

to refrain from dating anyone exclusively during their freshman year (much less be overly concerned with marriage). We should instead take the time to grow straight and tall like a young tree, finding our place in the sun. Father Mike counseled us to grow "in wisdom and in stature" toward the light of God, finding our place in the Son – that state of fruitful maturity which is our vocation.[153]

Palms

Historically, palm fronds have been read as words which bestow honor upon royalty. Why? Because palm trees applaud and cheer – they "do the wave" and make a clapping sound with the slightest breeze or movement. To witness this, one need only to hold a pine bough in one hand and a palm frond in the other then gently shake them. Which one seems more worthy of honoring a king?

King Kamehameha, ruler of the Hawaiian Islands, was honored with palms fronds by his subjects. Likewise, we are told that as Jesus entered Jerusalem the people "took branches of palm trees and went out to meet him, shouting 'Hosanna! Blessed is he who comes in the name of the Lord – the King of Israel!'"[154] We are also told in John's vision of heaven that a great multitude "stood before the throne and before the Lamb, wearing white robes and holding palm branches".[155] And finally, we are told that at the second coming of the Lord, palm trees will be joined in praise, for "all the trees of the forest will clap their hands." [156] So whenever I am in the islands and the palms begin to celebrate, I respond with the simple antiphon: "Hosanna!"[157]

Evergreens

Pope John Paul II often became immersed in thought as he looked out the window of his study upon the events of the Great Jubilee of the year 2000. During advent of that year, he shared one of these reflections

---

153 Luke 2:52 (Teenage years are intended to be a time when the hormonal mind and body, which are seeking independence prematurely, can be disciplined in preparation for one's vocation.)
154 John 12:13
155 Revelation 7:9; cf. 2 Maccabees 10:7; 1 Maccabees 13:51-52
156 Isaiah 55:12
157 A Hebrew acclamation of joy and triumph, meaning "Glory!" or "May God save us!"

with the pilgrims from Austria who had donated the Christmas tree for St. Peter's square:

> In the past few days, every time I have looked out of my study window at St. Peter's square the tree has uplifted my spirit. I always loved trees in my homeland. When one looks at them, in a certain way they begin to speak . . . In the flowering of spring, in the ripeness of summer, in the autumn fruits and in the death of winter, a tree tells of the mystery of life. . . . Like trees, human beings also need deeply anchored roots. Only those who are rooted in fertile soil have stability. They can reach up high to receive the sunlight and at the same time can resist the winds around them. But those who think they can live without foundations live an uncertain existence, like roots without soil.[158]

The idea of associating an evergreen tree with the birth of Jesus is credited to St. Boniface, an eighth century missionary to Germany.[159] He taught that the evergreen was a symbol of eternal life because its branches are always green and its shape points toward our heavenly home.

It is a little known fact that America actually has a living national Christmas tree. This exceptional honor has been given to a giant *sequoia* in King's Canyon National Park in California. Standing over 267 feet high and 40 feet wide, it is our only living national shrine, and also serves as a living memorial for U.S. veterans of war.

The only time I visited King's Canyon most of my days were spent trying to gain a perspective of how enormous and ancient this tree really was. As I sat at its base and pondered, or hiked along ridges which afforded new vantage points, I began to imagine that this great tree, estimated to be around 2000 years old, had germinated on that same beautiful spring day when Jesus was conceived by the Holy Spirit and began to grow in Mary's womb.

---

158 Pope John Paul II, *Audience for Pilgrims from Carinthia, Austria,* (on the occasion of the presentation of the Vatican Christmas tree, December 16, 2000).
159 When St. Boniface learned that the Germanic tribes were worshipping the tree of Thor as a god, he chopped it down. When he wasn't struck down himself by Thor, he gained credibility and a platform for teaching about the one true God.

Like many other tourists, I wanted to gather the giant cones which were strewn about the forest floor. But when I learned that these12-18 inch cones were actually from the *sugar pine*, I researched the *sequoia* and found that their cones were among the smallest in the evergreen kingdom. This, of course echoed one of Jesus' great parables: "The kingdom of heaven is like a mustard seed that someone took and sowed in his field; it is the smallest of all the seeds, but when it has grown it is the greatest of shrubs and becomes a tree, so that the birds of the air come and make nests in its branches."[160]

This idea of a small seed becoming a large tree is invaluable when trying to understand why the 21st century Catholic Church is not identical to the 1st century Catholic Church. As the famed author J.R.R. Tolkien once wrote, the desire to return to the time of Jesus and the Apostles, while understandable, is neither possible nor congruent with God's plan:

> The 'protestant' search backwards for 'simplicity' and directness – which, of course, though it contains some good or at least intelligible motives, is mistaken and indeed vain. . . . [The Church] was not intended by Our Lord to be static or remain in perpetual childhood; but to be a living organism (likened to a plant), which develops and changes in externals by the interaction of its bequeathed divine life and history with the particular circumstances of the world into which it is set. There is no resemblance between the mustard seed and the full grown tree. For those living in the days of its branching growth, the Tree is the thing, for the history of a living thing is part of its life, and the history of a divine thing is sacred. The wise may know that it began with a seed, but it is vain to try and dig it up, for it no longer exists, and the virtue and powers that it had now reside in the Tree.[161]

The mustard seed of the Church cannot be excavated any more than we can dig up the cone-seed beneath the sequoia, or the acorn beneath the oak. What can be found, however, are apostolic roots anchored in *humus* and founded upon rock.

---

160 Matthew 13:31-32
161 J.R.R. Tolkien, *Letter #306.*

Flowers

The most popular saint of the 20th century was St. Therese of Lisieux, a young Carmelite nun who died at age 24 and whose autobiography became an instant classic of Western spirituality. She often referred to herself as "The Little Flower", not only because flowers were among her favorite creatures, but because she learned from Jesus how to read them:

> Jesus deigned to teach me this mystery. He set before me the book of nature; I understood how all the flowers He has created are beautiful, how the splendor of the rose and the whiteness of the lily do not take away the perfume of the little violet or the delightful simplicity of the daisy. I understood that if all flowers wanted to be roses, nature would lose her springtime beauty, and the fields would no longer be decked out with little wild flowers. And so it is in the world of souls, Jesus' garden. He willed to create great souls comparable to lilies and roses, but He has created smaller ones and these must be content to be daises or violets destined to give joy to God's glances when he looks at his feet. Perfection consists of doing the His will, in being what He wills us to be. Just as the sun shines simultaneously on the tallest trees and on each little flower as though it were alone on earth, so Our Lord is occupied particularly with each soul as though there were no others like it. And just as in nature all the seasons are arranged in such a way as to make the humblest daisy bloom on a set day, in the same way, everything works out for the good of each soul.[162]

Another lesson St. Therese learned was spiritual heliotropism, that is, to live like those flowers which follow the light of the sun. This insight, that we should continually orient our lives to the Light, exposes her simple genius, for it is derived from her simple obedience to Jesus' command: "Learn from the way the wild flowers grow."[163]

---

162 St. Therese of Lisieux, *Story of a Soul*, 14-15.
163 Matthew 6:28

"Consider the lilies"

The lily is singled out by Jesus as a word of the Father's devotion and care for us, as a word of freedom from anxiety over what we are to wear, eat, or drink:

> Consider the lilies, how they grow; they neither toil nor spin; yet I tell you, even Solomon in all his glory was not clothed like one of these. But if God so clothes the grass which is alive in the field today and tomorrow is thrown into the oven, how much more will he clothe you, O you of little faith! And do not seek what you are to eat and what you are to drink, nor be anxious about it. For all the nations of the world seek these things; and your Father knows that you need them. Instead, seek his kingdom, and these things shall be yours as well.[164]

When he was 12 years-old, I took my nephew Colton on his first backcountry trip – a trip we had been preparing for it since he could walk. Shortly after we arrived at our site (and had reviewed NOPS base-camp procedures), he started chopping wood. He chopped all day, giving me a chance to explore the surrounding area. We were camped in the Park Range near Rabbit Ears pass in northern Colorado. At such a high elevation, the *glacier lily* emerges in late June at the edge of receding snow fields. Some send their shoots toward the sun through five inches of snow pack. This quality of certain flowers to persevere under extreme conditions was observed by St. Therese, who found it helpful in understanding her own trials: "Just as the flowers of spring begin to grow under the snow and to expand in the first rays of the sun, so the little flower whose memories I am writing had to pass through the winter of trial".[165] As The Little Flower noted, glacier lilies eventually break into the sunlight, but then, as if giving all glory to God, they bow in a profound gesture of reverence. After the lily has been pollinated and its petals fall, the fruit bearing stamen grows straight once again,

---

164 Luke 12:27-31
165 St. Therese of Lisieux, *Story of a Soul*, 30.

173

offering its seeds to heaven and increasing their range of dispersal as they are borne on the wind.

Roses

At times, a bouquet of roses can say more than spoken words because it can be easily read as a gift from the heart. In the natural realm, too, roses have the power to soften us. Aromas are not often read as words, but the *wild rose* has an exceptional clarity and tenderness. It is the most Marian of fragrances for reasons I will not be able to fully explain in this life. Not just because I was taught of roses and the rosary by my grandmother, whom I adored, but because of something more objective than that. The perfume of a wild rose emanates a gentle magnanimity from among hardened thorns, just as Mary's fragrant prayer of joy "proclaims the greatness of the Lord" in the midst of life's inevitable hardships.[166]

As one might expect, some of the best advice in the entire Old Testament speaks of emulating both little flowers we have just mentioned: "Listen, my faithful children: open up your petals, like roses planted near running waters. Send up the sweet odor of incense; break forth in blossoms like the lily. . . . Proclaim the greatness of his name".[167]

---

166 Luke 1:46
167 Sirach 39:13-14

CHAPTER 20

Animals

In the diagram of the six days of creation, we used the term *animals* to abbreviate the three types of creatures God made on the sixth day: "cattle, creeping things, and wild animals of all kinds".[168] Let us now read each of these categories in turn.

"Cattle"

The Hebrew word translated as *cattle* in Genesis 1 refers to any animal that has been domesticated: "By *cattle*, domestic animals are signified, which in any way are of service to man."[169] Clearly, some species are better suited than others to be our helpers or to be raised as livestock, which indicates that it was part of God's plan from the beginning was to provide us with animals to serve our needs. Consider how horses have benefited mankind. They seem to have been crafted to carry a rider or pull a wagon. Consider also how predisposed wolves were to domestication. The assimilation of dogs within the human family is not an accident, but a gift. Among other things, they alleviate loneliness for those who have become isolated. In their faithfulness, forgiveness, and joy, they are symbols of exemplary Christianity. Still, we must guard against the temptation to value pets as much as persons, thus becoming excessive in our devotion to them: "It is contrary to human dignity . . . to spend money on them that should as a priority go to the relief of human misery. One can love animals; one should not direct to them

---

168 Genesis 1:24
169 St.Thomas Aquinas, *Summa Theologica*, I.72.3.

the affection due only to persons."[170] Since the overvaluing of pets has reached epidemic proportions, let us now delineate a few divergences between pets and people.

It may offer some solace to realize our pets neither suffer nor die as we do. They don't suffer like us because they don't see that this could be the end of their life or dreams, that is, they cannot comprehend their own mortality or that their suffering might affect their future. We, on the other hand, are painfully aware of our own mortality, we understand that pain and suffering can go on for months, and we are stricken with the thought that our goals in life and our yearning for fulfillment hang in the balance. Pets certainly have emotions and memories, by which they develop preferences for certain people and learn from experiences, just not with the meaning and understanding that we have.

Additionally, pets don't experience humor as we do. They show might become excited and look like they are having fun, but only persons can be truly amused. Why? Because we understand what was supposed to happen but didn't. On different occasions as an adult, I have hiccupped bubbles, slipped on a banana peel, and stepped on a rake so that it hit me in the forehead. I laughed aloud when these things happened, because I could see that it was not what I intended. I could see the incongruity. When a raccoon watches a fisherman slip on a mossy rock, then sees all his gear explode into the air and begin to float downstream as he scrambles to collect it, it doesn't laugh because it doesn't understand. Only persons are entertained by things like funny home videos.

Finally, pets don't think as we do. They have brains which sort out the complexities of instinct, memory, and emotion, but they do not reason. Human beings, on the other hand, are flooded with ideas. Every waking moment, we are solving problems, weighing options, pondering questions, and imagining possibilities. Only humans get bored because we alone want more information: new thoughts and fresh insights.

"Creeping Things"

The greatest diversity of species on earth is found in among insects. In the fourteenth century, St. Theresa of Avila saw how worthwhile it was to mine the riches of creation, especially little creeping things: "In all the things that have been created by so great and wise a God there must be many secrets by which we can profit . . . I believe that in every little

170 *Cathecism of the Catholic Church*, #2418

thing created by God there is more than we realize, even in so small a thing as a tiny ant."[171] Indeed, the author of Proverbs invites us to do just that – read the ant then turn from the foolishness of being lazy toward the wisdom of being industrious: "Go to the ant, you lazybones; consider its ways and be wise."[172]

Like most children, I was fascinated by bugs as a boy. Perhaps because then I walked closer to the earth. But it wasn't until I began to go on backcountry retreats and learned to be still that I rediscovered them. At one camp, along the Na Pali coast of Kauai, I came upon a beetle the size of a lady bug which had a transparent sky-blue shell. The spiritual sense was immediately apparent. *Morally*, we should strive to be transparent, straight shooters who are sincere and genuine, never duplicitous or deceptive. *Allegorically*, we should see how Jesus was a man of surrender, completely transparent to His Father's will. And *anagogically*, we should remember that all our innermost thoughts and desires are seen by the Lord, and will be revealed on the last day.

At another backcountry site, this time in the Lamar Valley of northern Yellowstone, I came upon a creature I thought only lived in Africa, a dung beetle. About the size of a pecan, it was pushing elk scat backwards with its hind legs (just as its bigger cousins do with elephant scat) to use as a nursery for eggs and hatchlings. Similarly, even though the effort to provide for others can seem futile, a faithful Catholic knows it is not meaningless drudgery. God's always gives us opportunities to make our labor meaningful, transforming the dung of futility inherited through original sin into an occasion of fruitfulness and renewal. And even when it seems we are blindly moving backwards, He guides us along right path, for we endure by faith rather than sight, in the hope of one day being resurrected.

This hope of resurrection has no more poignant sign than that of another insect, the butterfly. Consider how a caterpillar is shackled to the earth and strenuously labors for its food, but upon entering the tomb of its cocoon that same creature is transformed, receiving a new body and emerging with wings. No longer bound to earth, it delights in the heavenly nectar of flowers. If one were to reference such a clear and potent word from God's first book, it might look something like the footnote below.[173]

---

171 St. Teresa of Avila, *Interior Castle*, 4.2.
172 Proverbs 6:6
173 The Most Holy Trinity, *The Book of Creation: "On the Glory of Resurrected Bodies"*, 33. (cf. 1 Corinthians 15:43)

"Wild Animals"

Grizzly Bears

A common reference for human mothers is the justifiable ferocity with which a grizzly mother defends her cubs. The message "Don't mess with my kids" is loud and clear. When a mother's offspring are threatened, the appropriate response is anger; but here we must distinguish good anger from bad. Good anger displays disapproval at an injustice while remaining ordered toward willing the good of others (like Jesus and the moneychangers), bad anger also displays disapproval but becomes disordered and does not will the good of others. This difference is noted by St. Paul: "Be angry but do not sin."[174]

The sign of a mother grizzly and her cubs can assist us in understanding the good anger which may arise when disciplining children. The sow shows her disapproval by giving her cubs a swat, but it is quite literally for their own good. Her role is to show them what to pursue and what to avoid in becoming a good and healthy bear. Proper discipline avoids two extremes: physical abuse (which results from bad anger), and disordered restraint (which results from not seeing that physical discipline is a good which should be willed to some children because it leads to happiness). Imagine a grizzly bear that let her cubs do as they pleased and was afraid to upset them. Spoiled cubs are dead cubs, just as spoiled children are miserable children. Permissive parenting does not will good to the child, for a disciplined life is a happy life.

Since proper discipline is widely neglected by parents in our day, it is not surprising that many adults are confused by the discipline of our Father in heaven. We are called to submit to God as a loving parent, but St. Paul teaches that even as adults we sometimes act like His disobedient and spoiled children; so for our sake He disciplines us to teach us to love more and behave better:

> My child, do not regard lightly the discipline of the Lord, or lose heart when you are punished by him; for the Lord disciplines those whom he loves, and chastises every child whom he accepts. Endure trials for the sake of discipline.

---

174 Ephesians 4:26

> God is treating you as children; for what child is there
> whom a parent does not discipline?[175]

St. Paul continues by explaining that understanding loving discipline requires some hindsight, a retrospective on the benefits of being justly punished by our human parents: "For they disciplined us for a short time as seemed good, in order that we may share his holiness. Now, discipline always seems painful rather than pleasant at the time, but later it yields the peaceful fruit of righteousness to those who have been trained by it."[176] Here the analogy concludes by emphasizing that discipline is an investment in the future of a person. Whether we are disciplining our kids or God is disciplining us, it is upsetting to be trained; but as parents of children and children of God we must learn see past the temporary pain to the permanent and "peaceful fruit" of a good and happy life.

Buffalo

In June of '96, I went on a three day retreat in the Lamar valley. As I was hiking out, I came over a rise and was confronted by fifty bison traveling single-file on the trail. The lead cow paused for a moment, then reeled around and took off down the long valley. The herd instantly fell into formation. Their twelve calves were gathered into the center, with three layers of adult defenses surrounding them. When I arrived at the trailhead about an hour later, I could see where they had finally stopped – more than two miles away.

A few years earlier, I was fishing the Firehole with a friend and noticed another herd of fifty bison ford the river then enter a forest, which had been burned and blackened during the great fires of '88. Anticipating there path, I went to the opposite edge of the forest, climbed a lodgepole, and waited. Thirty minutes later they began to emerge. Neither the lead cow nor the ranks of other mothers noticed me, and soon the entire family had surrounded my charred hideout. At first, the babies were nursing and playing, but soon needed a nap; and four of them lied down directly beneath me. One of these little golden calves still had a dried umbilical cord attached to its stomach. They napped for an hour or so, but each remained in touch with their mother by snorting a response to

---

175 Hebrews12:5-7
176 Hebrews12:10-11

her deep bellow. Then, they got up, nursed, played until they were tired, and took another nap as the adults and sub-adults grazed forward.

The point of these brief readings from Yellowstone is that children need various levels of protection. Sometimes they should be closely guarded, so that no evil can approach; other times they should be free to explore the world, but only under the watchful eye of family. Too often, American parents become duped into believing that kids just need food, water, and affection to grow. That is not true. Children need love which goes beyond affection to service, the service of knowing and willing what is good for them. A loving parent should know how to protect them from predatory evil as well as how to train them to eventually combat it on their own. Only negligent parents expose their children to evil by letting down their guard and becoming too lenient.

Lions

Nothing is more powerful sign of courage than "the lion, which is mightiest among wild animals, and does not turn back before any."[177] For this reason, the Book of Revelation refers to Jesus as the "Lion of the tribe of Judah".[178] But a lion is concurrently a word of demonic predation. As the first pope teaches, "Be sober, be watchful. Your adversary the devil prowls around like a roaring lion, seeking someone to devour."[179] All who have ever witnessed a mountain lion hunt mule deer, or just watched a pride of lions hunt on television, can immediately see what Peter was talking about: lions are sneaky and vicious. The devil and his demons, as well as anyone who has chosen their way, are predators who lie in wait, ready to "ambush like lions in a thicket."[180]

Wolves

Like lions, wolves can also be read as good or evil. In scripture they are spoken of pejoratively, but we have since come to read them in a fuller light. Since it is clear that they are predisposed to associate with human families and become domesticated pets, some anthropologists believe that wolves, more so than chimps, parallel human social structures. Nonetheless, a wolf can be as savage and merciless as any creature.

---

177 Proverbs 30:30
178 Revelation 5:5
179 1Peter 5:8
180 Psalm 10:9

Jesus points to wolves as signs of those who ruthlessly distort the truth. He warns us to beware of those who seem harmless but then assault the teaching of His Church: "Beware of false prophets, who come to you in sheep's clothing, but underneath are ravenous wolves."[181] The Church is not immune from attack, even from within the sheepfold. But if a wolf in sheep's clothing is bad, a wolf in shepherd's clothing is worse. St. Paul warns the bishops of the Church ("overseers" in some translations), that wolves can also emerge from within their own ranks:

> Keep watch over yourselves and over all the flock, of which the Holy Spirit has made you overseers, to shepherd the church of God that he obtained with the blood of his own Son. I know that after I have gone, savage wolves will come in among you, not sparing the flock. Some even from your own group will come distorting the truth in order to entice the disciples to follow them.[182]

A bishop is to be a shepherd of souls after the likeness of Jesus, "the Good Shepherd", but by perverting the truth he becomes a wolf disguised as a shepherd.[183] He may think he is leading the flock to greener pastures, but in the confusing fog of dissent he leads them instead to a precipice. One has only to compare the prophetic teaching of Pope Paul VI (who in 1968 warned that if contraception became widespread, marital infidelity and sexual promiscuity would as well), to those dissenting American priests and bishops who thought they knew better than the Magisterium, claiming morality was evolving and that we had become sophisticated enough to have sex without an openness to life.

Predation and violence are major themes advanced by wild animals. The message that something is wrong with the physical world is conveyed by the brutality of thieves, baby-killers, and home-wreckers. It is there whenever a wolf pack takes down an elk calf and begins eating it alive. On the other hand, non-violence and joy is conveyed by otters sledding, antelope kids playing tag, and buffalo calves bucking in wild bovine

---

181 Matthew 7:15
182 Acts 20:28-30
183 John 10:14

rodeos. Thus, earth is a place with signs of heaven, but also of hell "where there will be weeping and gnashing of teeth."[184]

The animal kingdom is full of jaws and claws but also of familial tenderness, signifying that evil has entered the world yet will not win the day. For all the savagery of nature, there remains a fundamental trajectory of good over evil, order over chaos. As St. Paul tells us, "where sin increased, grace abounded all the more".[185] So let us be attentive to the triumph of beauty over ugliness, tranquility over war, for at the second coming of Jesus (when sin and death are banished forever), mountain lions will lie in peace with mule deer . . . and wolves with elk.[186]

* * *

Discerning the massive divergence between the human person and the physical world is vital, especially when reading other animals. Injecting human dialogue and thoughts into animal behavior is quite normal, but we must guard against the tendency to assign our spiritual gifts to non-human creatures. Anthropomorphism is fine as long as it checked by reality. And even though an entire genus can exhibit such a dominate characteristic that we eventually create a word which reflects that characteristic, like when we call someone "crabby", unwarranted anthropomorphism causes confusion by misinterpreting God's words.

At the risk of belaboring this point, let us recognize that non-human animals *do not*: paint; sing new songs; synchronize movement to new songs (i.e. dance); create words; protect the rights of other species; own pets or slaves; worship creatures as gods; swear oaths or make covenants; project fear and anxiety into the future; use drugs to escape from reality; use contraceptives; blush; take vacations; make fires; wear clothes; fix broken bones; visit the moon; or pray for their enemies. Obviously this list could go on and on, but for our purposes it is an adequate segue into our next section: a reading from the human person.

---

184 Matthew 8:12; 13:42,50; 22:13; 24:51; 25:30
185 Romans 5:20
186 Cf. Isaiah 65:17ff.

Part IV

A Reading from the Human Person

* * *

Prologue

There is much confusion today about what it means to be a human person. Are we just highly evolved animals, or maybe just spirits trapped in a body? Are we bodily beings having a spiritual experience, or spiritual beings having a bodily experience? To some extent, we have already clarified how a spiritual soul makes us different from other bodily creatures (animals), as well as how having a body makes us different from other spiritual creatures (angels). But since it has become so popular to blur the line between humans and animals, or between humans and angels, it is essential to further discern the unique composition of "the human creature, who as it were shares in both orders, being composed of spirit and body."[1] Therefore, each of the following chapters will attempt to further concretize the distinct status of the human person as a body and soul composite.

---

1   *Lateran Council IV*, 1215 A.D. (cf. CCC, #327).

CHAPTER 21

Man the Philosopher

The word philosophy is a compound of the Greek words for love (philos) and wisdom (sophia). Wisdom can be generally defined as the understanding of causes: like what causes a child to be spoiled instead of giving, what causes a teen to develop addictions instead of character, or what causes a young couple to end up divorced instead of committed. Associating certain causes with certain effects allows one to make sound judgments and give good advice.

Natural Wisdom
One of my favorite examples of natural wisdom is the old adage, "Show me your friends and I'll show you your future." But at the forefront of natural wisdom is acknowledging an Uncaused Cause who has infused the physical world and the human person with first principles:

> Whoever reflects with an open mind on what is implied in the existence of the universe, cannot help but pose the question of the problem of the origin. Instinctively, when we witness certain happenings, we ask ourselves *what caused them.* How can we not but ask the same question in regard to the sum total of beings and phenomena which we discover in the world?[2]

---

2   Pope John Paul II, *General Audience,* July 10, 1985 (emphasis mine).

Discerning the existence of a Creator and His principles of truth, goodness, and beauty is the highest natural wisdom because it is based on first causes, yet it remains incomplete due to our fallen nature. If our wisdom is to encompass the big questions, this natural understanding of causes needs to be supplemented by a supernatural understanding of causes, especially as it pertains to good and evil.

Supernatural Wisdom

Wisdom on the supernatural level is an understanding of the ultimate causes of good and evil. To use the examples already cited, without an understanding of original sin, understanding what causes a child to be spoiled or a teen to develop addictions is limited; without an understanding of love as self-donation, understanding what causes divorce is limited.

If the gift of supernatural wisdom is not brought to bear on an issue, our view of what constitutes "sound" judgments can be as disparate as believing porn and same-sex marriage are basic human rights versus believing they are destroyers of civilization. Psychologists and parents who have received no insight from the supernatural realm can convince themselves that something as unnatural as homosexuality is natural, that a child does not need to be disciplined, or that guilt is bad . . . even when we've done something wrong.

Supernatural wisdom is "a spiritual gift which enables one to know the purpose and plan of God."[3] Knowing God's plan includes knowing why His first book has tattered pages and a broken binding, that is, it includes knowing the plan of the Devil, the ultimate cause of evil and falsehood.

The Devil is the father of half-truths, which is why he is likened to the fork-tongued serpent. For example, he might agree that we are animals with desires that God has made good, but then use this half-truth to overshadow that our desires are out of order and must disciplined to avoid becoming slaves to lust. Moreover, he might agree that it is good to fight the spread of AIDS, but then use this half-truth to promote condom distribution – an apparent good which causes promiscuity, which then causes sexual obsession, which then causes more opportunities for AIDS to spread. Recently, these fork-tongued tactics have been employed by a condom manufacturer whose advertising campaign promises to help

---

3   *Catechism of the Catholic Church*, appendix.

endangered species with each sale. This new company begins with the idea of safety for the human person and stewardship of the physical world, in order to sell the lie that contraception causes good, not evil.

In most instances, the serpent's goal is to convince us that God's plan is unnatural and unfulfilling. The supernatural gift of wisdom exposes his lies as apparent goods which are contrary to God's plan, a plan made known to us through the gift of faith in His Church.

One summer I took a group of ninth graders from Jackson Hole on a retreat to Santa Fe. On our last day there, we visited the Carmelite monastery about a half-mile from my parent's house. We were greeted by the mother superior, who remained out of sight, and after introducing everyone I asked if she had any words of wisdom for the young people gathered in the vestibule. Without missing a beat, she spoke with serene authority from behind the screen, "Yes . . . I do . . . Pray for the gift of faith."

After pondering her words for a few weeks, it became clear that she had struck upon the *sine qua non*[4] of understanding supernatural causes. The supernatural gift of faith is, in a certain sense, required to develop the supernatural gift of wisdom. Her advice was to "pray for the gift of faith" so that with faith we could pray for the gift of wisdom. As St. James assures us: "If any of you lacks wisdom, he should ask God, who gives to all generously and ungrudgingly, and he will be given it. But he should ask in faith, not doubting".[5] Mother Rose understood that faith unveils many purposes and plans, and many causes.

Several summers later, while on a solo retreat in Yellowstone, I was particularly focused on my lack of wisdom and began meditating on St. James advice. I resolved to ask for wisdom with unwavering faith and my daily prayer became very simple: "Sweet Jesus, grant me the gift of faith so that I may confidently ask for the gift of wisdom." About a week later, I was sitting by the Harlequin Eddies of the Yellowstone River, thanking God for a tangible improvement in making sound judgments and giving good advice, and as I began praying Morning Prayer from the Liturgy of the Hours, a passage jumped from the page: "I have openly sought wisdom in my prayers, and it has blossomed like early grapes."[6] I do not

---

4   The indispensable condition for something; literally "without which it is not".

5   James 1:5-6

6   Liturgy of the Hours, *Antiphon for Canticle of Zechariah*, Feast of Our Lady of Mount Carmel, July 16th.

consider myself a wise man, just a man who is slowly becoming wiser – simply because he asked.

Liberation from Error

One of the most serious problems we face in modern education is the marginalization of the quest to become wise. In advanced degree programs, for example, over-specialization has led many to become highly educated "experts" who lack wisdom. They might earn a PhD by studying the reproductive rate of Costa Rican tree frogs at elevations above 3,000 feet during el niño years, and be considered intelligent, but to go that deep into one subject is pretty shallow – unless, of course, that knowledge is situated within right reason and the big picture of God's plan. So what's the remedy? How can a person who wants to be a scientist or professor acquire wisdom? One solution is for Catholic colleges to revive the role of wisdom in their curriculums.

When I was a boy, my family took our VW bus through the vast mountains, canyons, and plateaus of the Rockies. There were often days when "it seemed as if those scenes of visionary enchantment would never have an end", and we would become so overwhelmed by the landscape that we were drawn into silence.[7] Then one of my parents would proclaim as a matter of fact, "This is God's country."

The motto of the newly founded Wyoming Catholic College is *Wisdom in God's Country* (which would have been a great title for this book). In the summer of 2007, I was invited to accompany the first freshman class on their inaugural backcountry trip into the Wind River Range.[8] All incoming students are required to complete a three-week NOLS wilderness course, which will hopefully translate into a comfort level that makes entering the wilderness less intimidating and, thus, more frequent. This is part of a larger plan to introduce the students to God's first book before they begin an academic curriculum based on liberal arts.

The foundation of liberal arts is traditionally called the Trivium: grammar, logic, and rhetoric. Grammar is needed to express oneself clearly, logic to express oneself coherently, and rhetoric to express

---

7   Merriweather Lewis, *The Journals of Lewis and Clark*, May 31, 1805.
8   By God's design, I was unable to go.

oneself persuasively.[9] These three disciplines can be associated with the transcendentals in that an individual's thoughts must be liberated from ambiguity and contradiction to be meaningful and *true* (the role of grammar); each series of thoughts must be liberated from disorder to be sequential and *good* (the role of logic); and each logical sequence of thoughts must liberated from sterility to be fruitful, inspiring, and *beautiful* (the role of rhetoric). It is fitting, then, that the crest of Wyoming Catholic College contains three words: *Veritas, Bonum, Puchrum* (Truth, Goodness, Beauty).

It might seem that logic should be associated more with truth than goodness, but not when we consider that individual thoughts can be true without being put with other thoughts in a way which makes sense. As we saw in Part I, individual creatures have identity, making them true, but without being coherently arranged with other creatures as they pass through time they do not adequately express goodness. Similarly, thinking errors arise from an inability to string thoughts together in a logical fashion. Consider the difference between someone explaining their tardiness by making bad excuses (which taken as individual thoughts might all be true), to someone who has "good reasons".

Thinking errors (logical fallacies) have become so rampant in our culture that even psychology has moved away from talking about how one is feeling to talking about how one is thinking. For instance, just because you *feel* like you are being treated unfairly doesn't mean you are. If you are punished for something like everyone else and knew the consequences beforehand, the punishment is fair. Counselors and therapists are rediscovering what Aristotle saw over two millennia ago: the intellect leads the will. Good thinking leads to good choosing. And good choosing to the art of living well.

In the study of a trade like engineering, medicine, or law, a student learns to provide an external service for wages and the common good of

---

9   The other liberal arts are known as the Quadrivium: arithmetic, music, geometry, and astronomy.

society.[10] In the study of liberal arts, on the other hand, a student is not bound by the pursuit of an external skill set, but is freed by the pursuit of an internal one: reason liberated from error.

Teaching students to make sense when they are thinking, writing, or speaking is a major step toward natural wisdom, but when a liberal arts college does not inform reason with faith and supernatural wisdom, it cannot see the fullness of truth, and therefore cannot fully liberate the student from thinking errors. I have known many graduates of liberal arts colleges who promote the distribution of condoms for high school students because they simply do not understand supernatural causes. But being informed by the fullness of truth is never enough. We must also have the courage to practice that truth, and the wisdom to practice it in a manner which causes others to be inspired. As St. Paul put it, "to practice the truth in love".[11] Wyoming Catholic College teaches students to do just that.

Colleges and universities where students learn a trade are necessary for the common good, but without a foundation in Catholic liberal arts a student might not learn how to think clearly or act with courage and charity. A greater service to the common good is always provided by one who supplements their job skills with the ability to understand natural and supernatural causes; thereby becoming a wise judge of things.

---

10   The "common good" is the totality of social conditions which allow us to seek fulfillment. This includes basic needs like food, shelter, clothing, as well as basic rights such as having a family, receiving an education, freedom of religion, and health care. All charitable service and honest work contribute to the building up of these conditions: from the person who picks up the garbage every week or makes sure that homes have electricity, to the person who works in an emergency room or the jail.

11   Ephesians 4:15

CHAPTER 22

Man the Judge

The Wisdom of Solomon

Becoming a good judge of things is related to one's level of wisdom. When the Lord asked Solomon what gift he desired, the king responded, "an understanding mind . . . able to discern between good and evil."[12] The Lord then granted him "a wise and discerning mind" and the people "stood in awe of the king, because they perceived that the wisdom of God was in him, to execute justice."[13]   In order to "execute justice", Solomon needed supernatural wisdom, because it is impossible to fully discern between good and evil without it. Justice is served when those in authority make sound judgments based on what is objectively good and what is objectively evil.   Solomon was considered the wisest man in the world because he received supernatural wisdom from above, but never stopped reading from wisdom that was here below, for he often made reference to God's first book when giving advice and rendering judgments: "He would speak of trees . . . he would speak of animals, and birds, and reptiles, and fish. People came from all the nations to hear the wisdom of Solomon."[14]

Judging Others

The natural law dictates that we should be fair, but complex circumstances often make judging what is fair difficult.   Consider

12   1Kings 3:9
13   1Kings 3:12; 3:28
14   1Kings 4:33-34

191

the confusion in our culture regarding discrimination. Those who obstinately believe it is wrong to discriminate against someone have often not made the necessary distinctions; whereas the wise man sees that not all discrimination is unjust. An employer would be completely justified in discriminating against a convicted pedophile when screening applicants to work in a day care. In fact, he or she would be obligated to discriminate. Discrimination is not always wrong, which is why the Church teaches us to pray for homosexuals and avoid any "unjust discrimination" towards them; but at the same time teaches that if they are lobbying for marital rights discrimination is justified because they are violating the natural law.[15] The wise man also distinguishes between and making sound judgments and being judgmental.

A popular defense when confronted with wrongdoing is to say, "Who are you to judge me?" Indeed, we read in scripture that Jesus warns against judgment: "Do not judge, so that you may not be judged."[16] But here we must distinguish between the intellectual act of discernment, reflected in the phrase *use good judgment,* and determining another's status before God in order to assign eternal punishment, reflected in the term *judgment day.* The first type of judgment, to discern good from evil, we are all called to exercise. This becomes clear as Jesus continues His sermon, "Do not give what is holy to dogs; and do not throw your pearls before swine." By telling us to make right judgments in identifying what is holy and unholy, Jesus is not telling us to condemn others, only to assess there behavior so as to avoid profaning holy things. The second type of judgment, to condemn and assign eternal punishment, is the exclusive domain of God, who alone can accurately judge what is in someone's heart. Only God knows with certainty a person's intentions or what past injustices in their own life may be mitigating circumstances. We can certainly judge if a person is guilty or innocent of certain actions and sentence them to some type of punishment, like prison, but we can never judge whether they deserve eternal punishment or what circumstances might diminish their moral responsibility before God.

Let us now turn to the application of right judgment and discrimination in the formation of human laws.

---

15   *Catechism of the Catholic Church,* #2358.
16   Matthew 7:1

Civil Law

Civil laws are valid insofar as they extend natural law to specific circumstances. If our view of civil law is that it is merely a social contract invented by the weak to protect themselves against the strong, our view of justice can easily become subjective. In America, the natural moral law found within each of us is the objective truth upon which we. have based our nation's idea of what is just and unjust:

> When the founding fathers of this great nation enshrined certain inalienable rights in the Constitution – and something similar exists in many countries and in many international declarations – they did so because they recognized the existence of a "law" – a series of rights and duties – engraved by the Creator on each person's heart.[17]

If civil laws are to reflect our natural rights and duties, they must have an objective basis. One may have noticed that St. Augustine and St. Thomas Aquinas, who achieved the most elevated synthesis of faith and reason in their respective millenniums, have been cited more than others in this book. That is because their genius is still relevant. Their insights into the relationship between natural law and civil law, for example, forcefully impacted the civil rights movement of the 1960's.

When Dr. Martin Luther King Jr. protested the unjust discrimination and violence against blacks in Birmingham, Alabama, he was arrested and thrown in jail. There he composed a letter in response to allegations that he was not a law abiding citizen:

> One may well ask: "How can you advocate breaking some laws and obeying others?" The answer lies in the fact that there are two types of laws: just and unjust. I would be the first to advocate obeying just laws. One has not only a legal but a moral responsibility to obey just laws. Conversely, one has a moral responsibility to disobey unjust laws. I would agree with St. Augustine that "an unjust law is no law at all." Now, what is the difference

---

17   Pope John Paul II, *World Youth Day: Vigil of the Assumption of Mary*, August 14, 1993; Cherry Creek State Park, Colorado.

between the two? How does one determine whether a law is just or unjust? A just law is a man-made code that squares with the moral law of the law of God. An unjust law is a code that is out of harmony with the moral law. To put in the terms of St. Thomas Aquinas: "An unjust law is a human law that is not rooted in eternal law and natural law."[18]

Dr. King then cites the example of unjust taxation laws suffered by the American colonies, and their right to oppose them with demonstrations like the Boston Tea Party. He also cites the example of Nazi Germany's unjust laws against Jews.

It is essential to see that without the objective moral law there would be no basis to convict the perpetrators of the Holocaust. If moral relativism is true, then the Nazis were just doing what was subjectively true for them, even though it might not be true for us. Their general defense at the Nuremberg trials was that they were obeying the civil laws of their country. In order to convict them, the court needed to establish they had violated natural law by committing "crimes against humanity".

Since natural law is available to us all through the right use of reason, those who perpetrate unjust laws cannot hide behind their legality: "Human law has the nature of law in so far as it partakes of right reason ... But in so far as it deviates from reason, it is called an unjust law, and has the nature, not of law but of violence."[19] What is remarkable here is that St. Thomas sees unjust laws as legislated violence. Certainly this was true in Nazi Germany, but doesn't the law protecting a woman's "right" to kill her unborn child have the same violent nature?

Legalizing same sex marriage is another example of an unjust law which does violence. In this case, the violence does not directly threaten the life of the individual, but the life of society, the foundation of which is the natural family. As the Bishop of Honolulu recently wrote regarding a proposal to legalize same sex marriage in Hawaii, our duty is to promulgate the truth of natural law, even when that discrimination is considered by many to be unjust:

---

18   Martin Luther King Jr., *Letter from a Birmingham Jail*, April 16, 1963.
19   St. Thomas Aquinas, *Summa Theologica*, I-II.93.3.2.

The truth is that God made complementary sexes, that he gave the power of procreation to be used responsibly by a man and woman, and he wants both father and mother, when possible, to contribute to the healthy nurturing of children. This special role of man and woman has been recognized for millennia by societies as *marriage*, the stable, committed relationship of man and woman giving themselves to each other totally and bearing the fruit of that love in the procreation and education of children. This is a truth that goes beyond religions, because it is built into the very nature of our human being. It is a reality that has been safeguarded by the laws of societies in virtually all cultures of the world. In many places throughout our country and the world, and now here in Hawaii, some are attempting to distort this natural relationship by claiming the right of persons of the same sex to marry. They point out that it is discriminatory to allow opposite-sex couples to marry but to disallow the same for same-sex couples. And they are correct! It is discriminatory, making distinctions between one and another. But not all discrimination is unjust. Some is quite justified because it is based on reality and truth. While every person, no matter his or her sexual orientation, is worthy of dignity and respect and has certain inalienable rights given by the Creator, there is no right for people of the same sex to call their unions marriage.[20]

I have quoted the Bishop at length to highlight how judgment informed by right reason has a unique clarity; and also to highlight how right reason is protected from error by the apostolic Church. The domain of the Magisterium extends to matters of natural law, that is, to discerning justice from injustice, true rights from false rights.

Ecclesial Law

Catholicism is often criticized for having so many rules. Kneel down. Stand up. Do this. Don't do that. But consider how unfair it would

---

20   Most Reverend Larry Silva, Bishop of Honolulu, January 12, 2010.

be to dishonor God with unworthy words and actions, or to disrespect our neighbor with false teaching. Like civil law, ecclesial law attempts to implement natural law, and the Code of Canon Law is a book which ensures that God and neighbor are given their due.

Consider two examples from canon law. First, giving God what He deserves means respecting the sacred order of celebrating His sacraments. If Jesus celebrated the first mass with unleavened bread and wine, it is not lawful to use doughnuts and grape juice. Second, giving our neighbor what he deserves means respecting his right to be told the truth. If one desires to teach the Catholic faith, it is only fair that he or she profess allegiance to the faith so that students and parents can be confident that what is being taught is the truth about God and His Church.

Ecclesial law is also similar to civil law in establishing a hierarchy of just punishments. In civil law, first degree murder is punishable by life in prison or death, whereas traffic violations only carry a fine. Likewise, in ecclesial law the intentional killing of an innocent human being is the worst possible offense. One notable difference, however, is that a civil law can be passed which violates natural law and promotes the intentional killing of an innocent human being, like legalized abortion, whereas a comparable ecclesial law cannot be passed. Abortion will always incur the penalty of exclusion from God's family until one formally repents of that sin. It will never be left to judge for ourselves.

CHAPTER 23

Man the King

By reading the human person we learn who we are, what relation we have to others, and how we came to be. Other animals do not know these things anymore than a word on a page understands its significance, its function within a sentence, or its relationship to the author. As we become more aware of ourselves and others, we also discover that we have a heart which cannot be taken from us but is ours alone to give. No one can make us love someone we choose not to. We can be tortured, imprisoned, or forced to do things against our will, but in the recesses of the heart we reign as kings of our own little kingdoms.

Magnanimity

The word magnanimous is a compound of the Latin words *magnus* (great) and *animus* (soul). Being magnanimous means believing we are called to do great things with our lives. It is the good kind of pride which must be distinguished from the bad kind. Bad pride says "I am great and do great things!", whereas good pride says "God is great and has called me to do great things for Him with the talents He has given me." Bad pride is a lack of humility; good pride is rooted in humility (much like the glory of wildflowers is rooted in good soil). As St. James affirms, "God resists the proud and gives grace to the humble."[21] But humility must not be taken too far. A realistic assessment of our gifts is essential, for everyone is called to develop their God-given talents into a great and beautiful life:

---

21 James 4:6

It is a sign of humility if a man does not think too much of himself, through observing his own faults; but if a man has contempt for the good things he has received from God, this, far from being a proof of humility, shows him to be ungrateful.[22]

Without making these distinctions, the desire for greatness can stray into sinful pride or false humility. This is why JP II often guided young people toward true greatness:

Do not be content with anything less than the highest ideals! Do not let yourselves be dispirited by those who are disillusioned with life and have grown deaf to the deepest and most authentic desires of their heart. You are right to be disappointed with hollow entertainment and passing fads, and with aiming at too little in life.[23]

Unfortunately, the "highest ideals" are often presented to youth in terms of material greatness rather than spiritual greatness. Material possessions, though not sinful in themselves, can easily be idolized by young people. The material self can also be overemphasized, especially since American culture "tends to promote the cult of the body . . . to idolize physical perfection and success at sports."[24] Sports are good insofar as they teach young people discipline, perseverance, fairness, sacrifice, self-control, and courage, but they cannot make a person great. And I can think of no better way to illustrate this point than to recall my favorite Olympic moment, and the Marine who won gold in 1964.

True Greatness

Billy Mills was born an Oglala Sioux on the Pine Ridge reservation in South Dakota. Orphaned at 12 years old, he attended a boarding school where he excelled in track and received a scholarship to run at the University of Kansas. After graduating, he became a lieutenant in the Marine Corps and qualified for the 10,000 meter run at the 1964 Olympics in Tokyo. Mills was not expected to medal. During the race he

---

22 St. Thomas Aquinas, *Summa Theologica*, II-II.35.1.3.
23 Pope John Paul II, *Message for World Youth Day, 2002*.
24 *Catechism of the Catholic Church*, #2289 (emphasis in original)

took the lead then fell behind several times, all the while telling himself he could win. With 300 meters to go on the final lap he was pushed and stumbled, with 100 meters to go he was in third place and trailing by 10 meters. Then, with only 50 meters to go, he seemed to be shot from a cannon and won decidedly. In the excitement of that final stretch, the commentator cried out hysterically, "Look at Mills! Look at Mills! Ahhhhhh! Mills is coming on!" Billy Mills ran his best time by almost a minute, that's one full lap, and set a new Olympic record. No American before or since has won the event.

Because of his discipline and perseverance, some consider Billy Mills a hero. And while the apostle Paul draws an analogy between those who discipline themselves to succeed in Olympic competition and those who strive for heaven, he emphasizes that a true hero is someone who is disciplined for eternal glory, not just temporary glory:

> Do you not know that the runners in the stadium all run
> in the race, but only one wins the prize? Run so as to win.
> Athletes exercise discipline in every way. They do it to win
> a perishable crown but we an imperishable one."[25]

The life of Billy Mills is not commendable just because he won a gold medal, but because he went on to help the poor by raising over 200 million dollars for Christian Relief Services, and to help young people be magnanimous by teaching them a simple principle: "My life is a gift to me from my Creator, what I do with my life is my gift back to the Creator."[26]

No matter what physical or intellectual talents a young person possesses, the goal of living a truly great life will always be a spiritual quest, a quest to find fulfillment and happiness. JP II addressed this universal desire at World Youth Day in Toronto:

> It is Jesus in fact that you seek when you dream of
> happiness; he is waiting for you when nothing else you
> find satisfies you; he is the beauty to which you are so
> attracted; it is he who provokes you with that thirst for
> fullness that will not let you settle for compromise; it is

---

25   1Corinthians 9:24-25

26   Billy Mills, *Makata Taka Hela* (respects the earth, loves his country).

he who urges you to shed the masks of a false life; it is he who *reads in your hearts the desire to do something great* with your lives, the will to follow an ideal, the refusal to allow yourselves to be ground down by mediocrity, the courage to commit yourselves humbly and patiently to improving yourselves and society, making the world more human and more fraternal.[27]

Many young people have "the courage to commit" but they do not know what to commit to. There are so many contradictory opinions of what is great in the sight of God they cannot see which opinion is right; and if there is no way of knowing which convictions are objectively true, then one's idea of greatness is based on the blind faith of fideism. Youth can see that there is nothing worse in the modern world than to seek to be magnanimous but be wrong about God's will. Islamic extremists believe they give glory to God, but instead make the world *less* human and *less* fraternal. Here again we find the incomparable value of right reason and the Magisterium of the Church. The assurance of truth regarding who God is and what God wants should infuse every young Catholic who searches for meaning with undaunted courage.

Fear

Fear is the enemy of courage, and the heart is where we conquer it. The Bible is said to include the phrase *do not be afraid* 365 times – one for each day of the year – and Jesus himself uses the phrase at least eighteen times. Fear, it seems, is one of our biggest problems. But since the Bible also commands us to *be afraid*, we must distinguish good fear from bad.

The book of Proverbs begins by saying, "The fear of the Lord is the beginning of wisdom."[28] This refers to the respect we owe to God as our Father who knows what is good and what is evil. As Pope Benedict XVI teaches, "To be without *fear of God* is equivalent to putting ourselves in his place, to feeling we ourselves are lords of good and evil".[29] The beginning of wisdom is a trust that God is a good and loving Father who knows what leads to our happiness. In the Gospel of Matthew, Jesus tells

---

27 Pope John Paul II, *Message for Vigil of Prayer*, World Youth Day; August 19, 2002 (emphasis mine)
28 Proverbs 1:7
29 Pope Benedict XVI, *Angelus*, June 22, 2008.

us that true greatness consists of three things: observing and teaching all of His commandments; being humble like a child; and striving to be the servant of all.[30] Good fear persuades us to act heroically and animates the courage we need to follow these ideals, that is, to live according to The Way.

Bad fear, on the other hand, does not trust that God is a loving Father. It dissuades us from acting heroically and making a gift of oneself by paralyzing us with irrational thoughts of being unfulfilled by The Way. It is a form of being our own God, for it is a fear that our life will not be great if we surrender to Him. Psalm 112 incorporates both concepts of fear: "Blessed is the man who fears the Lord, who greatly delights in his commandments! . . . His heart is firm, trusting in the Lord. His heart is steady, he will not be afraid."[31]

Heroic Virtue

With our free-will comes the ability to sin and behave cowardly, but also the ability to be great-hearted. To be really honest about both the depravity and sanctity we are capable of, we only need to recall the differences in parenting styles that children experience: some are cowardly, some are heroic. But perhaps an additional example, from a concentration camp no less, really gets to the heart of the matter; for there we find the depths of cowardice and the summit of heroism.

I remember at first being somewhat unmoved by the tour of the concentration camp called Auschwitz. Rooms full of eyeglasses, for example, just made me reflect on how during World War II there was only one shape of lens, round. Other rooms stacked with shoes and clothing just reminded me of rooms where I worked at the Samaritan House homeless shelter. Without knowing it, I seemed to be searching for something which would make it all seem real. Eventually, I was drawn to a small exhibit under glass which listed the personal effects of some of the prisoners. My eyes fell upon a hand-written entry in that inventory: one Sacred Heart of Jesus medal. Thoughts about how much my own medal meant to me began to resonate deeply, piquing my sensitivity to the fact that a real person had arrived there half a century earlier. Auschwitz was slowly becoming a reality – and the next room I entered removed the scales from my eyes completely.

---

30   Matthew 5:19; 18:4; 20:26
31   Psalm 112:1, 7-8

I had been traveling with two particularly kind sisters that day who were among my closest friends. They had grown up in the idyllic setting of a small farm near the Great Bear sand dunes in northwest Michigan. Both had been home-schooled and almost always wore their long hair in a single thick braid. In hindsight, the three of us had been drifting toward the horror of what happened at the death camps all day, but when we entered that next room it finally hit close to home. Piled four feet deep, ten feet wide, and twenty feet across, were the braids of hair from thousands of women and girls whose heads had been shorn before they entered the gas chambers. These were not possessions like clothes, but pieces of God's own children – children who were thought to be less than human by other humans. Auschwitz had become personal.

A short time later, the devastating reality of man's inhumanity to man was conquered by hope when we visited the cell where a Catholic priest had been starved then murdered. St. Maximilian Kolbe was a Franciscan who spread the Gospel by example, and by printing a weekly newspaper. A clear threat to Nazism, he was arrested and brought to Auschwitz. Shortly thereafter, a prisoner escaped and in retribution the Nazis selected ten men to be killed by starvation. One of them was a man with a wife and family. Maximilian volunteered to take his place and for the next two weeks he led the nine other men in prayer, helping them overcome bitterness and hatred as they slowly starved to death. He was the last man standing; and in order to make room for more victims was killed by lethal injection on August 14, 1941. The man with a wife and family, whom he had saved, attended St. Maximilian's canonization ceremony on October 10, 1982.

To be magnanimous is to be brave-hearted, overcoming bad fear with good fear, spinelessness with backbone. As King David put it, "Be strong, let your heart take courage".[32] The coward makes life a gift *for* oneself, the hero makes life a gift *of* oneself. Those who choose to exercise such heroic virtue take the words of the New King David to heart: "whoever loses his life for my sake will save it."[33]

We are indeed enthroned as kings of our own hearts, the lords of whom we choose to love; but if we desire to enter eternal glory and the kingdom of heaven, we must surrender our own kingdoms by laying our crowns at the feet of Jesus, who is "King of kings and Lord of lords."[34]

---

32   Psalm 31:25
33   Luke 9:24
34   Revelation 19:16

CHAPTER 24

Man the Artist

As we saw in Part I, the heart expresses beauty in works of art and the art of living; and both illustrate differences between us and other animals. A beaver, for example, instinctively builds the same dam over and over without trying to make it more stylish or giving it a personal touch: "Indeed, *art* is a distinctively human form of expression; beyond the search for the necessities of life which is common to all living creatures, art is a freely given superabundance of the human being's inner riches."[35] The inner riches of the human person, while bearing a likeness to God's, are at the same time radically dissimilar.

One radical difference is that a human artist cannot make a sculpture or painting that has the power to then create original sculptures or paintings, or even invent other mediums of art. Divine creativity is far beyond our own in the very fact that God created a creature that is a little creator, us. Clearly, no matter how advanced the science of robotics becomes, man will never produce something which is truly creative.

Another radical difference is that a human artist cannot produce a painting on a canvass in their studio while simultaneously creating the canvass and studio as well. A sunset is painted on clouds which are themselves being sculpted and are dynamically situated within an environment of sounds, scents, and motion. The colors of a human painting don't breathe from the canvass like God's sky. Even high definition 3D video with surround-sound cannot affect the senses like divine art. The sweet smell of decaying leaves on an autumn breeze, as

---

35   *Catechism of the Catholic Church*, #2501

mountain jays chatter through the forest and bull elk bugle from every direction, is an example of how God alone creates *sensurround* art.[36]

Nonetheless, human art is in some ways similar to divine art. Creation as a whole is beautiful because every creature has been ordered to act in harmony with every other creature, which is analogous to playing beautiful music:

> Think of a musician tuning his lyre. By his skill he adjusts high notes to low and intermediate notes to the rest, and produces a series of harmonies. So too the wisdom of God holds the world like a lyre and joins things in the air to those on earth, and things in heaven to those in the air, and brings each part into harmony with the whole. By his decree and will he regulates them all to produce the beauty and harmony of a single, well-ordered universe.[37]

Beyond the orderly meter of the song of creation, we must emphasize that beauty emerges from the way God plays that song. For us, too, playing beautiful songs is not just a matter of striking the strings of a guitar that is in tune, producing various chords, but rather skillfully striking the strings with one's God-given aptitude for heartfelt expression. It is the difference between a song played with precise mechanical attention to the notes and that same song played with gifted phrasing and harmony.

Hearing or seeing the phrasing in God's works of art is not always easy. Some creatures taken individually appear drab, like certain gulls or reef fish, but when gathered in a flock or school become poetry in motion. Other creatures must be examined closely, for they seem dull from a distance. Wasps and yellow jackets are examples of paintings which are rarely admired from the right perspective. (Granted, they are difficult to appreciate until they are lying dead on a windowsill or stuck to the grill of a car.) Human works of art also have a distance from which their beauty becomes more evident. A good exercise is to find the vantage from which you think an artist contemplated his work: the distance from the canvass or clay perhaps.

---

36   Mountain jays are also known as Steller's jays.
37   St. Athanasuis, *Office of Readings*, First Friday in ordinary time

The Beautiful

Regarding *works of art*, let us recall that truth and goodness are signs of intellect and will, but that the signature of the heart is beauty. Certainly we can make things that are what they are and do what they do (thus becoming true and good), but the full-flowering of creativity is something which brings truth and goodness to a higher level. A rifle or wineglass is good insofar as it is functional (shooting accurately or holding liquid), but when given an artistic touch, perhaps by the checkering of the wood, the etching of the glass, or the simple balance of form, it becomes beautiful.

Many works of modern art express little truth in that they cannot be identified, and little goodness in that they have no order; therefore, they have little beauty and do not inspire. Since the transcendentals of being are both unified and distinct, art moves away from beauty as it fails to incorporate the true and the good. Sometimes, however, beauty can be found in the artist's attempt to make something beautiful. The crayon drawing of a child may not be an objectively beautiful work of art, but it is nonetheless worthy of display at the museum of Mom's refrigerator because something of the artist always shows itself – in this case, the beauty of innocence, purity, and potential for self-giving.

Regarding *the art of living*, let us recall that to identify and choose the right thing to do is a matter of intellect and will, but to embrace an inspiring way of doing it is a matter of the heart. Compare the difference between picking up a piece of trash and grumbling about how people are so inconsiderate, to joyfully offering up that small action for the salvation of souls.

Poetry

Poetry is a unique form of the beautiful, for it transcends the syntax of prose by joining words with integrity, proportion, and radiant economy. The following poem represents this sublime power of poetry to rise above the prosaic, yet is easily accessible:

> Do you remember, my sweet, absent son,
> How in the soft June days forever done
> You loved the heavens so warm and clear and high;
> And, when I lifted you, soft came your cry, –
> "Put me 'way up, – 'way up in the blue sky"

> I laughed and said I could not, – set you down
> Your gray eyes wonder-filled beneath that crown
> Of bright hair gladdening me as you raced by,
> Another Father now, more strong than I,
> Has borne you voiceless to your dear blue sky.[38]

The author of this poem could have written a few pages of prose on how his young son had died (or how he knew of a father whose son had died), but for all its power to expose, prose cannot so poignantly wed the grief and hope of the Father's heart.

Artists can penetrate the deepest realities of the human condition, both good and evil, and every form of art that sincerely pursues beauty can reveal more of a given reality than everyday experience:

> In so far as it seeks the beautiful, the fruit of an imagination which rises above the everyday, art is by its nature a kind of appeal to the mystery. Even when they explore the darkest depths of the soul or the most unsettling aspects of evil, artists give voice in a way to the universal desire for redemption.[39]

Some artists may indeed be giving voice to the "desire for redemption", but that does not mean that all art is beautiful. All too often, modern forms of art place subjective expression above objective reality. This misuse of God-given talent then becomes more a disclosure of the falsehood, disorder, and ugliness found within the artist's soul than an unveiling of being or penetration of mystery.

Modern Art

As we've said, to the extent that creativity neglects to integrate what is objectively true and good, it drifts from being objectively beautiful. This is why so much of modern art is illegible and unintelligible, yet is misread as beautiful simply because it is considered "honest", "courageous", or "provocative". The following considerations may provide a foundation for a more realistic appraisal of beauty in modern art.

---

38 George Parsons Lathrop (1851-1898), *The Child's Wish Granted.*
39 Pope John Paul II, *Letter to Artists*, #10

First, some modern art shifts from exposing deeper objective truth to exposing the lack of conformity with reality in the mind of the artist. The artist may be praised as "honest" for expressing tormented feelings or intellectual confusion, but is it really beautiful to overemphasize the subjective or promote skepticism? Second, some modern art shifts from highlighting some aspect of objective goodness to highlighting rebellion and disorder. The artist may be praised as "courageous" for breaking away from objective moral norms; but is it really beautiful to defy the order in the universe by exalting chaos or relativism? And third, some modern art shifts from evoking magnanimity – that greatness which is based on what is true and good – to provoking a disturbed or meaningless emotional response. The artist may be praised as being "provocative" for causing a reaction; but is it really beautiful to create something mostly for "shock effect", or for the sake of idolizing individual expression without reference to integrity, proportion, and clarity?

One of the hallmarks of beauty is its power to provoke creativity in the form of prayerful communion and charitable service. *Provocation* is a compound of the prefix *pro* (on behalf of) and the word *vocation* (calling), which is derived from the Latin verb *vocare* (to call). Any work of art may be "provocative", but beautiful art must be distinguished from that which calls us to the futility of nihilism or atheism, as that which speaks *on behalf of our calling* to love God and neighbor with gifts from the heart.

My Muse

When God's creativity is read from the human person in the form of talent or physical beauty, it often provokes a creative answer. To behold a woman singing, painting, or playing the guitar stirs a man's heart, bypassing the intellect in a certain sense. If the woman happens to be physically beautiful as well, it is all the more ravishing. But even if she is not, her inner beauty becomes radiant through artistic creativity. Such an encounter can then summon a response of music or poetry within the man, and the woman becomes his muse.

In my lifetime, only one woman I dated ever had such an effect. At times she thought I was her soul-mate and wanted to spend her life with me, but in the end the weeds of anxiety over living the American dream choked out the Catholic dream of living the gospel faithfully. I don't know what happened to her, but for a brief time our hearts shared a timeless embrace . . . an eternal moment of gift and mystery . . . and

I hope she went on to give the world as much joy as her gifts would afford. But more than anything, I will always be thankful for the love and creativity she induced from my heart. One of the poems I wrote for her contained a verse about how everything had become imbued with her being, and how every creature began to speak her name:

Are all the flowers hers now,
All the birds and colors of the sky?
Will every poem speak of her somehow,
Every deer bounding by?

Who she was as a person inspired me to create works of art (however poor) but also to create a better man, to make something more of myself. This reply to *beauty in the human person* reaches its summit when one is inspired by the perfect human muse, God's perfect creature, the Blessed Virgin Mary.

When a heart is captivated by *The Immaculata*, every rose begins to emit her perfume and every face shines with the smile of her Son – even the air we breathe begins to speak of her. And how appropriate this rapture truly is, for among all the artistic endeavors in the universe, Mary stands alone as the masterpiece of divine and human creativity. Her art of living teaches us that a full appreciation of beauty is inseparable from acknowledging the divine font from which it flows. Any visit to a wildlife refuge, art gallery, or holy shrine should redound to the glory of God in imitation of Mary – the master of all masters in crafting one's life into something beautiful.

Something Beautiful for God

Every Catholic has a vocation as an artist. As John Paul II reminds us, "all men and women are entrusted with the task of crafting their own life: in a certain sense, they are to make of it a work of art, a masterpiece."[40] Life becomes a work of beauty to the extent that it harmonizes with right reason and the fullness of God's will. A holy life can be so inspiring that others wish to emulate that life. This is especially true of great saints like Francis of Assisi and Teresa of Calcutta.

Inspired by Jesus and Mary (as well as her parents), Mother Teresa simply wanted to make her life "something beautiful for God."[41] This

---

40   Pope John Paul II, *Letter to Artists*, 2.
41   Mother Teresa, *Light for Our Times: On Purity*, #49 (CD ROM).

one eighteen year-old heart, full of love, became so beautiful that by the time she died over 4,000 women had been inspired to live every day exactly the way she did, serving the poorest of the poor for the glory of God. The Missionaries of Charity now serve in 134 countries, and untold millions think of this great saint as a mother. Yet for all that, she would say with complete sincerity that the key to the art of living is simplicity: "The whole thing has been nothing extraordinary, nothing special. It has been just a simple surrender, a simple yes to Christ."[42] A simple yes to The Beautiful: that is the art of living well . . . that is the art of compassion.

If I was asked to identify my favorite place in Jackson Hole, it would neither be up in the mountains nor down in the river bottoms, but in the very heart of the valley – a vast plain known as Antelope Flats. From there one can survey the full circumference of peaks which make up the "hole", but there is also the sense of open space; and perhaps that is why it speaks to me. Much like the Front Range of Colorado from the vantage of Cherry Creek, the Teton Range is to the west of the plain, running north and south. A perfect morning for me is to pray the Liturgy of the Hours with the universal Church, and then pray spontaneously as the sun lights up the Grand, then the lower peaks, and finally the valley floor where buffalo calves and antelope kids celebrate a new day. One July morning, however, was not so sweet for a baby pronghorn. He was only 50 yards from my truck by the time it was light enough for me to see, and seemed confused. After I glassed around for his mother, it became apparent that he was lost. He ran over to the nearest doe he saw, about a quarter mile away, but was rejected. He became more and more panicked as each doe he thought might be his mother refused to accept him. The last time I saw him he was running at near full speed away from any antelope for miles around.

When a story like this bothers us it is precisely because we have a capacity for compassion, an expression of the heart not possible for other animals. Bulldogs, for example, would be just as interested in chewing their bones after witnessing this event as they had been before. Certainly there have been cases where animals have adopted the young of others, but they are rare and instinctual – another example of an exception that proves the rule. We alone take in and care for orphans of all species. And while one may argue that there have also been cases where human parents have rejected and exploited their children in ways that an animal

---

42   Mother Teresa, *Total Surrender*, 5.

could literally not even imagine, those compassionate souls who have given their entire lives in the service of orphans and outcasts prove the same point: we are without equal in the animal kingdom.

Further clarity is provided by the example of a robin raising her chicks. She instinctively gives the worm to the strongest, whereas the weakest is usually pushed out of the nest, falls to the ground, and dies. The spiritual powers of the human person, on the other hand, are able to transcend instinct and exercise compassion. Our intellect sees that some offspring need extra care, our free-will chooses to provide it, and our heart goes out to them. Far from letting "nature" take its course, what is natural for us is to intercede on behalf of those with special needs.

In the Footsteps of Father Damien

Much like St. Maximilian Kolbe and Mother Teresa, St. Damien of Molokai was a poet who wrote his life as a sacred sonnet. He willingly stepped into a world of contrast, where physical and moral ugliness engendered despair, but glorious beaches and cliffs filled with seabirds brought inspiration. With artistic vision, he saw beyond the leprosy, alcoholism, and sexual depravity to the deeper reality that serving the poor was serving Jesus. The poor then became his muse and summoned from him the great refrain of compassionate creativity: "There is no greater love than to lay down one's life for one's friends."[43] He could see, like so many other saints, that laying down one's life out of love for God is the greatest love, the greatest creativity, the greatest willing of good to another:

> To desire *unlimited good* for another person is really to desire God for that person: He alone is the objective fullness of the good, and only His goodness can fill every man to overflowing.[44]

By crafting his life as a gift of self, St. Damien wrote words of compassion that went beyond the prosaic needs of the body to feed the poetic needs of the soul. And so that small peninsula, originally set aside to be a lepers' colony, with the arrival of Kamiano became transformed into an artist's colony.

---

43 John 15:13
44 Karol Wojtyla (Pope John Paul II), *Love and Responsibility*, 138.

CHAPTER 25

Man the Procreator

In spite of the speculations of psychological evolutionists, love cannot be reduced to chemical reactions, however complex. It may include psychological attraction toward talent and trait, but as we've seen, free-will is an absolute pre-requisite. No matter how much affection an animal displays toward us or another of their kind, they are never offering a gift which they are free not to give. Rather, it is a preference induced by programmed instincts and conditioned responses. This is not intended to minimize the gift of animal friendship, but to distinguish it from human love.

The most profound utterance of love in the physical universe is the birth of a child. Even those without the light of faith intuit that a newborn baby has a special dignity – a little miracle that has been endowed with something divine, something more than what is produced by animal reproduction. The child's spiritual potential to bring love and creativity into the world, perhaps as an artist, doctor, or missionary, is read as hope for the future. And even when those gifts have been marred, leaving the child with special needs, this inherent dignity remains.

Since only human offspring have the capacity to love, it follows that God's plan is for them to be generated through an act of love. The physical processes of sexual intercourse are within the domain of science, but what sex means is a matter of faith. Human sex is a sign of covenant communion with a profound spiritual sense: *allegorically* it signifies that Christ is a devoted bridegroom who has become one flesh with His mystical body, the Church; *morally* it signifies love which is faithful and fruitful making husband and wife one flesh; and *anagogically* it signifies our becoming one with His body and blood in the Eucharist, which is a foretaste of the personal and eternal communion of heaven.

Nothing is more personal than making a gift of oneself to someone who reciprocates that gift; and this is the very definition of covenant communion. Sexual intercourse is a word which should communicate a whole-hearted gift of self, but whenever sex is not accompanied by life-long marital commitment and openness to new life, that is, by fidelity and fecundity, it is a word which says *I give myself to you* and *I don't give myself to you.* It is then an outright contradiction, a lie in the language of the body. Since a contradiction is meaningless, contraceptive sex and homosexual sex are sinful acts, privations of the truth and meaning which out to be there.

Contraception

As we saw in Part II, "Be fruitful and multiply" are the first words that God addressed to man and woman in sacred Scripture.[45] After man's fall from grace, the covenant with all creation was renewed through Noah and the imperative repeated: "Be fruitful and multiply."[46] Finally, when God established the chosen people of Israel as the means by which He would gather the tribes of the earth into one kingdom, the command was repeated yet again: "Be fruitful and multiply."[47] These are not insignificant events in salvation history, but moments when God's will for His family is being reiterated with the utmost clarity. As such, they should be given special attention. So the question must be asked: how can the use of contraception be seen as anything but disobedient to this proto-commandment?

From the time of Christ to 1930, every Christian denomination agreed that both nature and scripture taught that contraception was unnatural and contrary to God's will.[48] Since then, almost every non-Catholic denomination has reversed their interpretation of these books. Contradicting previous doctrine shows just how necessary it was for God to empower the Magisterium to protect the faith from error. A similar reversal has occurred among many denominations with regard to homosexual sex.

---

45 Genesis 1:28
46 Genesis 9:1
47 Genesis 35:11
48 Cf. Genesis 38:9-10

Homosexuality

Like contraception, God's first book is unequivocal regarding homosexuality being unnatural and contrary to His will. Preventing a sexual act from being procreative is antithetical to the fundamental trajectory of living things: the generation of new life. God's second book teaches that this disordered desire for others of the same sex can be the result of disordered thoughts regarding God and His benevolence (i.e. laws of nature and natural law). In St. Paul's *Letter to the Romans*, the refusal to acknowledge the Creator and the goodness of His laws suppresses the duty to give thanks, making the soul vulnerable to the disordered desires of gay and lesbian sex:

> For the wrath of God is revealed from heaven against all ungodliness and wickedness of those who by their wickedness suppress the truth. For what can be known about God is plain to them, because God has shown it to them. Ever since the creation of the world his eternal power and divine nature, invisible though they are, have been understood and seen through the things he has made. So they are without excuse; for although they knew God they did not honor him as God or give thanks to him, but they became futile in their thinking and their senseless minds were darkened. . . . For this reason God gave them up to degrading passions. Their women exchanged natural intercourse for unnatural, and in the same way also the men, giving up natural intercourse with women, were consumed with passion for one another. Men committed shameless acts with men and received in their own persons the due penalty for their error. . . . They know God's decree, that those who do such things deserve to die – yet they not only do them but even applaud others who practice them.[49]

Those who reject God the Creator tend to reject man the procreator. And even though the cultural, genetic, and psychological factors which may or may not contribute to homosexual tendencies remain unclear, what is clear is that scripture leaves no doubt about the sinfulness of

---

49   Romans 1:18-20,26-27,32

homosexual actions. In addition to the passage above, consider the following: "Do you not know that wrongdoers will not inherit the kingdom of God? Do not be deceived! Fornicators, idolaters, adulterers, male prostitutes, *sodomites*, thieves, the greedy, drunkards, revilers, and robbers – none of these will inherit the kingdom of God."[50]

Furthermore, St. Jude teaches us that the people of Sodom and Gomorrah who "indulged in sexual immorality and pursued unnatural lust, serve as an example by undergoing a punishment of eternal fire."[51] He then goes on to say that such people are "waterless clouds . . . fruitless trees . . . for whom the gloom of darkness has been reserved forever."[52]

It is clear from these New Testament passages that active homosexuality is sinful, but mangling sacred texts is growing in popularity. Once again, this highlights the logical necessity of a Magisterium to interpret scripture and creation infallibly; for without it, the spirit against God will continually prompt contradictory interpretations, especially regarding the intended fruitfulness of sexual activity.

Fruitfulness

For a man, there is a lot of sacrifice involved in providing for the daily needs of his family, but the sweat of his labor exists alongside the joy of reaping the fruit of that labor. For a woman, there is a lot of sacrifice involved in giving birth, but the blood and water of her labor exists alongside the joy of bearing the fruit of that labor. Original sin had the effect of making man suffer where he is fruitful (in the labor of providing for his family) and woman suffer where she is fruitful (in the labor of childbearing).[53] Both are labor pains, but with the vision provided by faith we see that these pains are given meaning by Jesus' sweating blood in the Garden, and by the blood and water flowing from His side on the cross. Suffering where we are naturally fruitful can now be united to Jesus' suffering on the cross and become supernaturally fruitful, procreating sons and daughters of God.

The idea of remaining open to life and having to raise a large family may seem intimidating, with too many sacrifices to be truly fulfilling. But over and over we are confronted with choosing love or fear, with trusting

---

50   1Corinthians 6:9-10 (emphasis mine)
51   Jude 7
52   Jude 1: 12-13
53   Genesis 3:16-19

214

God or convincing ourselves that God's way is not as good as our way. Meaningful self-sacrifice is essential to living a joyful and meaningful life. Sex according to God's plan does not minimize the joy of intimacy, but maximizes it according to the law of freedom; for it is His law which brings us happiness, fulfillment, and an abundance of gifts for which to be thankful. Children are worth the sacrifice.

CHAPTER 26

Man the Religious

As we saw in Part I, recognizing goodness in creation should be co-extensive with recognizing the need to give thanks. For all who immerse themselves in nature, the language of goodness is also a language of faithfulness:

> For you . . . God's faithfulness is a daily experience, constantly repeated in the observation of nature. You know the language of the soil and the seeds, of the grass and the trees, of the fruit and the flowers. In the most varied landscapes, from the harshness of the mountains to the irrigated plains under the most varied skies, this language has its own fascination which you know so well. In this language, you see God's fidelity. . . And you, experts in this language of fidelity – a language that is ancient but ever new – are naturally people of gratitude.[54]

Gratitude

In becoming aware of our status as creatures, we see that we are just as dependent upon God for our existence as a giraffe; thus, the first application of natural law should be to give God thanks for that gift. So how is it that some neglect to give thanks even before a meal? Perhaps since so few of us grow our own food or make our own clothing there is a

---

54 Pope John Paul II, *Homily for Jubilee of Agricultural World*, November 12, 2000.

disconnect between what we eat and wear, and the Source of what we eat and wear. When our culture was primarily agrarian rather than urban, being thankful for favorable weather and good health was an ordinary part of life. The Catholic prayer known as *The Blessing before Meals* must have been easier to relate to in an agricultural setting: "Bless us O Lord, and these your gifts, which we are about to receive from your bounty, through Christ our Lord. Amen." Nonetheless, a posture of gratitude for gifts received should be present no matter where one lives. Even in those settings where the language of goodness is less accessible, the Church would remind us of this simple truth: "Prayer is lived in the first place beginning with the realities of creation."[55]

The creatures of the physical world are gifts which should be received with gratitude, but they are also examples of prayerfulness:

> Every creature prays. Cattle and wild beasts pray and bend the knee. As they come from their barns and caves they look up to heaven and call out . . . The birds too rise and lift themselves up to heaven: they open out there wings, instead of hands, in the form of a cross, and give voice to what seems to be a prayer.[56]

Simply by doing what they were created to do, non-human creatures follow God's will and offer a prayer of thanks and praise: "By their mere existence they bless him and give him glory."[57] The entire life of a bird or animal is a prayer, and even though it is not freely offered it is still exemplary.

For the creatures of the physical world, praying at all times is unconscious and effortless, but "we cannot pray at all times if we do not pray at specific times, consciously willing it."[58] Toward that end, the daily prayer of the entire Church, known as *The Liturgy of the Hours*, gives structure to prayer throughout the year.[59] The seven scheduled prayer times are comprised of psalms, readings, and canticles, but Morning Prayer and Evening Prayer are naturally the two pillars. Why? Because

---

55 *Catechism of the Catholic Church*, #2569, (emphasis in original).
56 Tertullian, *Office of Readings*, Third Thursday of Lent
57 *Catechism of the Catholic Church*, #2416
58 *Catechism of the Catholic Church*, #2697
59 The word *liturgy* originally meant public duty, which is significant, but now it refers to a prescribed form of public religious worship.

for all the beautiful sonatas of the physical world, dawn and dusk hold pride of place. Consider, for example, how common it is to find birds singing at dawn and dusk, and how during these hours of transition all of creation seems to collaborate in order to create an atmosphere of gratitude. These are quintessential moments of gift and mystery: "The ends of the earth stand in awe at the sight of your wonders, the lands of sunrise and sunset you fill with your joy."[60]

The Liturgy of Creation

Several years ago, I was having a typically delightful conversation with my friends Annie and Emily, who are always interested in speaking of God and beauty, literature and art, but mostly in sharing a good laugh. Since it was the night before the Feast of St. Francis (October 4th), and since St. Francis always seems to have a gift for me on his feast day, I was telling the girls that I had planned a trip to Yellowstone for early the next morning. They were excited to talk of the great saint and his love for creatures, but less enthused about my early departure. One of the comical things about teenagers (especially when they are twins who react in unison) is that even the thought of someone else getting up early seems to deflate them. In any event, I rose at 3 a.m. and drove the two-hour trip to Hayden valley in Yellowstone. Along the way I prayed that my heart would be open to whatever the day might bring. At first light, I pulled over next to the Great River and prayed the psalm which begins the Liturgy of the Hours everyday:

> Come let us sing to the Lord and shout with joy to the Rock who saves us. Let us approach him with praise and thanksgiving and sing joyful songs to the Lord. The Lord is God, the mighty God, the great king over all the gods. He holds in his hand the depths of the earth, and the highest mountains as well. He made the sea; it belongs to him, the dry land too, for it was formed by his hands. Come, then, let us bow down and worship, bending the knee before the Lord, our maker. For he is our God and we are his people, the flock he shepherds. Today, listen to the voice of the Lord.[61]

---

60   Psalm 65:8
61   Psalms 95:1-7

Then, near a frost-covered bison family which had bedded down on the river bank, I added, "Jesus, open my heart to the great book of creation. Teach me to be thankful for your gifts and to trust you like the buffalo."

A few minutes later I was alone at an overlook we call Wolf Butte and began to glass around. There were no tourists or road noise like in summer, and as the new day lit a firestorm in the eastern skies, the smooth baritone of timber wolves drifted up from the valley floor. Soon tenors joined in, a pack of coyotes from the hills behind me. Geese and ravens began to punctuate the chorus . . . and time stood still. A grizzly sow and her two plump cubs processed across the river bottom, and as the wolves continued to howl a pair of pure white trumpeter swans took flight, heralding His coming all the while. A congregation of 700 buffalo then came to drink their fill of gift. As they crossed the Great River in search of new pastures, some were not twenty yards from where two wolves were dispassionately lying in the grass, foreshadowing The Day when the wolf will lie down with the lamb.

Not everyone will experience such magnificent lessons from the wilderness, but on every farm and at every city park there are creatures which confirm that giving thanks to God, in an orderly and public manner, is natural: "Worship is inscribed in the order of creation."[62]

Public Worship is Natural

Since creatures are gifts we sometimes receive from God as a community, like rain, but other times as an individual, like a fish, our gratitude should be expressed both publicly and privately. Contrary to popular opinion, the idea that God deserves to be thanked publicly on given days is derived from our natural sense of justice. For the ancient Israelites, this meant keeping the seventh day of the week holy: "Among all the benefits of God to be commemorated the first and foremost was the gift of creation, which was called to mind by the sanctification of the Sabbath."[63]

---

62   *Catechism of the Catholic Church*, #347
63   St. Thomas Aquinas, *Summa Theologica*, I-II. 100.5.2. "Inter omnia autem beneficia Dei commemoranda, primum e paecipuum erat beneficium creationis, quod commemorator in sanctificatione sabbati." (author's translation)

Observing a day of thanks is usually associated with religion rather than right reason. This duty, along with the other obligations found in the Ten Commandments, are all too often viewed as supernatural revelation but not as natural revelation. As we saw in Chapter 6, this confusion can arise whenever first principles are reiterated in scripture. So while it is true that God wrote the Decalogue on stone tablets and gave them to Moses on Mount Sinai, it is also true that they did not contain anything beyond reason: "The commandments of the Decalogue, although accessible to reason alone, have been [supernaturally] revealed."[64] Because reason has been obscured by sin, God chose to reissue natural law in the scriptures as a reminder of the justice naturally found within our hearts: "From the beginning, God had implanted in the heart of man the precepts of the natural law. Then he was content to remind him of them. This was the Decalogue."[65]

The first three commandments of the Decalogue are prohibitions against injustice toward God, the remaining seven against injustice toward one's neighbor. St. Thomas clarifies further by teaching us that "the first three precepts are about acts of religion, which is the chief part of justice."[66] One of the grave thinking errors of our time is the belief that these acts of religion are unnatural, yet it is precisely our *natural* ability to observe *natural* law which obliges us to be fair to our Creator: first, by putting Him above all else and not succumbing to idolatry; second, by respecting the sacredness of His name; and third, by remembering to keep certain days holy to offer Him thanks.

Thanking God in a respectful manner is foundational to the Catholic obligation to attend mass every Sunday: "The celebration of Sunday observes the moral commandment inscribed by nature in the human heart to render to God an outward, visible, public, and regular worship".[67] For the sake of clarity, public religious worship on particular days is a matter of natural revelation whereas the specific celebration of mass on Sunday is a matter of supernatural revelation. Intentionally missing mass is first and foremost an injustice, because the Sunday obligation is rooted in the natural call to recognize "the many gifts we

---

64   *Catechism of the Catholic Church*, #2071
65   St. Thomas Aquinas, *Summa Theologica*, I-II. 100.5.2. "Inter omnia autem beneficia Dei commemoranda, primum et paecipuum erat beneficium creationis, quod commemorator in sanctificatione sabbati." (Author's translation)
66   St. Thomas Aquinas, *Summa Theologica*, II.II.122.1.
67   *Catechism of the Catholic Church*, #2176

receive, and thus to discover gratitude, for only in a grateful heart can the great liturgy of gratitude be celebrated: the Eucharist."[68]

It is becoming more and more common to hear someone say that they "feel" closer to God when hiking in the mountains or relaxing at the beach than they do at a religious service or mass. This intuition of the sacred in natural beauty is understandable, even more since our fallen nature makes us prone to becoming confused about our duty to give thanks; but worshipping the Creator alone, respecting His name, and setting aside time to give thanks publicly is as much a part of being fair as not lying or committing adultery. The Ten Commandments are natural law written in stone.

Rites of Communion

Between 1831 and 1839, four delegations of Flathead Indians attempted to reach St. Louis to ask the Jesuits there for a priest, a "black robe" who could celebrate the Eucharist, "the great prayer" as they called it. Their desire to give thanks to God according to the pattern He had revealed was so profound that they kept sending groups of men on the 1200 mile journey no matter how often they were killed along the way. The Flatheads had been prepared for supernatural revelation by natural revelation. They understood that it was unjust to invent their own way of celebrating the mass because they often observed sacred rituals in nature.

Sage grouse, for instance, perform their annual mating ritual at prescribed places called *leks*, small clearings where year after year the community congregates to do what is pleasing to God. Although performed by mere instinct, these natural rites of communion can enlighten those who are tempted to view supernatural rites of communion as unnatural.

During the 40 days between His resurrection from the dead and His ascension into heaven, Jesus supernaturally revealed to the first bishops the ritual for commemorating the Last Supper, the first rite of Communion. As an apostolic Church, we thank God according to the prescribed pattern He revealed to them. Through the millennia Catholic ecclesial laws apply natural law to liturgical rites in order to protect the sacred character of those rites, ensuring that God is being given the respect He deserves.

---

68   Pope Benedict XVI, *General Audience,* June 8, 2005.

Being Spiritual vs. Being Religious

We often hear people claim to be spiritual but not religious. Even so, attempting to be spiritual apart from being religious is unnatural and unreasonable. Being authentically spiritual is an attempt to have a right relation with God and answer life's big questions; and because both of these are matters of supernatural revelation, intended for all, our quest for God and meaning is ultimately a religious quest:

> In many ways, throughout history down to the present day, men have given expression to their quest for God in their religious beliefs and behavior: in their prayers, sacrifices, rituals, meditations, and so forth. These forms of religious expression, despite the ambiguities they often bring with them, are so universal that one may call man a religious being.[69]

The perception that organized religion is less "spiritual" because it institutionalizes rites and beliefs is a collapse of reason. Sacred traditions reflect what is thought to be good in the eyes of God and are preserved out of our natural sense of justice. In other words, private spirituality which never participates in public worship – by petitioning, praising, and thanking God according to designs revealed for the people – is simply unjust.

Without religion, man is in an unnatural state: either embracing a subjective spirituality, which idolizes the individual self; or embracing atheism, which idolizes futility. Everyone has a god; the question is whether that god is the true God or an idol. And while a religious person can certainly go through the motions of organized religion without engaging the heart, rendering their worship sterile, to be a sincerely spiritual person one must also be deeply religious.

---

69   *Catechism of the Catholic Church*, #28

CHAPTER 27

Man the Gardener

In the Book of Genesis, Adam is commissioned to be responsible for the Garden of Eden, "to till it and keep it" or "to cultivate and care for it."[70] Indeed, as the only creature made in God's image and likeness, we have all been given a certain creative authority over the rest of creation. As he contemplates God's act of entrusting the earth to us, the psalmist writes: "You have given them dominion over the works of your hands; you have put all things under their feet, all sheep and oxen, and also the beasts of the field, the birds of the air, and the fish of the sea".[71]

Our dominion over creation is plainly stated in scripture, but that does not mean it is a merely a matter of religion; the fact that the physical world has been entrusted to us is a conclusion which can be drawn by reading nature with right reason: "The law written by God in nature and capable of being read by reason leads to respect for the Creator's plan, a plan which is meant for the benefit of mankind."[72] And what precisely is the Creator's plan? Essentially, it is for men and women "to govern the world in holiness and justice", giving nature and neighbor the respect they deserve.[73]

In trying to define an authentic ecology, therefore, we should stress "the importance of giving attention to what the earth and its atmosphere are telling us: namely, that there is an order in the universe which must be

---

70   Genesis 2:15
71   Psalm 8:6-8
72   Pope John Paul II, *Homily at Zamosc Poland* (June 12, 1999); Cf. Chapter 6
73   Wisdom 9:3

respected".[74] Laws of nature and natural law are what give the universe order – they are the grammar of the Creator's goodness – and wherever these laws have not been respected, the effects are clear: "The earth lies polluted under its inhabitants for they have transgressed laws".[75] It is a grave injustice for the book of creation to have it's pages torn or it's binding bent, because there is something about a good book which calls for respect – all the more when the book is God's.

Reading and respecting God's first book requires that we first read creatures as individual words and then understand those words in the context of the broader narrative. As we've seen, naming things and understanding them with our intellect is then followed by responding to their truth with our will: "The book of Genesis teaches that human dominion over the world consists in naming things. In giving things their names, man must recognize them for what they are and establish with each of them a relationship of responsibility."[76] In other words, the intellect reads things as individual parts of a plan and the will chooses to follow that plan.

Since establishing a "relationship of responsibility" must be based on truth, if the intellect misreads creatures it adversely affects the will, causing confusion and stimulating irresponsible responses. Two of the most common irresponsible responses are: (1) the domination of nature; and (2) the idolatry of nature.

Some wrongly believe that creatures are merely for us to dominate and consume; but just because God has "put all things under our feet" does not mean we should trample them. Domination must be distinguished from dominion: domination is irresponsible tyranny, whereas dominion is responsible stewardship. Others wrongly believe we do not have a right to the earth's resources and should just leave things alone, enshrining nature like a museum. The former view is a disordered emphasis on nature's goodness and usefulness, the latter a disordered emphasis on nature's beauty and transcendence. The truth of the matter, however, is that we are called to both develop *and* preserve the environment, to both till *and* keep the garden: "If this vision is lost, we end up either considering nature an untouchable taboo or, on the

---

74   Pope John Paul II, *Message for World Day of Peace* (January 1, 1990), #15.
75   Isaiah 24:5 (To care for and respect the land, *malama'aina* in Hawaiian, is a universal call to honor the creatures of the universe according to the Creator's plan.)
76   *Compendium of the Social Doctrine of the Church*, #113.

contrary, abusing it. Neither attitude is consonant with the Christian vision of nature".[77] Thus, Catholic environmentalism can be summed up in two closely related phrases: *stewardship without worship, use without abuse.*

Idolatry, by definition, is to put something before God and His plan, or to worship something in place of God. To refute those who view the physical world as an "untouchable taboo", we need only to recall that God made the physical world as our home, "not creating it to be a void, but designing it to be lived in."[78] Although the creatures of the physical world are sacred, it is idolatrous to place them above or on the same level as the human person, even more so to worship them as gods.

Animal Rights

Current trends which place human beings on an equal level with other living things are sometimes seeking to justify immoral behavior by portraying humans as amoral, as animals who act on instinct alone. But those who recognize that the dignity of the human person is derived from our being created in the image and likeness of God should not hesitate in affirming that God created us with more value than other creatures. If Jesus Himself was unequivocal on this point, we should be as well: "How much more valuable a person is than a sheep!"[79] "How much more important you are than birds!"[80]

Animal rights extremists usually downplay the differences between the human animal and other animals, but in the very act of defending the rights of other species they demonstrate how unique we really are. Do other animals defend the rights of other species? Of course not! We alone violate rights, and we alone recognize and defend rights. Being free to accept or reject God's plan presupposes that we are not preconditioned by instinct to act one way or the other. Once again, we

---

77   Benedict XVI, *Caritas in Veritate* (Charity in Truth), #48.
78   Isaiah 45:18
79   Matthew 12:12
80   Luke 12:24 (Precisely because we have the capacity to love and be loved, we must insist on our primacy in environmental concerns. We are the focal point of the universe, the center, but this view has become easier to see as well as more challenging over the past century: easier because our explorations have discovered absolutely no evidence of life elsewhere in the universe; and more challenging because we have discovered the universe to be so vast that we can seem insignificant.)

cannot have the capacity for freely choosing goodness without having the same capacity for freely choosing evil.

The most balanced statement I have ever read on the subject of man and his relationship to animals is from the Catechism of the Catholic Church:

> God entrusted animals to the stewardship of those whom he created in his own image. Hence it is legitimate to use animals for food and clothing. They may be domesticated to help man in his work and leisure. Medical and scientific experimentation on animals is a morally acceptable practice if it remains within reasonable limits and contributes to caring for or saving human lives. It is contrary to human dignity to cause animals to suffer or die needlessly. It is likewise unworthy to spend money on them that should as a priority go to the relief of human misery. One can love animals; one should not direct to them the affection due only to persons.[81]

God's plan is for us to benefit from animals without being cruel, and to be their protectors and caregivers without putting them before our neighbor. To combat the error of elevating the physical world above the human person, and to focus our attention on stewardship of neighbor, Pope John Paul II adopted the term *human ecology*:

> In addition to the irrational destruction of the natural environment, we must also mention the more serious destruction of the *human environment,* something which by no means is receiving the attention it deserves. Although people are rightly worried – though much less than they should be – about preserving the natural habitats of the various animal species threatened by extinction because they realize that each of these species makes its particular contribution to the balance of nature in general, too little effort is made to *safeguard the moral conditions for an authentic "human ecology".*[82]

---

81   *Catechism of the Catholic Church*, #2417-2418.
82   Pope John Paul II, *Centesimus Annus*, #38 (emphasis in original).

Human Ecology

A person's conscience is formed within the "moral conditions" of family life. Since conscience is the arbiter of natural law, if the family is not in accord with natural law (as is the case with same-sex unions) conscience breaks down; and if conscience breaks down, morality breaks down. Learning to read and respond to the natural law of justice is the key. Basic injustices such as pride, anger, greed, lust, envy, gluttony, and sloth can all lead to violence against human and non-human environments. Thus, a natural and stable family life is the cornerstone of authentic environmentalism:

> The first and fundamental structure for "human ecology" is *the family*, in which someone receives his first formative ideas about truth and goodness, and learns what it means to love and to be loved, and thus what is actually means to be a person. Here we mean the *family founded on marriage*, in which the mutual gift of self by husband and wife creates an environment in which children can be born, develop their potentialities, and become aware of their dignity . . .[83]

When laws are promulgated which threaten the family, they necessarily threaten the well-being of society. The Bishop of Honolulu recently responded to proposed legislation which would redefine marriage to include homosexual unions. His statement illustrates that laws which endanger the natural order, whether of the physical world or the human person, are unjust and harmful:

> In these days in which we lament decisions we made regarding our environment and are paying the price for those decisions, let us not make decisions now that ignore our social environment or experiment with its well-being. Love and friendship are realities that

---

83   Pope John Paul II, *Centesimus Annus*, #39 (emphasis in original). We would be negligent not to mention the more subtle form of environmental worship: the idolatry of one's own family. As Jesus warns, "Whoever loves father or mother more than me is not worthy of me, and whoever loves son or daughter more than me is not worthy of me." (Matthew 10:37) This form of narcissism can be especially insidious within large families.

all people can share, regardless of sexual orientation. Marriage, however, is a sacred bond between a man and a woman, and we need to do all in our power to preserve, strengthen, and nurture it.[84]

The foundation for all moral and social development is a proper understanding of the human person within the context of family. God has commissioned us to be stewards of all creatures, not just some, so it is a contradiction to implement curriculums or pass laws which promote respect for the physical world but undermine respect for the human person. When schools implement curriculums which promote homosexuality and contraception under the guise of alternative life-styles, respect for the human person begins to erode. When legislators pass laws which violate the right to life of the unborn by allowing abortions, violate the very definition of marriage by allowing same sex unions, or violate the dignity of the human body by allowing the distribution of pornography, respect for the human person erodes even further. As Pope Benedict XVI wrote in His most recent encyclical, our educational and legislative systems must be based on an *integrated* human ecology – an ecology which recognizes that moral and social ecosystems must also be safeguarded:

> The book of nature is one and indivisible: it takes in not only the environment but also life, sexuality, marriage, the family, social relations: in a word, integral human development. Our duties towards the environment are linked to our duties towards the human person . . .[85]

Among these duties, the primary duty is to protect the inalienable right to life. If our reasoning about human ecology is to remain consistent, we must protect *the first environment* of the human person, the mother's womb. Unfortunately, within the Catholic Church in America there exists a false dichotomy between environmental activists and pro-life activists. Those environmentalists who overreact to population growth, viewing the elimination of an unborn child as one less consumer

---

84   Most Reverend Larry Silva, Bishop of Honolulu, January 12, 2010. (Cf. Man the Judge)
85   Pope Benedict XVI, *Caritas in Veritate*, #51.

on earth, should be asked, "How can nature be effectively defended if justification is claimed for acts which strike at the very heart of creation, which is human life? Is it really possible to oppose the destruction of the environment while allowing, in the name of comfort and convenience, the slaughter of the unborn?"[86] On the other hand, those pro-lifers who overreact to environmental protections, viewing all preservation initiatives as the hidden enemy of the unborn, should be asked, "What type of garden would you have this child grow up in? How can you be opposed to violence against the human person, but not violence against the physical world?" Respect for the dignity of the human person should extend to the rest of creation, and vice versa. As JP II clarifies: "To choose life involves rejecting every form of violence . . . [including] the violence of mindless damage to the natural environment."[87]

Another duty toward the human person is the restriction of drug use "except on strictly therapeutic grounds".[88] Frequently the objection is made, "Why did God put medicinal plants on earth if not for us to use?" The Creator has indeed made "plants to serve man's needs" and "leaves for healing", but the valid use of drugs for healing or palliative care does not include selfish escapism.[89] Recall that sin is often a truth taken too far. Medicinal plants can be used or abused because they have consistent properties, just as wood can be *used* to build a house or *abused* by being carved into an idol. Specific drugs like morphine or marijuana are *used* in hospitals to alleviate pain or other symptoms, but the danger of them being *abused* and idolized, because of the way they make one feel, is so clearly imminent these drugs must be regulated by law.

We would be remiss not to single out marijuana as one the great false lights of our time. Opposing the legalization of marijuana is another example of discrimination which is just – precisely because it ravages the garden of the soul and, by extension, the garden of the family, society, and nature. Often characterized as harmless or liberating when

---

86   Pope John Paul II, *Homily at Zamosc, Poland* (June 12, 1999).
87   Pope John Paul II, *Message for World Day of Peace,* January 1, 1999. Laws designed to protect the natural environment could eventually help protect unborn babies from the hypocrisy of abortion. For example, the federal protection of bald eagles includes eggs in their nest. The penalty for killing adult or egg is the same because the law recognizes the embryonic form as an individual being, just as in many states if one murders a pregnant woman it is considered a double homicide.
88   *Catechism of the Catholic Church,* #2291
89   Psalm 104:14; Ezekiel 47:12

used recreationally, it is anything but re-creative; rather, it engenders hedonism and narcissism. I have never met a person that smokes weed who remains capable of truly free love, of laying down there life for God and neighbor. It is the *me* drug, the *license* drug, which is presented by the spirit against God as the *love* drug and the *back to nature* drug. It is a masterful lie. Any survey of the sixties revolution or individuals who have started abusing this substance reveals its inherent endorsement of selfish pleasure.

Aestheticism

A final duty toward the human person is to make provisions for aesthetic experience. Our national park system (which some believe is America's best idea) was established primarily "for the benefit and enjoyment of the people." Legislation which preserves natural beauty ought to ensure not only that the physical world is being respected, but that the spiritual needs of the human person are as well. Those who want nature preserved for its own sake, without reference to its benefit for people, should be reprimanded, because "the aesthetic value of creation cannot be overlooked. Our very contact with nature has a deep restorative power; contemplation of its magnificence imparts peace and serenity."[90] We need to grant reasonable access to natural beauty because that is what the Creator intended, stewardship without worship.

The most recent addition to our national parks and monuments is a prime example. Established by the executive order of President George W. Bush, Papahanaumokuakea Marine National Monument encompasses the entire Hawaiian island archipelago. It is the largest preserve in America and the largest marine preserve in the world. Studies are underway which will ensure that sea turtles and monk seals are protected, fishing populations are maintained for commercial and recreational purposes, and the "deep restorative power" of these islands is made available to all.

The management of our national parks and monuments is generally a well balanced effort to serve the needs of human and non-human environments. Still, public initiatives cannot preserve either environment unless accompanied by individual initiatives; that is, personal reforms which address the underlying moral crisis, resolving the tension between proper use and abuse.

---

90   Pope John Paul II, *Message for World Day of Peace*, January 1, 1990, #14.

Consumerism

Reduce, Reuse, Recycle is the motto of Jackson Hole's cooperative effort toward protecting the environment. As Catholics, we are called to "encourage and support the *ecological conversion* which in recent decades has made humanity more sensitive to the catastrophe to which it has been heading."[91] Recycling in particular is a great achievement of the environmental movement, but it can also create the false impression that everything can be replaced or converted into new resources. It can actually mask the underlying issue of unbridled consumerism, a disorder which "makes people slaves of 'possession' and immediate gratification with no other horizon than the multiplication or continual replacement of the things already owned with others still better."[92] *Recycle* must be complemented by *Reduce*.

A person is not fulfilled by his material possessions or by how many achievements, experiences, and pleasures he can amass, but by who he is. A person is not a human *having*, but a human *being*:

> To *have* objects and goods does not in itself perfect the human subject, unless it contributes to the maturing and enrichment of that subject's *being*, that is to say, unless it contributes to the realization of the human vocation as such.[93]

And what is the human vocation? In simplest terms, it is to love God and neighbor in the freedom of His plan, and be loved by them in return. Once again, to will the good of another must be guided by what is truly good, not just apparently good. The lifestyles of the rich and famous, or the more general pursuit of the American dream, are all too often characterized by a disordered pursuit of possessions and pleasure, turning things which are good into evil by pursuing them to an extreme:

> It is not wrong to want to live better, what is wrong is a style of life which is presumed to be better when it is directed towards "having" rather than "being", and which wants to have more not in order to be more but in order to

---

91   John Paul II, *General Audience,* January 17, 2001 (emphasis in original).
92   Pope John Paul II, *Sollicitudo Rei Socialis,* #28
93   Pope John Paul II, *Sollicitudo Rei Socialis,* #28

spend life in enjoyment as an end in itself. It is therefore necessary to create lifestyles in which the quest for truth, beauty, goodness, and communion with others for the sake of common growth are the factors which determine consumer choices, savings, and investments . . .[94]

By contrast, Jesus promotes lifestyles where "choices, savings, and investments" are directed by the perspective of eternity: "Do not store up for yourselves treasures on earth, where moth and rust consume and where thieves break in and steal; but store up for yourselves treasures in heaven . . . For where your treasure is, your heart will be also."[95] He also warns that fulfillment in this life cannot be found in gathering possessions and over-indulging in pleasures; in fact, these disorders can supplant the possessions and pleasures of eternal life. Contrary to the motto "whoever dies with the most toys wins" is the reality that whoever dies in God's will wins: "Take care! Be on your guard against all kinds of greed; for ones life does not consist in the abundance of possessions."[96] "What profit would there be for one to gain the whole world, but suffer the loss of his own soul?"[97] Death is one of the many certainties in this life . . . another is that no one takes anything with them.

Nonetheless, if the goods we rightfully desire are within God's plan for the development for human person, they are necessarily within God's plan for the development of the physical world.

Asceticism

The most fulfilling lifestyle is one which follows God's plan, the plan of freedom from all forms of slavery. The true environmentalist chooses a lifestyle based on love and responsibility for *all* of creation:

Modern society will find no solution to the ecological problem unless it takes a serious look at its lifestyle. In many parts of the world, society is given to instant gratification and consumerism while remaining indifferent to the damage these cause. As I have already

---

94   Pope John Paul II, *Centisimus Annus,* #36.
95   Matthew 6:19-21
96   Luke 12:15: cf. Hebrews 13:5: Matthew 6:24
97   Matthew 16:26; cf. James 1:10-11

stated, the seriousness of the ecological issue lays bare the depth of man's moral crisis. If an appreciation of the value of the human person and of human life is lacking, we will also lose interest in others and in the earth itself. Simplicity, moderation and discipline, as well as a spirit of sacrifice, must become a part of everyday life . . .[98]

A true environmentalist, then, is not so much an activist as a model of virtue. And who is more attentive to living a simple, moderate, disciplined, and sacrificial life than one committed to vows of poverty, chastity, and obedience? Who leaves a smaller "carbon footprint" than a devout religious? Consequently, those laypersons wise enough to integrate simplicity and penance into their state in life are the antidote to consumerism, hedonism, and narcissism. This is not to say that curriculums and laws are not important, just that without moral rectitude they have a limited efficacy. Pope John Paul the Great was particularly aware of how a disciplined lifestyle is the ultimate solution to the environmental crisis:

As nature reawakens to new life at this beginning of spring, I would also like to stress the value of penitential practices as a deeper education in respect for the environment according to God's plan. One might suspect that fasting and other forms of self-denial proposed by the Church's pedagogy imply contempt for creation. But this is not the case! On the contrary, they presuppose a high regard for the material world and can be seen as *antidotes to intemperance and greed,* opposing the sense of having and of enjoying at all costs, which spurs man to make himself the absolute master of everything around him. How can we deny that one of the negative results of this "culture of domination" is a distorted use of nature which disfigures its face, jeopardizes its balance and does not even stop at the threat of ecological disaster? On the other hand, the ascetic virtues help man to open himself to God and to his brothers and sisters, and they direct him to see material things in the proper perspective. They teach him *to use them without abusing them,* to use

---

98   John Paul II, *Message for World Day of Peace,* January 1, 1990, #13

them in solidarity and not with selfishness, looking not only to immediate enjoyment but also to the future.[99]

Our current culture is more "aware" of the global environmental crisis than any previous culture, yet we produce more waste and are more fixated on self-gratification. Unless we harness our desires, we will continue to fall headlong into taking more than we need, thinking only of ourselves and becoming addicted to pleasure. In so doing, we are not reducing ourselves to the level of other animals but to the level of demons, who instead of turning their faces to God turned their backs – choosing license over freedom.

The more we are liberated from these disordered desires for power, pleasure, and possessions by way of prayer, fasting, and almsgiving, the more we are gainfully employed in "the continuation of God's work of creation rather than the unbridled exploitation of creation."[100]

The Beaver

My first backcountry trip was when I was six years old and my brother seven. Our mom had hired an outfitter to take the three of us on horseback into the Maroon Bells Wilderness Area in the Elk Range of central Colorado. For three days my brother and I were free to explore, fish, and because we were little boys, throw rocks. Anyway, as far back as I could remember I had been trained to relieve myself in water, so when nature called one morning while we were fishing at a beaver pond, I just went in the creek. A short time later my mom gave me a lecture on why that wasn't appropriate – then she showed me where the outfitter and his wife had been getting water for us to drink just downstream. The point is we are the only creature who can easily upset nature if we do not engage our ability to read.

In the *Seven Teachings* of the Ojibwa (Chippewa), the beaver is read as a word of wisdom. Beavers are the engineers of the animal kingdom, capable of altering their environment on a scale rivaled only by humans; thus, they speak to us of the proper development of the physical world. They are symbols of wisdom in that their industry provides for their own needs as well as the needs of others. In the application of their

---

99 Pope John Paul II, *Angelus Message,* March 24, 1996, #1. (emphasis mine)
100 Pope John Paul II, *Homily at Zamosc, Poland,* June 12, 1999 (emphasis mine).

gifts, water spreads over the earth – creating habitat for otters, fish, and countless forms of microscopic life.

Building for the common good is natural for us too, but unlike the beaver we can do what is unnatural and become pillagers, intentionally disrupting the balance of nature. We can evangelize as responsible stewards or vandalize as selfish brutes. The following two examples from the Greater Yellowstone Ecosystem contrast these abilities.

In the twentieth century, greedy mining executives harvested every single elk in the Rocky Mountain National Park region. Later, generous stewards reintroduced this majestic species from the abundant herds of Yellowstone. In this century, fuel executives are drilling for natural gas in western Wyoming and in some cases disrupting the largest big game migration in the lower forty-eight: the two hundred mile annual trek of 50,000 pronghorn antelope. Generous stewards of the land are now trying to reconcile the extremists: acquisition of natural gas as a resource is fine, but any major disruption of the pronghorn migration corridor or the mating rituals of sage grouse must be rejected.

The resources of the physical world are here for us to use responsibly and develop aesthetically. When the physical world is tilled correctly it can inspire an appreciation for the gift of human creativity. A well designed city, a well planned neighborhood, or well landscaped backyard can be worthy of aesthetic contemplation; therefore, it is important to be educated in the ways of the Master Gardener. Through words like the beaver, we can see how to design things with respect for skylines, contours of the land, and next-door neighbors.

Agronomy

The young man who delineated first principles so readily when I began to study philosophy is also commendable in his understanding of stewardship.[101] The farm he was raised on in Idaho has implemented a method of agronomy which is less abusive to soil. By using a *no till drill,* seeds are planted with minimal disruption of the land. This allows organic matter to build up, which in turn encourages worm populations to rise to levels where they can become natural aerators of the land. When the soil is tilled naturally there is less erosion, less carbon emissions, and less pollution of runoff water. His family is among those who have heeded

---

101 Cf. Chapter 8

the call "to substitute new techniques of agricultural production for antiquated methods and adapt them prudently to their own situation."[102]

My friend Mark has also become an expert in the area of global warming and the social structures which contribute to ecological imbalances. He is a husband and father now, and I'm sure will be an exceptional steward in that environment as well. For isn't raising children similar to cultivating a garden, where pruning and fertilizing, herbicides and pesticides, sowing and reaping all play a role?

* * *

There is both cause for concern and cause for hope regarding the ecological crisis, because the environments of the physical world and the human person are both fragile and resilient. A century of over zealous suppression of fires combined with severe drought in 1988, causing seventy percent of Yellowstone to burn. This was initially thought to have caused irreversible damage, but over the past twenty years, as the mature logdepole forests in other parts of the Rockies were devastated by pine beetle, the saplings of Yellowstone, which are immune to the beetle, have grown into the healthiest lodgepole forest in America. Similarly, a half-century of attacks on objective truth and the value of self-discipline scorched young Catholics in the 60's and 70's. This too was initially thought to have caused irreversible damage, but over the past thirty years, as other parts of society were being devastated by thinking errors, youth inspired by John Paul II became immune to relativism and have grown into the healthiest stewards on the planet – eager to exercise creative dominion over the earth, the family, and their own soul.

---

102 Vatican II, *Gaudiem et Spes*, #87

Part V

The New Heavens and Earth

* * *

Prologue

The Book of Genesis reveals that on the seventh day of the week God rested from all the work He had done. But after Jesus rose from the dead on the first day of the week, the Catholic Church moved that temporal day of rest to Sunday to symbolize the eternal day of rest as well. Moving the Lord's Day to Sunday emphasizes both the first day of the week and the "eighth day", the day of time and the day of eternity, the day of creation and the day of re-creation, the first day and the last day. The following chapters, therefore, will attempt to illustrate: how the "eighth day begins the new creation": how Mary is cast in this story, and how we might "stir up one another to love and good works . . . as [we] see the Day drawing near."[1]

---

1   *Catechism of the Catholic Church*, #349; Hebrews 10:24-25

CHAPTER 28

The Day of Creation

After all the theology we've discussed, it may be useful to return to that simple yet profound philosophy of the common man, that "cowboy logic" if you will.[2] As a boy, one of the first quotes I can remember being stuck in my mind was from the protagonist of *How the West Was Won*. When asked if he believed in God, the old cowboy responded: "Seein' a deer bound across the crik, smellin' the pines after a rain, or listenin' to an owl on a moonlit night . . . well . . . a man'd have to be a fool to think there wasn't a hand in all that." That's the first statement of being – there was a hand that made these things – and everyone but the fool can read it. This may have been what David had in mind when he expressed the foolishness of atheism: "The fool says in his heart 'There is no God.'"[3]

The Fool

Jesus tells us in the Sermon on the Mount that "whoever says, 'You fool!' shall be liable to the hell of fire."[4] But here again we must distinguish between being judgmental and exercising good judgment. In biblical usage, a fool is one who is dishonest before creation and fails to rise above the convoluted arguments of atheism. Everyone learns from nature, and while some read better than others, the fundamental truths about God, the universe, and ourselves have been available to all.

---

2   The old country western group *The Sons of the Pioneers* had a song whose title went right to the heart of the matter: "Only God Can Make a Tree."
3   Psalm 14:1
4   Matthew 5:22

Unfortunately, the age-old temptation to be one's own God, following the paths of self-determination and self-deception, is also found in every heart:

> The fool thinks that he knows many things, but really he is incapable of fixing his gaze on the things that truly matter. Therefore he can neither order his mind nor assume a correct attitude to himself or to the world around him. And so when he claims that "God does not exist", he shows with absolute clarity just how deficient his knowledge is and just how far he is from the full truth of things, their origin and their destiny. . . . If human beings with their intelligence fail to recognize God as Creator of all, it is not because they lack the means to do so, but because their free will and their sinfulness place an impediment in the way.[5]

Man certainly gets in his own way, but we also get in each other's way. It is crucial to be realistic about how often our words and deeds are not in keeping with our belief in God and, therefore, become stumbling blocks to our neighbor. No one is born an atheist, it emerges primarily from poor thinking and poor example:

> For atheism, taken as a whole, is not present in the mind of man from the start. It springs from various causes, among which must be included a critical reaction against religions and, in some places, against the Christian religion in particular. Believers can thus have more than a little to do with the rise of atheism. To the extent that they are careless about their instruction in the faith, or present its teaching falsely, or even fail in their religious, moral, or social life, they must be said to conceal rather than to reveal the true nature of God and of religion.[6]

---

5   Pope John Paul II, *Fides et Ratio*, #18-19.
6   Second Vatican Council, *Gaudiem et Spes*, #19

An Appeal

Because I and other believers have often been a stumbling block to non-believers, I make the following appeal. In the name of all Catholics, both dead and alive, as the most insignificant member of the Church, I beg forgiveness for the scandalous sins of any pope, bishop, priest, deacon, religious, or lay person. I beg you to pardon us . . . then begin to read the beauty of nature, the saints, and the Messiah. Suspend for a moment the ugliness of sin, and consider the splendor of creatures:

> Ask the animals, and they will teach you; the birds of the air, and they will tell you; ask the plants of the earth, and they will instruct you; and the fish of the sea will declare to you. Who among all these does not know that the hand of the Lord has done this? In his hand is the life of every living thing and the breath of every human being![7]

Consider also the heroic lives of Catholic saints, the most loving and generous souls ever to walk the face of the earth. Who can compare, for example, with that American who inherited 20 million dollars in the nineteenth century (which today would be worth 500 million) then gave it all to educate Black and Native American children, taking vows of poverty, chastity, and obedience in order to become a nun.[8] Finally, consider Jesus, not as He is poorly imitated and frequently disobeyed by members of His Church, but as the most influential man in history, as the brother and savior who can reconcile us to our Father in heaven. Trust Him for a moment, and trust His words: "Ask and it will be given to you. Seek and you shall find. Knock and the door will be opened for you!"[9]

There is No Excuse

In the end, it is for God to sort out how obstacles might mitigate the misguided thoughts of the atheist. I have made this appeal in good will, however, because Scripture attests to the fact that denying the Creator is inexcusable:

---

7   Job 12:7-10
8   St. Katherine Drexel
9   Matthew 7:7

For what can be known about God is evident to them, because God made it evident to them. Ever since the creation of the world, his invisible attributes of eternal power and divinity have been able to be understood and perceived in what he has made. As a result, they have no excuse.[10]

Those who have chosen the path of self-determination have immersed themselves in sin and are prone to self-deception. Fools delights in foolishness and say in their pride, "He will not punish. There is no God . . . He does not see."[11] The last thing such people wish is to have light shined on their muddled thinking and deeds of darkness. Nevertheless, believers are called to be that light with the full understanding that it may provoke a violent response: "Better to meet a bear robbed of her cubs than to confront a fool immersed in folly."[12] For the sake of those who might return to the light, we are called to persevere with charity and with profound confidence that the existence of God is as clear as words on a page. According to St. Bonaventure, anyone who ignores these words and excuses themselves from giving thanks and praise to God has become deaf, dumb, and blind:

The book of creation clearly indicates the primacy, sublimity, and dignity of the First Principle [First Cause or Creator] and thus the infinity of His power. . . . Whoever, therefore, is not enlightened by such splendor of created things is blind: whoever is not awakened by such outcries is deaf; whoever does not praise God because of all these effects is dumb; whoever does not discover the First Principle from such clear signs is a fool. Therefore, open your eyes, alert the ears of your spirit, open your lips and apply your heart so that in all creatures you may see, hear, praise, love and worship, glorify and honor your God lest the whole world rise against you.[13]

---

10 Romans 1:19-20
11 Psalm 10:4,11
12 Proverbs 17:12 (This should help us understand why the crowd wanted Jesus crucified, why some fight so hard to have God removed from the public arena, and why gay and lesbian activists are so militant.)
13 St. Bonaventure, *The Soul's Journey to God*, I.14-15.

The whole created universe will rise up on the last day to testify against those who deny the truth, goodness, and beauty of God – and their testimony will always be the same: "You saw me. You touched me. You smelled me. You heard me shout that God had made me!"

CHAPTER 29

The Day of Rest

The weekly day of rest should be a day of repose, renewal, and reading – a day of giving God the respect He deserves. Several summers ago, I was visiting the ranch of some friends of mine from the Northwest. One Sunday morning, they were trying to get a steer ready to show at the county fair, which was later that week. I began to help, recalling the warning of Jesus to not be too rigid when observing Sunday rest: "Does not each of you on the Sabbath untie his ox or his ass from the manger and lead it out to give it water?"[14] When the steer obstinately refused to cooperate, I gradually began to realize that we weren't doing work that was necessary (giving it food and water), but work that was unnecessary and could be done the following day (bathing, grooming, and showmanship practice). There have been literally millions of Jews and Christians throughout history who would rather die than to break God's commandment of refraining from unnecessary work on the Lord's Day, yet there we were with a rope around the neck of a steer, pulling with all our might. After an hour of struggling with the poor beast, some ranch hands from nearby came to help and the steer was roped to the back of a pickup. With legs locked, he dug in and refused to take a step, preferring to plow furrows in the ground with his hooves. As Catholics we should have known better: "Six days you shall do your work and on the seventh day you shall rest, so that your ox and your ass may have rest."[15] But it seemed this animal was the only one among us who was

---

14   Luke 13:15
15   Exodus 23:12

obeying God, the only one who would prefer death to disobeying. Sure enough, after resisting for a few more minutes, the steer lay on his side and died of exhaustion. He had testified against us.

One way to look at Sunday rest is that it should be a day which is free from trying to get ahead (whether by doing laundry or landscaping), and free from the business we are in the business of doing (whether student or salesman). In a word, it should be a day of leisure.

Leisure

Leisure is often confused with laziness or even license, our so-called "free-time". But authentic leisure has nothing to do with mindless inactivity or self-indulgence; it is rather an active and sober appreciation of God, family, neighbor, and nature:

> Through Sunday rest, daily concerns and tasks can find their proper perspective: the material things about which we worry give way to spiritual values; in a moment of encounter and less pressured exchange, we see the true face of the people with whom we live. Even the beauties of nature – too often marred by the desire to exploit, which turns against man himself – can be rediscovered and enjoyed to the full. As the day on which man is at peace with God, with himself and with others, Sunday becomes a moment when people can look anew upon the wonders of nature, allowing themselves to be caught up in that marvelous and mysterious harmony which, in the words of Saint Ambrose, weds the many elements of the cosmos in a "bond of communion and peace" by "an inviolable law of concord and love." Men and women then come to a deeper sense, as the Apostle says, that "everything created by God is good and nothing is to be rejected if it is received with thanksgiving, for then it is consecrated by the word of God and prayer." [16]

Authentic leisure allows us to hear everything speak of God's goodness. It is a state of contemplative repose which locates recreation

---

16   Pope John Paul II, *Dies Domini (The Day of the Lord)*, #67; 1 Timothy 4:4-5

that is truly re-creative. It is the difference between sitting in front of an inane T.V. show and sitting by a lake.

The Lord's Day has been called the weekly Easter, but I suspect that many of us in America could also benefit from a comparison to a weekly Thanksgiving, a holiday which approximates much of what Sunday rest is all about.[17] Think about how we celebrate Thanksgiving Day. It is not usually thought of as a holyday (the original meaning of *holiday*), but we innately perceive that giving thanks for the good things in life is best done by setting time aside to be with family and friends, sharing the fruits of our labor without being burdened by labor.

Lectio Divina

The Latin phrase *lectio divina* means divine reading. It is an approach to scripture whereby the Holy Spirit prompts us to pause and reflect on certain words before we continue, if we continue at all. The emphasis is on absorbing a few words rather than groping for many.

By God's design, we need time to eat as well as time to digest. The same is true when we are fed by scripture; we need time to read and to ruminate, to peruse and to ponder:

> It is not for nothing that so many pages of scripture are opaque and obscure; but these forests are not without deer which recover their strength in them and refresh themselves by roaming about and feeding, by resting and ruminating. O Lord, bring me to perfection and reveal to me the meaning of these pages.[18]

Like deer that browse on vegetation and then retire to chew things over where they will not be disturbed, we need to digest the words we are fed where it is peaceful. But where is that place? Where should we go to read "the meaning of these pages"? Mother Teresa gives us the answer with utmost clarity:

---

17 In 1863, the presidential proclamation of Abraham Lincoln established the last Thursday of November as a day when "the gracious gifts of the Most High God . . . should be acknowledged as with one heart and one voice by the whole American People."
18 St. Augustine, *Confessions*, XI. 3.

In the silence of the heart, he speaks to us. If you have silence of the heart, you can hear God everywhere: in the person that needs you, in the birds that sing, in the flowers, in the animals and fishes. Why? Because even that crow is praising God, that stupid crow – I can hear it well. We can see and hear God in that crow, but we cannot see and hear him if our heart is not silent, if our heart is not clean. We need to find God, and he cannot be found in noise and restlessness. See how nature, the trees, the flowers, and the grass grow in perfect silence. See the stars, the moon, and the sun, how they move in silence. We need silence to be able to touch souls. Let us adore Jesus in Eucharistic silence. For the more we receive in silent prayer, the more we can give in our active life. You will never learn to pray until you keep silence. The fruit of silence is faith. The fruit of faith is prayer. The fruit of prayer is love. And the fruit of love is service.[19]

Love expresses itself in service, but it all begins with silence.

Silence

Silence of the heart is indispensable when assimilating scripture, and equally so when we seek to be restored by natural beauty. A vacation or Sunday which is filled with activity can be anything but restorative. The "been there, done that" approach will never yield the fruits of aesthetic contemplation because the words of nature are inaudible if the soul is not still: "The ear of the heart must be free of noise in order to hear this divine voice echoing in the universe."[20]

Earlier we spoke of the primacy of being over having, and here we come upon a similar concept: each of us is a human being not a human doing. Pope John Paul II addressed this issue in his letter on living well in the third millennium: "Ours is a time of continual movement which often leads to restlessness, with the risk of *doing for the sake of doing*. We

---

19   Mother Teresa, *Total Surrender*, 106-108.
20   Pope John Paul II, *General Audience*, Aug 2, 2000, (emphasis in original)

must resist the temptation of trying to do before trying *to be.*"[21]   Our impulses and drives to get things done must be tempered by silence if we truly desire to "do everything for the glory of God."[22]

A first step in becoming a person who reads well is to recognize the strategy of the enemy. The father of lies wants to keep us too busy to notice we are too busy. As T.S. Eliot put it:

> Distracted from distraction by distraction,
> Filled with fancies and empty of meaning.[23]

The devil wants to distract us from the realization that we are being distracted: usually by meaningless pleasures or by working too much. Mary, on the other hand, wants to help us become aware of our distractions so that we might move past them and have peace. She does this principally through the gift of the rosary. By exposing and healing restless conditions in the soul, the rosary prepares the heart for *lectio divina.* Divine writing is best understood through divine reading; thus, those who refuse to be still and be filled with the Spirit – at the very least on the Lord's Day – have "turned their backs, not their faces" to the meaning of God's books.[24]

---

21   Pope John Paul II, *Novo Millenio Ineunte (At the Beginning of the New Millennium)*, #15

22   1Corinthians 10:31

23   T.S. Eliot, *Four Quartets "Burnt Norton"*, III.

24   Jeremiah 7:24

CHAPTER 30

The Day of Priesthood

Scripture teaches that there is "one mediator between God and man" and that this God-man "offered one sacrifice for sins, and took his seat forever at the right hand of God."[25] The question arises: if Jesus is the one Mediator, why did He commission the apostles to be mediators of His gospel, His sacraments, and His teachings? And if the sacrifice of His body reconciled us with the Father, why are we called to offer our own bodies "as a living sacrifice"?[26] The simple answer is that Jesus *obtained* all the graces of redemption when He suffered and died the cross, but His plan is for those graces to be *distributed* throughout history by secondary and subordinate mediators, us. So while it is true that the universe has already been redeemed and "the gospel has been announced to every creature", it is also true that we have been commissioned: "Go into the whole world and preach the gospel to every creature".[27] The key to understanding this idea of *already, but not yet* is from the perspective of eternity.

The Perspective of Eternity

From God's viewpoint, there is no past, present, or future. That's why scripture can say that the redemption and renewal of all things is

---

25   1 Timothy 2:5; Hebrews 10:12
26   Romans 12:1
27   Colossians 1:23; Mark 16:15

already done, in the process of being done, and not yet perfectly done. In one sense, Jesus has already restored all things by dying on the cross in His human nature, because His divine nature remained united to the Father and Holy Spirit *outside of time*; in another sense, He is in the process of restoring all things through us *within time*; and in yet another sense, He will restore all things fully only at His second coming at the *end of time*, "so that what is mortal may be swallowed up by life."[28] This is also how we can understand St. Paul writing that we "have been saved", "are being saved", and "will be saved".[29]

"the revelation of the sons of God"

As the Son of Mary, Jesus shares our human nature so that we might become His brothers and sisters. As the Son of God, He has the power, in the Spirit, to draw us into His divine nature so that we might be adopted by the Father as *sons in the Son*. Divine adoption is not only participation in God's Trinitarian family life, but also in the priestly ministry of Jesus.

The disobedience of God's first-born son Adam is an unrepeatable historical fact that had a universal effect; and we distribute the fruits that disobedience throughout history whenever we disobey and commit sin. Likewise, the obedience of Jesus, the New Adam, is an unrepeatable historical fact which had a universal effect, and we mediate the fruits of that obedience throughout history whenever we commit grace. The fallen Adam brought about a universal slavery to death and decay which we spread by concealing God's plan. The risen Christ brought about a universal freedom from corruption which we spread by revealing God's plan. In Christ, then, we have been adopted and ordained as ministers of the Father's will. We have become "God's co-workers".[30] This is why St. Paul writes in his *Letter to the Romans* that the physical world is waiting for our ministry, for us to exercise the adoption and priesthood we have received:

> Indeed, the whole created world eagerly awaits the revelation of the children of God. Creation was made subject to futility, not of its own will but by the will of him [Adam] who subjected it; yet not without hope, because

---

28   2 Corinthians 5:4
29   Ephesians 2:8; 1 Corinthians 1:18; Matthew 24:13
30   1 Corinthians 3:9

creation itself will be freed from its slavery to corruption and share in the glorious freedom of the children of God.[31]

The physical world did not bring sin upon itself by rejecting God's plan, for it did not have the free-will to do so. Rather, Adam chose to reject God and the entire physical world suffered the consequences of his sin. Why? Because he stood at the head of the physical world and the human family in his priestly role as first born son.[32] As the Catechism states, "God created everything for man, but man in turn was created to serve and love God and to offer all creation back to him."[33]

Adam failed to be the priest God wanted him to be, and through his disobedience creation was enslaved by futility (just as by Jesus' obedience all of creation was liberated and given meaning). Though the physical world is *already* free from the futility of death and decay brought about by Adam's sin, it is *not yet* fully free. It yearns to be liberated within time by all those who have been adopted into the one priesthood of the New Adam, the New First-Born Son, the New High Priest of Creation.

Whenever we participate in His mission to imbue all things with meaning through the exercise of our priesthood, we are making the new heavens and earth present here and now:

> What is the new heaven? You may ask. It is the firmament of our faith in Christ. What is this new earth? A good heart, a heart like the earth, which drinks up the rain that falls on it and yields a rich harvest. In this new creation, purity of life is the sun, the virtues are the stars, transparent goodness is the air, and the depths of the riches of wisdom and knowledge, the sea. Sound doctrine, the divine teachings, are the grass and plants that feed God's flock, the people whom he shepherds; the keeping of the commandments is the fruit borne by the trees.[34]

---

31   Romans 8:19-21
32   First born sons were the priests within God's covenant family until they betrayed Him by worshipping the golden calf at Mt. Sinai. Only the tribe of Levi did not worship, so God instituted the Levitical priesthood as a temporary solution.
33   *Catechism of the Catholic Church*, #358
34   St. Gregory of Nyssa, *Office of Readings*, Fifth Monday of Easter

The new heavens and earth have begun, but the liberation from meaningless death and decay is imperfect while time and space remain. Until that coming of perfect liberation, physical evils like sickness and tsunamis will exist alongside physical goods like health and harvests. St. Paul explains further as his *Letter to the Romans* continues:

> We know that all creation is groaning in labor pains even until now; and not only creation, but we ourselves, who have the first fruits of the Spirit, we also groan as we wait for adoption, the redemption of our bodies."[35]

We have already been adopted, but while we are in the process of being adopted destructive forces will exist alongside constructive forces, causing us to groan as we wait to be eternally adopted. In this life we must labor and suffer along with the rest of nature through the residue of evil; however, "in accordance with his promise, we wait for new heavens and a new earth, where righteousness is at home."[36] This promise of eternal adoption into a peaceful home should "protect us from all anxiety as we wait in joyful hope for the coming our Savior".[37]

Every baptized person shares in the ministry of Christ's priestly sacrifice on the cross by spreading the fruits of that sacrifice.[38] Let us now distinguish between the two participations in this one priesthood of Jesus: the ministerial priesthood and the common priesthood of all the faithful.

The Ministerial Priesthood

The ministerial priesthood is reserved for men who have been ordained to act as representatives of Jesus, the head of the mystical body. They do this in a special way by commemorating His suffering, death, and resurrection in the mass. As Jesus commanded His first priests at the first mass, "Do this in memory of me."[39] When a ministerial priest celebrates the Eucharist, he makes Jesus' sacrificial offering to the

---

35 Romans 8:22-23 (Again, the perspective of eternity allows us to reconcile "already" with "not yet", understanding that we have been adopted, we are being adopted, and we will be adopted.

36 2 Peter 3:13

37 *Communion Rite,* from the Order of Mass.

38 *Catechism of the Catholic Church,* #1546-1547

39 Luke 22:19

Father present by acting in the person of Christ (*in persona Christi*). We common priests then join our lives to that offering in the power of the Holy Spirit.

The Common Priesthood

Whenever we offer our own suffering (or anything good in our lives) along with Jesus offering to the Father, we who have received redemption and the hope of resurrection are mediating the redemption and resurrection of the physical world:

> For all their works, prayers and apostolic undertakings, family and married life, daily work, relaxation of mind and body, if they are accomplished in the Spirit – indeed even the hardships of life if patiently borne – all these become spiritual sacrifices acceptable to God through Jesus Christ. In the celebration of the Eucharist these may most fittingly be offered to the Father with the body of the Lord. And so, worshiping everywhere by their holy actions, the laity consecrate the world itself to God.[40]

Moreover, even in the sacrifice of living a moral life we are mediating the graces of redemption: "The moral life is spiritual worship. We 'present our bodies as a living sacrifice, holy and acceptable to God' within the Body of Christ that we form and in communion with the offering of his Eucharist."[41] Obeying the Ten Commandments is the foundation of living a moral life, but obedience to natural law should be elevated to include obedience to supernatural law: the Beatitudes. When Jesus revealed the Beatitudes during His sermon on the mount, He opened "a new horizon of justice" and therefore, a new horizon of priesthood.[42]

The Eucharist

Jesus was unequivocal in the revelation that bread and wine are changed into His body and blood at mass, becoming our spiritual food and drink: "For my flesh is true food, and my blood is true drink.

---

40   Vatican II, *Lumen Gentium*, #34
41   *Catechism of the Catholic Church*, #2031 (Romans 12:1)
42   Pope Benedict XVI, *Angelus Message*, February 14, 2010.

Whoever eats my flesh and drinks my blood lives in me and I in him."[43] His blood is the fountain of youth and His body the antidote to the futility of death and decay. Our gratitude for having meaning restored to our lives is expressed in the sacrament of the Eucharist:

> The Eucharist is a sacrifice of thanksgiving to the Father, a blessing by which the Church expresses her gratitude to God for all his benefits, for all that he has accomplished through *creation, redemption, and sanctification*. Eucharist means first of all "thanksgiving".[44]

First, we give thanks for our *creation*, because it is a gift. And one of the things we come to know is the existence of another will, a will which keeps the universe in order. Go push on a *koa* tree and see. We cannot call down lightning or hold back the tide by just willing it. Human license and potential for evil is limited. There is much to be thankful for when willed that much good, that much law. Second, we give thanks for our *redemption*, because through it we have been shown the deepest meaning of love. The incomparable suffering of Jesus was the incomparable act of love. All sacrifices we make for others, especially for the procreation and education of children, can now become meaningful as acts of redemptive love. And third, we give thanks for our *sanctification* because receiving Jesus' own body and blood helps us to grow in holiness like nothing else can.

It is sometimes said that man is redeemed by wilderness, and insofar as we hear God speak, acknowledge His will, and are inspired to live by that truth and goodness it is a valid point. However, we are not "bought back" from the slavery to corruption by the natural beauty of wilderness, but by Jesus. So it is more appropriate to say that wilderness is redeemed by man. We become procreators of the new heavens and earth by offering daily sacrifices and bringing them into the Eucharist as we receive His body and blood. Employing a modern scientific discovery, Pope Benedict XVI explains the restorative power contained in that which we receive:

---

43 John 6:55-56
44 *Catechism of the Catholic Church*, #1360 (emphasis mine)

The substantial conversion of bread and wine into his body and blood introduces within creation the principle of a radical change, a sort of "nuclear fission," to use an image familiar to us today, which penetrates to the heart of all being, a change meant to set off a process which transforms reality, a process leading ultimately to the transfiguration of the entire world, to the point where God will be all in all.[45]

We enter into this transformation of reality to the degree that we intercede on behalf of the land, the sea, the sky, and all that is in them. Even a simple prayer of gratitude releases a creature from futility. The physical world is longing to become meaningful by being read as a word from God – perhaps by entering into His plan of salvation as a medicine, building material, or pigment – then being offered up by a human person.

On a hike or retreat, this *mediation of meaning* has great potential when built into periods of silence; and even more so when an excursion is attended by a ministerial priest who understands how moments of stillness at mass permit us to gather these gifts and present them with a pure heart.

Moments of stillness at mass also allow us to gather and present our sufferings, so that they too might be released from futility.

Suffering is Redemptive

As we discussed earlier, human beings suffer differently than other creatures. Other animals, for example, don't imagine how long pain might last or project how an injury might affect their future. Regrets, painful memories, or thoughts of loved ones do not pass through the mind of a mongoose that lies dying on the side of the road, but they do for a person. The prospect of suffering in this life can be an occasion of anxiety, but as the first pope tells us, learning to trust the Creator even in suffering is based on reading His faithfulness: "The season of judgment has begun . . . let those who suffer as God's will requires continue in good deeds, and entrust their lives to a faithful creator."[46] Attentiveness to nature builds unwavering trust in the midst of life's trials precisely because we can see God's goodness. Seeing that God is good helps us

---

45   Pope Benedict XVI, *Sacramentum Caritatis (The Sacrament of Charity)*, #11
46   1 Peter 4:17, 19

understand that He would not allow us to suffer unless He could bring good out of it. And since we all suffer, it is worthwhile to know how we can make our suffering meaningful.

As we discussed in *Man the Procreator*, the sufferings endured by parents have been made meaningful by Jesus' sweating blood in the Garden (man's labor), and the blood and water which flowed from His side on the cross (woman's labor). Similarly, His scourging at the pillar, crowning with thorns, and bearing of the cross has made our own pains, humiliations, and trials meaningful because they too contributed to our redemption. Any suffering we experience can now become meaningful and contribute to the renewal of the universe when it is united to His redemptive sacrifice. To begin each day with a *morning offering*, so that we might "suffer as God's will requires", is an exemplary exercise of our common priesthood:

> Most Sacred Heart of Jesus, through the Immaculate Heart of Mary I offer you my prayers, works, joys, and sufferings of this day in union with the holy sacrifice of the mass throughout the world. I offer them in thanksgiving for your blessings, in reparation for my sins, for the intentions of all my relatives and friends, and in particular for the intentions of the Holy Father. Amen.

The Gift of Self

The summit of meaningful suffering and self-donation is Jesus' revelation at every mass: "This is my body which will be given up for you." But in direct opposition to this sacrifice is the obstinate refusal to offer one's body as a living sacrifice. Abortion, for example, is the ultimate contradiction of Jesus' sacrifice because it withholds the gift of one's body for an innocent child; saying in effect, "This is my body which will *not* be given up for you". The difference could not be greater: giving one's life for another's sake, versus taking another's life for one's own sake. Abortion does severe psychological damage not only because it is murder, but because strikes at the very core of feminine genius and creativity. It is the antithesis of what it means to be a woman – a person who gives of herself and suffers well for the sake of others.

Let us now expose some other situations where we withhold the gift of self out of pride, fear, or confusion and actually become contraceptive in our vocation.

The Contraceptive Priest

Receiving Holy Communion is not just a passive acceptance of a gift, for rather "than just statically receiving the incarnate *Logos*, we enter into the very dynamic of his self-giving."[47] The gift of self offered to us by Jesus should be reciprocated by our own gift of self through a commitment to love as He loves, in truth. Communion with Jesus without a commitment to the life and rejuvenation of His Church is a lie in the language of the soul, just as sex without commitment to marriage and fruitfulness is a lie in the language of the body. To turn away from the commitment "to be a holy priesthood, to offer spiritual sacrifices acceptable to God through Jesus Christ" is a form of spiritual contraception. [48]

The education and upbringing of children involves sacrifices, and this is especially true when a father carries out his duty to "bring them up in the discipline and instruction of the Lord."[49] In the entire New Testament, fathers are given direct advice on how to treat their children only twice, and both times it is the same: a father should not provoke or exasperate his children so that they do not become bitter or lose heart.[50]

While intended for natural fathers, this advice can be applied to spiritual fathers as well.[51] As the former bishop of Cheyenne noted in his meditations on ministerial priesthood, "one act of rudeness, one moment of impatience, one sharp or unkind word can undo years of dedication, hard work, and devotion."[52] Natural and spiritual fathers alike must guard against all meanness, above all that which emerges from being a workaholic or alcoholic. Spiritual fathers must also guard against taking the idea of being another Christ (*alter Christus*) too far and losing perspective on one of the most important differences between themselves and Jesus: namely, that Jesus never needed to say He was sorry. Ministerial priests, like all fathers, often need to.

The ministerial priest marries the Church and as a spiritual father consummates that relationship in the procreation and education of spiritual children, but if he lacks the courage to form those children in truth, goodness, and beauty his ministry becomes somewhat sterile.

47   Pope Benedict XVI, *Deus Caritas Est*, #13
48   1 Peter 2:9
49   Ephesians 6:4
50   Colossians 3:21; Ephesians 6:4
51   Cf. 1 Corinthians 4:15
52   Most Reverend David L. Ricken, DD, JCL, *Be Thou My Vision: Meditations on the Priesthood*, 14.

Whenever a pastor convinces himself that he knows better than the Magisterium he withdraws from his mission to teach, lead, and sanctify; and whenever the accolades and celebrity of being a pastor become more important than this mission, he can be likened a man who wants only the pleasure of sex with his wife, not the sacrifices involved in conceiving and raising more children. Just as a natural father's use of contraception during intercourse with his wife withholds that which is fruitful, a spiritual father denies new life when he withholds the splendor of truth about God and His Church. Common priests (men or women) also impede the conception and development of life in Christ whenever they refuse to proclaim or accept the whole truth.

Unfortunately, for both contraceptive pastor and contraceptive parishioner, the infallible teaching of the Magisterium is frequently seen as an impediment to happiness rather than the great catalyst of fulfillment it actually is:

> All too often the Church's doctrine is perceived as a series of prohibitions and retrograde positions, whereas the reality, as we know, is that it is creative and life-giving, and it is directed towards the fullest possible realization of the great potential for good and for happiness that God has implanted within every one of us.[53]

To will the fullness of goodness to another is to will the fullness of truth, a truth which is made known to us by the Church. This is not easy. For instance, the common idea that receiving Holy Communion in a state of mortal sin can actually help a person conceive Jesus in their heart is contrary to the doctrine that a state of mortal sin acts as a contraceptive of the Eucharist and is sacrilegious. At first glance, the Church's teaching seems to be less than charitable, but if we consider that whoever "eats the bread or drinks the cup of the Lord in an unworthy manner will be guilty of profaning the body and blood of the Lord", helping a person avoid profaning the Eucharist is most charitable.[54]

As the reading from the *Feast of the Martyrdom of St. Stephen* illustrates, it requires courage to will the good of God's will to others, it requires

---

53   Pope Benedict XVI, *Letter to the Bishops of Scotland*, February 5, 2010.
54   1 Corinthians 11:27

magnanimity to choose love over fear: "Love inspired him to reprove those who erred, to make them amend; love led him to pray for those who stoned him, to save them from punishment."[55]

Whether we are a pastor or parent, teaching our children to lead objectively fulfilling lives sometimes involves being disliked, unappreciated, or wrongly labeled as oppressive. Nonetheless, we must take heart and never shy away from proclaiming the fullness of truth. As St. Boniface exhorts us, "Let us neither be dogs that do not bark nor silent onlookers . . . Let us preach the whole of God's plan".[56] We would do well to recall that the Holy Spirit often enters hearts as the Gospel is being proclaimed, as St. Peter shows us, and to recall what St. Paul wrote to Timothy: "be urgent in season and out of season, convince, rebuke, and exhort, be unfailing in patience and in teaching."[57] Yet for all that, zeal for souls must be tempered by great wisdom in order to discern the proper pedagogy – words or works: "A Christian knows when it is time to speak of God and when it is better to say nothing and to let love alone speak. He knows that God is love and that God's presence is felt at the very time when the only thing we do is to love".[58]

* * *

Each of the faithful cooperates in the redemption and sanctification of the universe. The one redemptive sacrifice of Jesus, by which we have been reconciled to the Father, has been drawn into eternity. Whenever mass is celebrated, that one sacrifice is drawn back into time by the God-given power of a ministerial priest. Common priests then gather to offer the physical world, their own lives, and the lives of others to the Father in the Spirit. Jesus has revealed the path of fruitful love to us by patiently enduring suffering and sacrificing His life; now our own sufferings and sacrifices can become fruitful and contribute to the renewal of all things as we make our offering "through Him, with Him, and in Him."[59]

---

55   St. Fulgentius, *Office of Readings*, Feast of the Martyrdom of St. Stephen, December 26.
56   St. Boniface, *Office of Readings*, June 5.
57   Acts 10:44; 11:15; 2 Timothy 4:2
58   Pope Benedict XVI, *Deus Caritas Est (God is Love)*, #31
59   *Communion Rite*, from the Order of Mass.

CHAPTER 31

The Day of Light

Sacraments communicate the life and light of Jesus; they are His principal means of distributing the graces of salvation obtained on the cross: "The seven sacraments are the signs and instruments by which the Holy Spirit spreads the grace of Christ the head throughout the Church".[60]

The photograph on the front cover symbolizes the confluence of natural life and supernatural life. The rainbow seems to flow down the canyon wall and merge with the waters of the Great River. Likewise, the graces of the sacraments merge with our nature, perfecting our natural traits and temperaments. Even in the midst of our radical freedom to cascade into darkness, sacraments flood our hearts with light, transforming us into sons and daughters of God. And the more we are transformed, the more the physical world can be transformed.

Sacraments are Signs

Let us distinguish between ordinary signs (like the creatures of the physical world or human gestures and words), and the seven extraordinary signs we call sacraments.[61] For example, the gesture of extending one's hand with palm facing outward or the spoken word "Stop" are both signs suggesting that one stops, but neither of them causes one to stop. What makes sacraments different from these ordinary signs is that they actually cause what they signify to happen: like if a policeman held up his hand and it actually caused oncoming traffic to brake, or a mother said, "Stop

---

60   *Catechism of the Catholic Church*, #774
61   Let us also distinguish between the seven sacraments and *sacramentals* like the miraculous medal, the rosary, and the brown scapular.

that right now!" and it actually caused her children to stop fighting in the back seat. Thus, when a Catholic bishop says, "Be sealed with the gift of the Holy Spirit", or a Catholic priest says, "I absolve you of your sins in the name of the Father and the Son and the Holy Spirit", a person's soul is actually strengthened or forgiven, accordingly. Sacraments make use of ordinary signs like gestures, words, and creatures of the physical world, but as these ordinary signs are empowered by God to actually do what they symbolize to do, they become *efficacious* signs.

Reading the power embedded within the seven sacraments begins with seeing even the simplest things as words of God's first book. Quoting a modern theologian, the editor of the *Catechism of the Catholic Church* brought this idea to light:

> "The simple things around us have largely lost their power to speak to us. And we, who no longer hear what they have to say, are like illiterates trying to read the book of creation." If we are to hear the language of sacraments, we must first of all learn the language of things.[62]

Physical life vs. Spiritual Life

The seven sacraments are supernatural gifts of life for the soul. And just as the body undergoes natural phases, these infusions of supernatural light correspond to the soul's spiritual phases: "There is thus a certain resemblance between the stages of natural life and the stages of the spiritual life."[63]

Physical	Spiritual
Birth	Baptism
Sustenance	Eucharist
Strength and Maturity	Confirmation
Vocation and Fruitfulness	Marriage/Holy Orders
Sickness and Death	Anointing of the Sick/Confession

---

62 Christoph Cardinal Shonborn, *Living the Catechism of the Catholic Church*, II.10. (quoting Hans Urs von Balthasar)
63 *Catechism of the Catholic Church*, #1210

The following comparisons are not intended to give a comprehensive definition of any of the sacraments, only to expose them as consonant with the life of the body: "Such comparisons aid our understanding, since we can grasp a point more easily when we have an analogy."[64]

Baptism

We must first be born before entering the other stages of natural life. Similarly, we must first be born again in baptism before entering the other stages of supernatural life. In baptism, water is a *material* sign that both symbolizes and actually causes a cleansing of sin, and the formula "I baptize you in the name of the Father, and the Son, and the Holy Spirit" is a *spoken* sign that both symbolizes and actually causes a soul to be adopted. Through baptism we become part of God's family and make a commitment to holiness, either on our own or by our parents and God-parents. The universal call to holiness is stated plainly by St. Paul: "This is the will of God, your sanctification."[65]

Eucharist

Baptism is both one of the colors of the rainbow and the prism which refracts those colors, whereas the Eucharist is both one of the colors and the light which is the source of that refraction. Baptism initiates the sevenfold light and therefore has priority, but the Eucharist *is* the Light and therefore has primacy. Every sacramental grace flows from His "eucharistic sacrifice, the source and summit of the Christian life."[66]

The Eucharist is food and drink for the soul, providing us with the nutrition we need to grow, heal, and sustain energy; but receiving His body and blood is also like receiving supernatural DNA to graft us on to His mystical body, corresponding to the old adage, "You are what you eat."

Reconciliation and Anointing of the Sick

Plato defined death as the separation of the body from the soul, and the author of Ecclesiastes defined it as the moment when "dust returns to the earth as it was and the breath returns to God who gave it."[67] Since

---

64 St. Hilary, *Office of Readings,* Fourth Wednesday of Easter.
65 1Thessalonians 4:3
66 Vatican II, *Lumen Gentium,* #11
67 Plato, *Phaedo,* IV; Ecclesiastes 12:7

the soul is spiritual entity, the moment when it is permanently separated from the body is outside the domain of science. At times, the body seems to undergo a temporary "death", like when a person's body has no vital signs but is then revived by means of cardiopulmonary resuscitation (CPR). Forty years ago, the maximum time of bodily lifelessness before being revived was about five minutes, now it is over two hours. The beginning and end of human life are questions of the Spirit because science can neither tell us when "breath comes into the mother's womb" nor when "breath returns to God".[68]

Spiritual death, defined as the separation of the soul from Christ's mystical body, can also be permanent or temporary. In order to understand this idea, we must first distinguish between two types of sin, mortal and venial. As St. John teaches in his first letter, "There is sin that is mortal . . . but there is sin that is not mortal."[69]

Mortal sin is also known as serious, grave, or deadly sin, because it kills the "state of grace" that gives us life in God's family.[70] For a sin to be mortal, we must freely choose to do something that is known to be a serious sin. Committing a deadly sin by rejecting God's plan puts us into a "state of sin". To overcome this condition of death, we must demonstrate a desire to embrace God's plan – and God's plan is for us to have our sins forgiven through the sacrament of confession.

The day Jesus rose from the dead He appeared to His first priests, the apostles, and gave them authority to forgive sins in His name: "He breathed on them and said, 'Receive the Holy Spirit. If you forgive the sins of any, they are forgiven; if you retain the sins of any, they are retained'".[71] We are following God's plan when we contritely confess our grave sins to a priest by name and number, and perform the required penance. Restored to a state of grace, we can then celebrate His other sacraments on earth and have the hope of enjoying Him forever in heaven. This sacrament is called Confession (because we confess our sins), Penance (because we perform some degree of restitution), and Reconciliation (because God, who alone can forgive sins, has given power to His priests to reconcile us with His family). Therefore, just as one's body may undergo temporary death yet be revived through cardio-

---

68 Ecclesiastes 11:5; 12:7
69 1John 5:16-17
70 If this happens, one should sincerely ask God for forgiveness and, trusting in His infinite mercy, firmly resolve to go to Confession as soon as possible.
71 John 20:22-23

pulmonary resuscitation, one's soul may undergo temporary death yet be revived through Confession, Penance, and Reconciliation: CPR for the soul.

Non-mortal sin, known as venial sin, does not place us in a state of sin and cut us off from God's family, but it does weaken our state of grace and makes us more likely to commit a mortal sin. Venial sins are like germs of the soul, yet the Church only requires that we confess mortal sins, and only once per year. The Church recommends, however, that we confess venial sins on a regular basis, for how could anyone consider themselves in good health if they washed away germs only once per year? Just as doctors prescribe general principles of health and healing, the Church prescribes that we maintain a steady diet of prayer and get plenty of silence so that we are less likely to be re-infected.

Anointing of the Sick is closely related to confession but corresponds more to permanent bodily death. This sacrament has a medicinal quality in that it relieves spiritual pain, preparing the soul for redemptive suffering and eternal rest.

Confirmation

We all have hormones at birth, but puberty stirs up those hormones so that the body may become strong and fertile. Similarly, we all receive the gifts of the Holy Spirit in baptism, but confirmation stimulates those gifts so that the soul may become strong and fertile in defending, proclaiming, and witnessing to the faith.

Marriage/Holy Orders

Boys and girls should eventually become men and women, but becoming a man or woman is just as much a question of spiritual maturity as it is of bodily maturity. Once a person's body has matured and become fertile, the soul must mature as well. Marriage and Holy Orders are sacraments of procreation which correspond to the natural stage of vocation and fruitfulness. Regardless of whether someone has been called to marriage, priesthood, religious life, or single life, or whether one's occupation is a teacher, coach, or soldier, it is only when life is seen as a gift for others, which is the essence of fatherhood and motherhood, that one becomes a man or woman. Many physically mature adults, even parents, have never matured spiritually.

Illuminating the Whole Person

Since God is the fullness of truth, goodness, and beauty, we might expect Him to impart His *being* in the sacraments in a way that is consistent with those transcendentals; that is, in a way that resonates within the thinking, choosing, and creating creature. During his very first homily as pope, Pope John Paul the Great proclaimed: "The absolute and yet sweet and gentle power of the Lord responds to the whole depths of the human person, to his loftiest aspirations of intellect, will, and heart."[72]

The sacraments administer the "power of the Lord" through words which communicate with the intellect, will, and heart: Spoken words, like traditional formulas and prayers, communicate intelligible truth (known as *form*); Material words, like water, wine, bread, and oil, communicate instantiated goodness (known as *matter*); and Artistic words, like harmony of movement, rhythm of gestures and responses, and colors of vestment and voice, communicate inspiring beauty (which could be called *manner*). Thus, sacraments are meant to have intelligible form, instantiated matter, and inspiring manner.

When sacraments are not celebrated in an inspiring manner they are still efficacious because God is faithful; nonetheless, the art of celebrating (*ars celebrandi*) should never be neglected. Why? Precisely because a sacramental celebration should communicate the beauty of Jesus, for beauty is what inspires us:

> . . . a correct *ars celebrandi* is an attentiveness to the various kinds of language that the liturgy employs: words and music, gestures and silence, movement, the liturgical colors of the vestments. By its very nature the liturgy operates on different levels of communication which enable it to engage the whole person. The simplicity of its gestures and the sobriety of its orderly sequence of signs communicate and inspire . . .[73]

Consider, for example, the difference between celebrating a baptism with a styrofoam cup and the ancient tradition of a seashell. Consider also the difference between a celebrant who is impatient or an egocentric

---

72   Pope John Paul II, *Homily for the Beginning of His Pastoral Ministry*, October 22, 1978, #4.
73   Pope Benedict XVI, *Sacramentum Caritatis* (The Sacrament of Charity), #40.

entertainer, and one who understands that "by his bearing and by the way he says the divine words he must convey to the faithful the living presence of Christ."[74]

Seeing in the Dark

For the human person, life on earth includes being involved in a holy war. The father of darkness presents himself as a father of light, and part of the battle we all face is to discern true light from false. Take the example of the rainbow. This sign of God's covenant with fallen creation has been appropriated as the sign of His covenant with renewed creation, because the seven sacraments are weapons of light in our battle to remain faithful. Is it any wonder, then, that gay and lesbian activists under the influence of the Enemy have misappropriated the sign of God's sevenfold covenant with creation? And is there anything more contrary to the fruitfulness of sacramental communion than the fruitlessness of homosexual activity?[75] In addition to discerning real light from apparent light, a soldier of Christ learns that God not only allows real darkness so that He might bring good from it, but also periods of apparent darkness so that we might discover a deeper love and a deeper trust.

All believers undergo periods of apparent darkness, times when we mistakenly perceive a withdrawal of God's grace. Most marriages and most saints bear witness to those phases when things are spiritually cold and gray, as if God had removed all warmth and color from our lives.[76] Even Jesus on the cross experiences this sense of abandonment. But it is here that we must distinguish true darkness, which is a false light and a deception of the devil, from false darkness, which is a true light and gift of God.

False darkness is meant to purify us by deepening our trust and is similar to the discipline of a loving parent, "for what child is there

---

74   General Instruction of the Roman Missal, *The Duty of Those in Holy Orders,* I.93.
75   It is worth noting that the greatest stewards of creation in salvation history, St. Noah and St. Francis, are mocked by the American homosexual agenda. Noah received the rainbow on behalf of creation, and St. Francis, the patron of ecology, is ridiculed by the ideology of the city which bears his name – San Francisco.
76   The *dark night of marriage* should be understood in this light, for everyone who perseveres through this trial experiences love and commitment on a deeper level.

whom a parent does not discipline?"[77]   Any child given extra chores or denied favorite privileges surely perceives darkness, yet it is only an apparent darkness. As St. Paul teaches, "discipline always seems painful rather than pleasant at the time, but later it yields the peaceful fruit of righteousness".[78] When a child has grown and acquired wisdom they then understand the light emitted from parental discipline and apply it to there own children. When we as adults are disciplined as children of God, however, acquiring that wisdom is more difficult. God's discipline can seem as mysterious to adults as parental discipline seems to teenagers.

Seasons of abandonment make us feel like tears have become our bread and our "one companion is darkness."[79] When the prophet Jeremiah is disciplined by the Lord, he laments that his life seems desolate and bitter, but even though he *feels* that he has been "forced to walk in darkness, not in the light", he is able to *see* that "the Lord is good to those who wait for him, to the soul that seeks him."[80] Jeremiah knows that God will not actually abandon him, and that beyond the pain of the present trial the Lord must be acknowledged as faithful: "But I will call this to mind, as my reason to have hope: the favors of the Lord are not exhausted, his mercies are not spent; they are renewed each morning, so great is his faithfulness."[81]

Just as children learn to overcome fear with trust during the night, those experiencing a dark spiritual night must learn to stabilize their faith. The following three words from the physical world may offer solace and perspective in this spiritual combat. And like so many other creatures, each of them is a sign of trust.

Stars

The stars represent the saints; whose wisdom guides us through trials and teaches us how to endure. During any and all trials, it is essential to remember that we can see farther at night than during the day. And the darker the night, the brighter the stars shine.

The summer that I endured my darkest spiritual trial to date, I had absolutely no idea what God wanted me to do with my life . . . except trust Him. I was camped along the Snake River one night and had stepped out

77   Hebrews 12:7
78   Hebrews 12:11
79   Psalm 88:18; cf. Psalm 42:4
80   Lamentations 3:2,25
81   Lamentations 3:22-23

into the darkness to pray. At first, I couldn't believe my eyes. The stars seemed to be hanging from the heavens by invisible strings of various lengths, and were much closer to earth than usual. Two nights later, I was standing under the stars again, this time at the home of my friend Susie who lives just outside the Grand Teton National Park boundary. I mentioned what I had seen earlier that week and was relieved that she could confirm the spectacle, for she too had wandered outside that night. A long-time resident of the valley and wildlife biologist, she had neither seen nor heard of such a thing before. Neither one of us knew the scientific explanation for the phenomena – and still don't – but as is often the case, it didn't matter. Excitedly, we began to talk of God and His saints and she encouraged me to trust the Holy Spirit during my trial . . . then a giant meteor dashed from one end of the sky to the other and seemed to dissolve into The Grand. As I drove from her house that evening, I reflected that by the Spirit of God all the saints are made, and "by the breath of his mouth all the stars."[82]

Owls

At *Our Lady of the Mountains*, there is a stain glass window depicting Jesus praying in the garden of Gethsemane just before he was arrested and tortured. Above him, perched in a tree, sits an owl. The owl is wise because it sees well in the darkness and is attentive to the slightest movements or sounds. It is silent in flight and it can look forward and backward with equal facility. So too, the wise man can dilate the pupils of his soul, detecting the slightest movements of God. When he takes flight in prayer it is with great silence, drawing no attention to himself. Often, he examines how trustworthy God has been in the past, and with that confidence looks to the future. Balancing hindsight and foresight, he sees that God is faithful even in the apparent darkness of the present, and wisely surrenders as Jesus did, "not as I will, but as you will."[83]

Infrared Light

The scientific discovery of light which exists beneath the first color of the spectrum (infrared) is another example of the stimulus of science

---

82   Psalm 33:6
83   Matthew 26:39

for theology.[84] Because of this insight, we should discern more clearly than ever that God's light is present even when visible light is absent. Our eyes of faith should perceive that infrared graces are at work beneath the apparent darkness, because there is always more light than meets the naked eye.

---

84 Light which exists beyond the last color of the spectrum (ultraviolet) also provides insight, but here I will let the reader discern.

CHAPTER 32

The Day of Trust

In the twentieth century, historical criticism dimmed the light of scripture. This caused many to question its authorship and inerrancy, as well as the Church's ability to interpret it infallibly. Sunday should be a day to renew our trust that God intended His second book to be inspiring, and there is little more inspiring than understanding how scripture reveals Mary as the model of trust.

Following the example of Jesus, Peter, and Paul (among others), the Church has always and everywhere understood God's second book typologically. Typology is the study of similarities between Old Testament persons, places, things, and events, and New Testament persons, places, things, and events. Three examples should help illustrate that typology is the Rosetta stone of scripture. First, Jesus uses this interpretive method with the two men on the road to Emmaus, showing them how certain passages in the Old Testament prefigured Him: "Then beginning with Moses and all the prophets, he interpreted to them what referred to him in all the scriptures."[85] Second, St. Peter tells us how Noah and his family being saved through water prefigured us being saved through the water of baptism: "God waited patiently in the days of Noah during the building of the ark, in which a few, that is, eight persons, were saved through water. And baptism, which this prefigured, now saves you".[86] And third, St. Paul shows how Adam was God's firstborn son who stood sinless at the head of all humanity as "a type of the one who was to come".[87]

---

85   Luke 24:27
86   1 Peter 3:20-21
87   Romans 5:14

The New Eve

Jesus is the New Adam because He too was God's sinless firstborn, but St. Paul sees a further parallel between the disobedience of Adam, by which "many were made sinners", and the obedience of Jesus, by which "many will be made righteous".[88] The parallel of disobedience being reversed by obedience can also be extended to Mary and Eve, which is why the early Church Fathers held the conviction that Mary was the New Eve.

Along with Adam, Eve rejected her Father's plan; but along with Jesus, Mary fulfilled it. As St. Irenaeus taught in the second century, "the knot of Eve's disobedience was untied by Mary's obedience."[89] The espoused yet virgin Eve responded to an unfaithful angel by giving the fruit of her disobedience – the forbidden fruit – to Adam, causing our fall from grace; whereas the espoused yet virgin Mary responded to a faithful angel by giving the fruit of her obedience – the fruit of her womb, Jesus' body –to the second Adam, causing our restoration to grace. Mary's obedient "yes" to God's plan counteracted Eve's disobedient "no".

Fiat (Let it be)

On March 25th, nine months before Christmas, the Catholic Church celebrates Mary's response to the archangel Gabriel's announcement that God wished her to conceive His Son. *The Annunciation*, however, was not just a simple declaration, but rather a proposition, an invitation for Mary to freely accept or deny. Gabriel was asking if she would reverse the curse so that the cosmos could join in the symphony of Trinitarian glory and begin the liberation from the futility of death and decay. But even when the salvation of the world hangs in the balance, God respects our freedom. Mary would have to choose . . . and all of creation held it's breath until she uttered the *sine qua non* of true freedom, "Let it be done to me according to your word."[90]

The Marian Sky

By accepting the invitation to conceive the fullness of light and initiate the new heavens and earth, Mary's *fiat* echoed the first words of creation, "Let there be light!" Since part of God's plan was to have

---

88 Romans 2:19
89 St. Irenaeus, *Adversus Haereses*, III.22.4.
90 Luke 1:38 "Fiat mihi secundum verbum tuum."

Jesus, the sum of all light and grace, be mediated to us through Mary, she is called the Mediatrix of all graces. Her mantle is often portrayed as sky blue to symbolize that all the light we receive from her Son passes through her, just as sunlight passes through our azure atmosphere.

Jesus is the sum of all light and grace; and since part of God's plan was for that light to be mediated to us through Mary, she is called the Mediatrix of all graces. Her mantle is often portrayed as sky blue to symbolize that all the light we receive from her Son passes through her as sunlight passes through the sky.

Moreover, in the Old Testament Zion prefigures the Church, and the daughter of Zion prefigures Mary, the pure embodiment of the Church. The Church and Mary are similar in that we receive Jesus through them, but Mary alone is sinless. Thus, like the sun shines through a beautiful blue sky, the Son comes to us through the only perfectly beautiful member of the Church: "Out of Zion's perfect beauty He shines."[91] In sum, by God's will Mary was chosen to mediate the fullness of light, and by God's will she continues to do so.

The Marian Moon

Early Christians not only saw the moon as a symbol of the Church, but also of the Virgin Mary. The difference is that Mary does not wax and wane like the Church for she is free of original sin and never interferes with grace. Even when the moon as a symbol of the Church seems to be obscured by worldly phases – "the desire of the flesh, the desire of the eyes, the pride in riches" – the full moon witnesses to heroic trust as a symbol of Mary.[92] Mary is associated with the full moon, the moon pregnant with light, not only because she received within her womb the fullness of light, but also because she never disobeyed God.

From the moment of her immaculate conception by her parents Joachim and Anne, Mary has remained totally beautiful (*tota pulchra*) or, as St. Elizabeth would say at the Visitation, "Full of Grace." [93] But this salutation is more than a recognition of what happened when she was conceived or when she conceived Jesus; rather, it is her name, an icon of who she is as a person. As John Paul II has noted, "'Full of Grace' is the name Mary possesses in the eyes of God."[94]

---

91   Psalm 50:2
92   1 John 2:16
93   Luke 1:28
94   John Paul II, *General Audience*, May 8, 1996.

To the extent that our plans conform to God's plans, we too are filled with light, but for Mary alone there was never a discrepancy between His plans and her own. As Bishop Fulton J. Sheen noted:

> As the architect has in his mind a plan of the house before the house is built, so God has in His mind an archetypal idea [or blueprint] of every flower, bird, tree, springtime, and melody . . . every atom and every rose is a realization and concretion of an idea existing in the mind of God from all eternity. . . . A tree is truly a tree because it corresponds to God's idea of a tree. A rose is a rose because it is God's idea of a rose wrapped up in chemicals and tints of life. *But it is not so with persons.* God has to have two pictures of us: one is what we *are*, and the other is *what we ought to be.* . . . God has to have these two pictures because in each and every one of us there is some disproportion and want of conformity between the original plan and the way we have worked it out. . . . There is, actually, only one person in all humanity in whom God has one picture and in whom there is a perfect conformity between what He wanted her to be and what she is, and that is His own mother.[95]

Mary's fiat in response to the angel Gabriel is a reflection of her perfect harmony with God's will at every moment of her life. When the objection is raised that Mary is not often mentioned in scripture, our response should be that she is found on every page where there is an act of trust and obedience to God's will.

The Woman

The parallel between Eve and Mary, however, rests not only upon obedience reversing disobedience and transparency to His will, but on identifying the typological figure of a *woman* who is to have a role in crushing the head of Satan. The battle between the woman and Satan bracket the canon of sacred scripture. On one end, the following words of God to Satan are the first sign of hope, the initial good news after the fall that God has a plan to overcome sin: "I will put enmity between you

---

95   Fulton J. Sheen, *The World's First Love*, I.1. (emphasis in original)

and the woman, and between your offspring and hers."[96] On the other end, we find the woman (this time with the moon under her feet) giving birth to a son "who is to rule all the nations"; and we find Satan seeking to "to devour her child . . . and to wage war with the rest of her children, those who keep God's commandments and bear witness to Jesus."[97] The identity of the woman is revealed to us by Jesus at the climax of salvation history – when beginning and end are gathered to a highpoint. From the cross, Jesus reveals that His mother is *The Woman* who battles Satan, and also that we are "the rest of her children". He does this by addressing His mother in an unusual way, "Woman, behold your son", and then by presenting her to us unambiguously, "Behold, your mother."[98]

My brother's youngest son, Thomas, proclaimed himself a marine while still in kindergarten, yet for all the wars he wages with swords and lasers, he is also very devoted to his mother, Mary. He has always been fond of the moon, and as a soldier could relate even at an early age to Mary doing battle with the forces of darkness. To him she is the Warrior Queen.[99]

Coredemptrix

The term Coredemptrix literally means "The Woman with the Redeemer." The prefix "co" comes from the Latin "cum" meaning "with". A great deal of confusion can be avoided by distinguishing the two ways this prefix is applied in English. When we refer to a co-captain of a team there is a connotation of equality with the other captain, but when we refer to a co-pilot there is only the connotation of being *with and under* the pilot. This is how "co" is used in Coredemptrix. A simple definition of Mary as Coredemptrix, then, is that she uniquely cooperated *with and under* Jesus in redeeming mankind. Again, it must be emphasized that her cooperation in our redemption is not out of necessity, but simply because God willed it to be.

The objection could be made that the above definition is no more than what we all do in our common priesthood by "making up what is lacking in the sufferings of Christ for the sake of his body, the Church."[100]

---

96   Genesis 3:15 (This event is called the *protoevangelium* because it is the *first good news* that God reveals after the fall.
97   Revelation 12:4-5,17
98   John 19: 26, 27
99   The people of Poland venerate Mary under this title.
100 Colossians 1:24

In other words, we are all called to cooperate with God in redeeming mankind.[101] Pope John Paul II helps us distinguish, however, between our cooperation and the unique cooperation of Mary:

> The collaboration of Christians in salvation takes place after the Calvary event, whose fruits they endeavor to spread by prayer and sacrifice. Mary, instead, cooperated during the event itself and in the role of mother: thus her cooperation embraces the whole of Christ's saving work. She alone was associated in this way with the redemptive sacrifice that merited the salvation of all mankind. In union with Christ and in submission to Him, she collaborated in obtaining the grace of salvation for all humanity.[102]

Only Mary helped Jesus obtain the gifts of redemption, the rest of us merely help Jesus distribute those gifts "by prayer and sacrifice". Through the ministerial and common priesthood, we mediate that one act of reconciliation between God and creation whenever we unite our sufferings to the cross at mass, whenever we pray for our neighbor, and whenever we proclaim the gospel through exhortation or example. As St. Paul explains, this secondary and subordinate mediation is always as a follower of our one leader: "Christ always leads us in triumph, and *through us* spreads the fragrance of the knowledge of him everywhere."[103]

Whether in words or works, the gospel is proclaimed through our bodies which have become one body in "His body, the Church". And since the offering of His body is what saved us, it is important to discern where he got that body to begin with.

Mary first became the Coredemptrix at the Incarnation through her maternal role in giving Jesus human flesh and blood. Since the Trinity is beyond the physical realm, Jesus needed a body to suffer and die for us. We know from scripture that He was able to take our sins upon Himself because His divinity was united to our humanity in a human body. For example, St. Peter testifies that He "bore our sins in his body

---

101 Cf. 1Corinthians 3:9
102 Pope John Paul II, *General Audience*, April 9, 1997.
103 2 Corinthians 2:14 (emphasis mine)

on the cross" and St. Paul testifies that "we have been sanctified through the offering of the body of Jesus".[104] As Mary accepted God's will to have Jesus formed in her womb, she agreed to provide Him with the instrument of our salvation. Thus, Mary is first of all Coredemptrix because she gave Jesus his body, the body by which we are redeemed.

Like any good mother, Mary suffered in her heart everything that her Son suffered in His body. When Jesus was presented in the temple as a baby, Simeon prophesied that a sword would pierce Mary's heart as it did her Son's.[105] Next to the surrender of Jesus, the surrender of Mary at the foot of the cross was the most heroic exercise of human freedom in history. In the twelfth century, St. Bernard of Clairvaux challenged us to think clearly about the co-suffering of Mary:

> Who are you, and what is the source of your wisdom that you are more surprised at Mary's compassion than at the compassion of Mary's son? For if He could die in body could she not die with Him in spirit? He died through a love greater than has ever been known, she died through a love greater than any other since His.[106]

Any good mother would also say that they would gladly lay down their life to protect their child, and from the physical world we read that there is no mother more ferocious in defending her offspring than the grizzly bear. When her cubs are in danger, every fiber of her being is caught up in frenzied impulses of defense. Mary, however, in a supreme act of faith, let the wolves tear into her boy in complete trust. She surrendered her maternal rights of protection and "in keeping with the divine plan, endured with her only begotten son the intensity of his suffering, united herself with his sacrifice in her Mother's heart, and lovingly consented to the immolation of the victim which was born of her."[107]

On Passion Sunday, one week before Easter, the Church anticipates the suffering of Jesus on the cross. During my first spring semester at Franciscan University, that particular Sunday was memorable. I had been working on a research paper and had wandered into my back yard to get

---

104 1Peter 2:24; Hebrews 10:10
105 Luke 2:35
106 St. Bernard of Clairvaux, *Office of Readings*, Memorial of Our Lady of Sorrows, September 15.
107 Vatican II, *Dogmatic Constitution on the Church (Lumen Gentium)*, #58

some fresh air (and perhaps some fresh ideas), when I noticed that the moon was full but peculiar. I then realized that I was witnessing my first lunar eclipse. The earth had begun casting its shadow and the moon was gathering a maroon hue, like the color of dried blood. I thought about all my new friends on campus just across the valley, and felt the urge to call them. Then I thought how silly I was to think that anyone was in their dorm rooms; certainly they were all gathered outside reading these words too. The next day, I asked everyone I spoke with if they had seen the sign of the Coredemptrix. Out of all those inquiries, only one young man had witnessed the spectacle. And as one might expect, John Steele is a naturalist. Even with his corroboration, however, few were able to appreciate that on the Sunday we remember the bloodshed of Jesus and the gift of Mary's motherhood, "the full moon turned blood red".[108]

That day I realized how living in a place like Jackson Hole had made me attentive to nature. For there in the valley of the elk, seasons come and go not by dates on a calendar but by migrations, blossoms, and ripening fruit; aerial courtships and hibernations; the shedding of old antlers and the emergence of new. There the natural world speaks a little bit louder.[109]

The Mother of Nature

It was Mary's union with Jesus' sufferings at the foot of the cross that united her with the redemption and renewal of all things. As the successors of the apostles infallibly declared at the 22nd council in history, "in a wholly singular way, she cooperated by her obedience, faith, hope, and burning charity, in the work of the Savior in restoring supernatural life to souls. For this reason she is a Mother to us in the order of grace."[110]

The name Eve means mother of the living. The New Eve, because of her singular role in the restoration of the universe, has become the new mother of the living, our mother "in the order of grace". As St. Anselm teaches, every creature now falls under her universal motherhood.[111]

---

108 Revelation 6:12
109 The book which best explains this *calendar of creation* in Jackson Hole is by renowned naturalist and grizzly bear research pioneer Frank Craighead. It is appropriately titled, *For Everything There is a Season: The Sequence of Natural Events in the Grand Teton – Yellowstone Area.*
110 Vatican II, *Dogmatic Constitution on the Church (Lumen Gentium),*# 61
111 See *Appendix D* for St. Anselm's commentary on Mary's universal motherhood.

CHAPTER 33

The Day of the Word

In my early thirties, I began to earn an undergraduate degree in theology and was acutely aware of being the same age as Jesus during his public ministry. I sold my truck to help pay for school and return to a simpler style of living. The house I rented was on top of a hill which was separated from campus by a deep ravine. Armed with a machete and shovel, I began to build a switchback trail down the steep hillside so that I could walk through the oak trees to and from school. After I was about half-way finished, I discovered some old stone steps which went the rest of the way down to the street. Apparently, my neighborhood was a thriving community at the peak of the steel industry with paths leading in every direction. It took a few more days to clear the steps of broken glass and debris, but finally my trail was complete.

Throughout the fall semester, I hiked back and forth at least twice each day because I had purchased a meal plan at the school cafeteria. I was home before dark until daylight savings began but even then I was able to use the trail all winter because the leaves had fallen, allowing the street lights below to illuminate the slope. Toward the end of the spring semester, however, final exams interrupted my late-night library routine and I walked home before sundown every night. After the semester was over, I took a short break then returned for the summer session. The first night of summer classes I stayed at the library until it closed, then, as was my routine, went down the campus sidewalk and across the ravine; but as I began to climb the stone steps up the other side I noticed something was different, yet continued on. When I was almost to the top where the trail I built began, I realized I couldn't see anymore. In the days since my last nocturnal hike, the giant oaks had leafed out and now blocked all the light from below. I stood there for a moment letting my eyes adjust, but it didn't help. And just when I had resolved to descend the steps and walk home along the dangerously narrow and serpentine roadway, the trail flashed at my feet . . . then flashed again. Fireflies were illuminating the path. One small step and one small beacon after another they led me home, and I began to contemplate how blessed I was to be studying God's words full-time: "How I love your teaching Lord, I study it all day long . . . your word is a lamp for my feet, a light for my path." [112] And as the soft summer days passed, I also began to ruminate on what it meant for Jesus to be called "The Word".

"The Word"

When we love another person and desire that they love us in return, there is a sense of wanting to promise them the moon, as the saying goes. All we really have to offer, however, is ourselves and a few material possessions. But what if we could give everything in the universe to the person we loved, not just ourselves? What if the relationship between "I" and "Thou" was not limited to "I love you and give myself to you", but included all things and became "I love you and give myself to you, along with all that is true, good, and beautiful in heaven and on earth"? What if we had that power? Who would not express their love with everything that belonged to them? Who would not deliver the promised moon?

It is in this sense that our Father says "I love you" to us, His children; for within this one word – Jesus – all the gifts of the universe are present:

> In the beginning was the Word, and the Word was with God, and the Word was God. He was in the beginning with God. All things came into being through him, and without him not one thing came into being. [113]

Our Father speaks with colors and accents which resound through a myriad of mediums, but He also speaks just one word that gathers together the meaning of every other word. None of the words of creation

---

112 Psalm 119:97,105
113 John 1:1-3

or scripture escape the one and only Word who is His one and only Son. Jesus is what the Father said when brought the universe into existence – when "he spoke; and it came to be."[114] Jesus is the one transcendent song that contains every pitch and tone, the one eternal aria that resonates with every timbre, a single utterance which encompasses every occasion of truth, goodness, and beauty:

> For your Word is not speech in which each part comes to
> an end when it has been spoken, giving place to the next,
> so that finally the whole may be uttered. In your Word
> all is uttered at one and the same time, yet eternally. If
> it were not so, your Word would be subject to time and
> change, and therefore would be neither truly eternal nor
> truly immortal. . . . Therefore, it is by a Word co-eternal
> with yourself that you say all that you say.[115]

And all that the Father has to say is "I love you . . . I want you to possess the glory of eternal life . . . . . . Come and see."

During Christmas break one winter, I made a one-day retreat at the *Bosque del Apache National Wildlife Refuge* in central New Mexico. I went for a long hike in just a t-shirt as it was an unseasonably warm day. As evening fell, thousands of snow geese approached from the north where they had spent the day feeding. Their multiple v-shaped formations stretched a half-mile across the sky and the setting sun lit up the undulating lines as they adjusted altitude, forming and reforming flight groups. The configurations began to look like cursive handwriting searching for the right font and my heart became lost in the moment – to the point that I expected Him to write something in the sky like *Merry Christmas Jon!* or *Trust Me!* As they passed low overhead, the whirr of wings and deafening honks lifted me even higher, and I impulsively cried out, "O Love!" After the flocks faded into the horizon and silence slowly returned, I then realized that He had indeed written something in the sky, the name which is above all names.

A week later I was back on campus at Franciscan University and saw my dearest friend, Sister Teresa of the Two Hearts, off in the distance. Again I spontaneously blurted out, "O Love!" It seemed that within a

---

114 Psalm 33:9
115 St. Augustine, *Confessions,* XI.7.

short span of time I had received two beautiful letters signed by the Father: one from a courier of the physical world, the other from a courier made in His image. And both had inspired me to provide a brief yet heartfelt accompaniment to that one beautiful song He always sings.

The Poor

In our discussion of St. Damien of Molokai, we learned that love expresses itself in service. Since the day of the Word is the day of love, it is appropriate for it to be a day of service, of spiritual and corporal works of mercy.[116]

On one of her visits to the United States, Mother Teresa tried to help us understand that love and the service it prompts can be stifled by material possessions and their maintenance: "Here in America . . . you can easily be suffocated by things. And once you have them you must give time to taking care of them. Then you have no time for each other or for the poor."[117] When we have too many things to repair, clean, or tend to in some other way, setting time aside for family or works of mercy becomes difficult. Why? Because we become distracted from gratitude, and the generosity which flows from it. Instead of poorly expounding this idea myself, allow me to step aside and turn to one of the greatest teachers in salvation history:

> Recognize to whom you owe the fact that you exist, that
> you breathe, that you understand, that you are wise, and,
> above all, that you know God and hope for the kingdom
> of heaven and the vision of glory, now dimly . . . but then
> with greater fullness and purity. You' have been made
> a son of God, coheir with Christ. Where did you get all
> this and from whom? . . . What benefactor has enabled
> you to look out upon the beauty of the sky, the sun in its
> course, the circle of the moon, the countless number of

---

116 The seven spiritual works are: Admonish the sinner. Instruct the ignorant. Counsel the doubtful. Comfort the sorrowful. Bear wrongs patiently. Forgive all injuries. Pray for the living and the dead. The seven corporal works are: Feed the hungry. Give drink to the thirsty. Clothe the naked. Visit the imprisoned. Shelter the homeless. Visit the sick. Bury the dead. (The latter works are taken mainly from Jesus' parable about separating the sheep from the goats at the end of time. Cf. Matthew 25:31ff.)

117 Blessed Teresa of Calcutta, *Light For Our Times: "On Purity"*, 45. (cd)

stars, with harmony and order that are theirs, like the music of a harp? Who blessed you with rain, with the art of husbandry [raising livestock], with different kinds of food, with the arts, with houses, with laws, with states, with the life of humanity and culture, with friendship and the easy familiarity of kinship? Who has given you dominion over animals, those that are tame and those that provide you with food? Who has made you Lord and master of everything on earth? In short, who has endowed you with all that makes man superior to all other living creatures. Is it not God who asks you now in return to show yourself generous above all other creatures in for the sake of all other creatures? Because we have received from him so many wonderful gifts, will we not be ashamed to refuse him this one thing only, our generosity? Though he is God and Lord, he is not afraid to be known as our Father. Shall we for our part repudiate those who are our kith and kin. Brethren and friends, let us never allow ourselves to misuse what has been given us by God's gift. If we do, we shall hear St. Peter say, "Be ashamed of yourselves for holding on to what belongs to someone else. Resolve to imitate God's justice, and no one will be poor." Let us not labor to heap up and hoard riches while others remain in need. . . . Let us put into practice the supreme and primary law of God. He sends down rain unjust and sinful alike and causes the sun to rise on all without distinction. To all earth's creatures, he has given the broad earth, the springs, the rivers, and the forests. He has given the air to the birds, and the waters to those who live in water. He is given abundantly to all the basic needs of life, not as a private possession, not restricted by law, not divided by boundaries. It is common to all amply and in rich measure.[118]

The Universal Destination of Goods

America is a gift which is best understood under three categories: (1) the crops grown in the Midwest, which feed the hungry of the world;

---

118 St. Gregory of Nazianzen, *Office of Readings*, First Monday of Lent.

(2) the democratic principles founded in the East, which have become a model of freedom for other countries; and (3) the national parks established in the West, which could very well be "America's best idea." All three should help us gain the perspective that America was and is God's gift to all people: precisely because all people have been endowed by their Creator with the right to life, liberty, and the pursuit of happiness.

Native Americans saw their land as a private gift for their own particular nation, and this is partially true. With the coming of those nations who understood that God's plan was for His people to go out to other nations and bring them into His one universal tribe, the original purpose of the land as a gift for all nations, not just one, was restored: "The right to private property, acquired or received in a just way, does not do away with the original gift of the earth to the whole of mankind. The *universal destination of goods* remains primordial".[119]

Symbiosis

The word *symbiosis* is a compound of the Greek words for same (*syn*) and life (*bios*). The countless symbiotic relationships in the universe testify that sharing the same life with other creatures is part of God's plan:

> God wills the interdependence of creatures. The sun and the moon, the cedar and the little flower, the eagle and the sparrow: the spectacle of their countless diversities and inequalities tells us that no creature is self-sufficient. Creatures exist only in dependence on each other, to complete each other, in the service of each other.[120]

At the lowest point of my life, I found myself enrolled in a pontifical university in Detroit's inner city, but everything seemed dark and I couldn't concentrate. I seemed to be forsaken, friendless, and despised... a living mistake. But just as I thought I had hit rock bottom and was lamenting the fact that I probably would never earn a doctorate or write this book, He spoke to me in the silence of my heart: "Why not begin our book right now?" And so it was that I began writing, and the whole thing was outlined in three days.

---

119 *Catechism of the Catholic Church*, #2403 (emphasis in original)
120 *Catechism of the Catholic Church*, #340

I was fortunate enough to be living in an old rectory on ten acres of mature oak forest. Adjacent to the rectory was a parish opened only for Sunday mass, but the greatest thing on earth – the real presence of Jesus in the Eucharist – was still there in the tabernacle, making all things holy. And I had a key.

The property was well-kept. A path had been constructed with benches, stations of the cross, and a statue of St. Francis, but mostly the landscape was undisturbed. Hundreds of oaks stood firm, steady, and upright: "oaks of justice" as Isaiah would say.[121] My responsibilities as groundskeeper allowed me to observe the relationship between these great trees and their tenants – squirrels and hawks – and I began to meditate on the wonderful service these creatures provided for one another. Each gives to the other by instinct, not by choice, yet are nonetheless exemplary lessons in serving the common good.

Some of the acorns that fall from the oaks are carefully planted by furry little hands to be eaten later, but to insure that some are left stashed in the earth to germinate the hawks reduce the number of squirrels. For their part, the trees provide safety and even building materials for both: dead leaves for the squirrels; dead branches for the hawks. One of the profound lessons of this giving and receiving is the serenity with which each species goes about serving and being served. The squirrels seem to have a sense of when the hawks are hunting and when they preoccupied with nest building. The frenzied activity and constant shrieks of the hawks make their presence anything but discreet, but at times the squirrels seem completely at peace out in the open.

This is how a forest remains beautiful and diverse: each creature striving to live and reproduce yet serving the common good by simply doing what they were called to do. With each species giving and receiving what they should, a forest of justice emerges.

The cooperative and mutually beneficial relationships found to exist between animals and plants can also be found between members of the mystical body of Christ: "As it is, there are many members, yet one body. The eye cannot say to the hand, 'I have no need of you,' nor again the head to the feet, I have no need of you.'"[122] We who belong to "the family of faith" share the same life; thus, our relationships are

---

121 Isaiah 61:3
122 1 Corinthians 12:20-21

symbiotic.[123] Some of us make generous donations to support missions or the building of new churches, while others teach at those missions and churches. Some members have extraordinary gifts such as miraculous healing or speaking in tongues, while others are born leaders. As St. Paul teaches:

> God has appointed in the church first apostles, second prophets, third teachers; then gifts of power, then gifts of healing, forms of assistance, forms of leadership, various kinds of tongues. Are all apostles? Are all prophets? Are all teachers? Do all work miracles? Do all possess gifts of healing? Do all speak in tongues?[124]

Clearly, we all "have gifts that differ according to the grace given to us", so it is worthwhile to be reminded that without the gifts of others we cannot exercise our own.[125]

Since sharing gifts with our neighbor can be challenging, it is also worthwhile to recall that Jesus does not call us to like everyone, but to love them. Some neighbors have betrayed us, taken us for granted, or simply rub us the wrong way and we don't *like* them; but being a Catholic means we must will goodness to our neighbors by forgiving all injuries, appreciating their gifts, praying for them, and serving them as a fellow son or daughter of God. For those who serve with "forms of assistance" let them also remember that their strength and abundance are gifts of God; for those benefiting from this assistance, let them remember to be models of bestowing honor and showing gratitude: "Let the strong care for the weak, and the weak respect the strong. Let the wealthy assist the poor and the poor man thank God for giving him someone to supply his needs."[126] (Furthermore, since God is ready to pour out His grace into the heart of anyone who has fallen away and takes even the smallest step back toward the faith, we must strive for the same disposition, rejecting every temptation to be judgmental or condescending.)

---

123 Galatians 6:10
124 1 Corinthians 12:27-30
125 Romans 12:4-6
126 Pope St. Clement, *Office of Readings*, Fourth Friday of Easter.

The Name Above All Names

The goodness of the physical world reveals that God has the power and desire to help us, and the freedom of the human person reveals that we can ask for help. By calling upon the Lord for assistance, we are acknowledging that there is nothing in the universe more powerful than the name of Jesus.

My dad loves the ocean and all its creatures, and on our frequent trips to Hawaii he gave my brother and me a real appreciation of sand and surf. He would always make us read the water – looking for signs of riptides or side-currents – which helped us feel that we belonged, that we weren't just tourists.

One summer, along the *Na Pali* coast of Kauai, I dutifully studied the water for quite some time before determining it was safe then went out for a swim. It was the first evening of a five day backcountry trip. The following morning I was standing on that gorgeous beach within minutes of waking . . . and I let myself be distracted. In the mental fog of early morning, I entered the surf without taking more than a moment to read it. And as soon as I had pushed through the crashing waves and looked back to where I had been standing, I knew I was in trouble. During the short time it had taken me to swim beyond the impact zone, an undertow had pulled me thirty yards down the shoreline, and it now felt like a river was pushing me out to sea. I was in a rip current that was sweeping an arc through the crescent-shaped cove. I knew I needed to relax but the instinct to get back to shore was too strong and I began to fight the current. I was being sucked toward the cliffs near the edge of the beach but, ironically, the approaching rocks gave me hope. Even though thundering sets were crashing right on top of me, the cliffs of Hawaii are where I had learned the language of the sea. As I was pushed against them, I tried to let the surge lift me to a handhold or foothold, as I had done thousands of times before; but since I could only search for an exit in between walls of churning whitewash, I had little success. At that point I was only 15 yards from a large sea cave but the undercurrent was still swirling against the rocks and battling the incoming waves. Exhausted, I thought to myself that I had one last violent chance to wrestle out onto the jagged outcropping. No matter how many cuts and bruises I had to endure it was better than dying. Then, as if I was remembering something I forgot to buy at the grocery store, I realized that I had not even thought of asking God for help. My prayer was simple and to the point: "Jesus". At that moment, the undertow subsided, the waves relented, and the roiling froth on the surface of the sea fizzled to a relative calm. My feet touched the bottom and I walked out onto the sand in the sea cave and collapsed. I had never been so fatigued or so thankful.

CHAPTER 34

The Day of Fire

Few things are more fundamental to survival than fire. Its greatest asset may not be practical uses, however, but the soothing effect it has on the soul. In times of fear and anxiety, there is a natural inclination to build a campfire as a sign of hope and readiness.

Campfires

During my first summer working with special needs students, I was asked to join a backcountry excursion for a group of teenage boys who were severely emotionally disturbed. The leader of our trip had a master's degree in social work and was trained by the National Outdoor Leadership School (NOLS). Headquartered in Lander, Wyoming, NOLS is internationally recognized for excellence in wilderness basics, but they are somewhat negligent when it comes to the more salient elements of backpacking: silence, prayer, and fire. But since this was a trip for teenage boys at a public school, so much for the first two.

Our first afternoon brought a cloud burst which soaked every kid and every kid's gear. Morale was pretty low and these young men had already lost interest in earning any privileges. Being emotionally disturbed, they were in a downward spiral which was accelerating with every thought of spending the night in a wet sleeping bag. They were primed for an insurrection. I asked the trip leader about building a fire. NOLS instructors are not opposed to fire, only to irresponsible high-impact camping. They promote a *leave no trace* ethic, which is good, but sometimes they take it to an extreme, as if we are trespassing in the mountains. The more appropriate view is to realize that we belong here and yet should strive to leave as few traces as possible, especially when building a fire. In any event, our leader reluctantly agreed to carefully remove the topsoil and sod from an area about 3 feet in diameter, set it aside so it could be replaced in the morning, and dig a fire-pit. Within minutes, the boys had gathered wood, busted it down to size, and were being comforted by the security of a blazing fire. We all stayed up well past midnight, telling stories, drying out bags, and enjoying each other on a level which bridged the gap between staff and student – we were men around a campfire. Then we slept like logs. After that, we had a fire every night.

The following summer Bud and I co-founded the National Outdoor Pyrotechnic School (NOPS) on those three pillars which NOLS does not emphasize (silence, prayer, and fire). That was twenty years ago when we were young and strong, and built young, strong fires. We thought it was a hilarious play on words to banter about the essence of fire in the NOPS backcountry system with a litany of "nopes": *Do ya feel safe without a fire goin'? Nope. Do ya think we oughta give the bugs a break from the smoke? Nope. Do ya feel like prayin' in the dark tonight? Nope.* We never seemed to tire of adding to the list of mock questions about whether or not to have a fire. As we grew in backcountry wisdom, however, silence and prayer grew as well, so we adapted the name to the *National Outdoor Pneumatology School* in order to affirm our commitment to the Holy Spirit and to reflect our graduation from fire basics into the spiritual sense of fire.[127]

We then adopted the motto *studeamus ignem* (let us study fire) based on several lessons from scripture. For example: St. Peter's three-fold denial of Jesus along with his repentant three-fold affirmation of love (both while standing next to "a charcoal fire") taught us how fireside chats with the Lord can call to mind our many denials and renew our devotion; and St. Paul's reaction to being bit by venomous snake after being shipwrecked on Malta taught us that even when it seems danger has passed and we've arrived safely on shore, the devil can strike at any moment in this life and must be immediately cast into the fire.[128] We were also taught the more general lesson that fire is a sign of who God is and what God wants.

---

127 "Pneumatology" is the study of the Holy Spirit.
128 John 18:18; 21:9; Acts 28:1-5

Like God, a campfire is comforting and captivating, while at the same time demanding a respectful fear. It is at once mysterious, tremendous, and fascinating *(mysterium, tremendum, et fascinans)*. When God revealed His plan to Moses from the burning bush, as well as when He gave him the Ten Commandments on Mt Sinai, He spoke through fire. If we let the proper understanding of *leave no trace* disintegrate into a bias against backcountry campfires, we will never hear "the voice of God speaking from the midst of fire".[129] And we will never hear him speaking of illumination, purification, and punishment.

Illumination

The apostles first received the Spirit from Jesus on Easter Sunday, and fifty days later they received it in full measure. But since on Pentecost that Breath came not only as wind but "as tongues of fire" it is fitting that "Sunday, the day of light, could also be called the day of fire, in reference to the Holy Spirit. The light of Christ is intimately linked to the fire of the Spirit, and the two images together reveal the meaning of the Christian Sunday."[130] On the first day of the Church, Pentecost, the apostles were illuminated so that they could illuminate others in God's name; on the first day of creation, the angels were illuminated toward the same end. It would seem that Sunday is the preeminent day of illumination.

We learn from St. John's vision of heaven that part of angelic ministry is to have a certain authority over creatures of the physical world: "Then another angel came out from the altar, the angel who has authority over fire".[131] Another part of angelic ministry is to protect us from spiritual and bodily harm, and still another is to illuminate the books of creation and scripture. The power given to angels over the physical world and the human person is an example of how God appoints creatures to be instruments of His will.[132] Since these spiritual creatures chose once and for all to be "ministers who do God's will", good angels live as synonyms of Light and Fire.[133]

---

129 Deuteronomy 4:34?????
130 Acts 2:2-3; Pope John Paul II, *Dies Domini*, #28.
131 Revelation 14:18
132 Cf. Psalms 91:11-12; 103:20-21; CCC #308
133 Psalm 103:21; cf. Dionysius, *The Celestial Hierarchy*, XIII. (The highest angels are called *seraphim*, "the burning ones").

Purification

The fire of love given by the Spirit is a fire of purification and renewal. This idea is highlighted in the first part of a common Catholic prayer: "Come Holy Spirit, fill the hearts of your faithful and enkindle in them the fire of your love. Send forth your spirit and they shall be created, and you shall renew the face of the earth."

During the great Yellowstone fires of 1988, over two-thirds of Yellowstone was burned. However, when a lodgepole forest is in extraordinary need of regeneration it is precisely through fire that this is accomplished. The ordinary regeneration process takes place through pollination and seed dispersal, but certain cones of the lodgepole pine are made fertile by being exposed to intense heat. These *serotinous* cones regenerate the land when fire melts away their outer layer. Ostensibly, the blackened forest appears devastated, but on a deeper level it has been purified, cleansed, and renewed. Few people passing through a charred landscape think of beauty and rejuvenation, and few who are passing through fires of personal purification see long term benefits either. The waxy covering of *serotinous* cones is similar to the residue of sin which must be burned away if we are to sow seeds abundantly. This indicates how both our faith and works must be purified by fire.

St. Peter writes that our faith is tested through suffering: "you may have to suffer various trials, so that the genuineness of your faith, more precious than gold which though perishable is tested by fire, may redound to praise and honor and glory."[134] And St. Paul writes that our works are tested through suffering: "fire will test what sort of work each has done. If what has been built on the foundation survives, the builder will receive a reward. If the work is burned up, the builder will suffer loss; the builder will be saved, but only as through fire." [135] If our ultimate goal is to be saved, that is, to live in the pure light and fire of God, we must remember that in this life "he disciplines us for our good, that we may share his holiness."[136] In the next life too, we may still need to be purified in order to live in His presence. Dying in a state of grace assures entrance into heaven, but where there has not been sufficient restitution on earth for the evil we have done, the fires of Purgatory *purge* the soul of

---

134 1 Peter 1:6-7
135 1 Corinthians 3:13-15
136 Hebrews 12:10

impurities. Prayer, fasting, and almsgiving are self-imposed purifications which help us avoid these fires by making up for the damage our sins have caused the other members of His body.

Punishment

We are free to live in the illuminating and purifying fires of the Holy Spirit through prayer, fasting, and almsgiving; or the destructive fires of disordered desires for power, pleasure, and possessions. One leads to the joy of heaven where "God is a consuming fire", the other to the torments of hell where there awaits "a punishment of eternal fire."[137] In his typically succinct style, the poet T.S. Eliot brings this idea to light:

> We only live, only suspire
> Consumed by either fire or fire.[138]

We'll return to the idea of fiery punishment later in this chapter, but for now let it serve to complete our reflection on fire's spiritual sense of illumination, purification, and punishment. And may this fuller sense also serve to broaden our understanding of the words of Jesus as He discloses His earthly mission and desire, "I have come to set the earth on fire, and how I wish it were already blazing!"[139]

Building a Campfire

To ignite and sustain a campfire, air and wood must co-exist in a certain proportion. When the wood is stacked too tightly, there is not enough air. When the wood is stacked too loosely, there is not enough fuel. If the arrangement of wood represents our own efforts – prayer, fasting, and almsgiving – and the air represents the breath of God, building a strong campfire is analogous to building a strong spiritual life, especially as it pertains to prayer.

When we stack prayer upon prayer without trusting in the action of the Spirit, we become too active, too dependent on our own efforts. Jesus warns us against falling into this error: "In praying, do not babble

---

137 Hebrews 12:29; Jude 7
138 T.S Eliot, *The Four Quartets: "Little Gidding"*, IV.
139 Luke 12:49

like the pagans, who think they will be heard by their many words."[140] In this case, we have neglected the necessity of grace. On the other hand, when we believe that God will do everything without any cooperation on our part besides sitting still, we become too passive, too dependent on the Spirit. In this case, we have neglected our freedom to exercise virtue.

Instead, proper dialogue with God is both active *and* passive. He initiates prayer with the gift of grace and we are free to respond to that grace. He gives us the inclination to pray without imposing on free-will and then animates our prayer with His Spirit. What we offer in prayer has first been *passively* received like the gift of a tree, but then *actively* cut, gathered, and arranged to make a fire. The Lord provides fuel for us in the form of wood, and when we gather that "wood in abundance; the breath of the Lord, like a stream of sulfur, kindles it."[141] In other words, our efforts build upon what is already a gift and offer it back to the God. The human condition, therefore, is that of a "re-gifter".

The mystery of grace and virtue is that our fire can be blazing or smoldering depending upon His gift and our cooperation. One aspect of our cooperation with grace is making sure our prayers are combustible; because when we ask for things that are outside of God's plan, it's like trying to burn dirt: "You ask and do not receive, because you ask wrongly, in order to spend what you get on your pleasures."[142] If we ask for something *contrary* to the will of God, however, we still have hope because "the Spirit intercedes for the saints *according* to the will of God."[143] No prayer goes unanswered, but sometimes the answer is the simple grace of a push in the direction of asking rightly.

Nevertheless, since everything we do and say is tainted by sin, even when we ask rightly "the Spirit helps us in our weakness; for we do not know how to pray as we ought".[144] The residue of sin must be burned away before our offering can be brought to God, for nothing impure is allowed in His presence. Our prayers are unacceptable until the Spirit translates them into the dialect of heaven, which is to say, our words are unworthy until "that very Spirit intercedes for us with sighs too deep for words."[145]

---

140 Matthew 6:7
141 Isaiah 30:33
142 James 4:3
143 Romans 8:27 (emphasis mine)
144 Romans 8:26
145 Romans 8:26

A campfire leaves behind ashes which are visible reminders of our pride, presumption, and other sins associated with our fallen nature. As the smoke mysteriously rises, dissipates, and disappears into the spiritual realm it symbolizes that the Spirit has eternalized our prayers, making them fit for heaven where angels offer them as "incense" before the throne of God.[146]

The Wilderness Retreat

If it has not been stifled by busy-ness, within each of us there is a desire to be alone with God and His words. As David illustrates, the human heart yearns for peace and tranquility: "Oh that I had wings like a dove, I would fly away and be at rest; I would flee far away, and encamp in the wilderness."[147] The Gospels tell us that Jesus would often "withdraw to deserted places to pray" both on foot and by boat, both into the desert and into the mountains.[148] A wilderness retreat, therefore, is a direct imitation of Christ.

We've seen how "spiritual growth comes from reading and reflection" and how the key to doing this well is *lectio divina*.[149] Entering the wilderness is like going to the library, where silence is so conducive to analysis and application. In this silence, the language of creatures becomes so amplified it can readily be translated into a virtue. Accordingly, in the NOPS system we have two ground rules for ensuring periods of *lectio divina* will yield a rich harvest: set and setting.

First, get set. This means taking care of camp chores so that you will not be distracted for a long period of time. Gather wood, prepare for a sudden storm, hang things out to dry, and make sure you have your rosary and books *before* you try to settle. Get your mind focused on what you are about, making a firm resolve to be still, then get your heart set with a period of formal prayer, asking for the grace to accept with joy whatever comes your way – especially with regard to the weather. If it starts to rain, for example, reflect on how God wishes to water our souls with graces: "May my instruction soak in like the rain, and my discourse permeate like the dew, like a downpour upon the grass, like a shower upon the crops."[150] Be determined to receive rather than achieve, to

146 Revelation 5:8 (cf. 8:3-4: Psalm 141:2)
147 Psalm 55:7-8
148 Luke 5:16 (cf. Matthew 14:13, 23)
149 St. Isidore, *Book of Maxims*, Office of Readings, April 4.
150 Deuteronomy 32:2

participate rather than anticipate. Often He will teach us to trust and be still by altering our plans. The goal here is surrender and freedom from anxiety, also known as holy indifference: "To take whatever he gives, and to give whatever he takes, with a big smile. You are free then."[151]

Second, find a beautiful setting. With the confidence that He is the great giver of gifts, put yourself in an occasion of grace that is as comfortable and glorious as possible. Sometimes the gift is subtle like a mayfly hatch or the trek of caterpillar, other times it's dramatic like a bison herd fording a river or the twilight playfulness of a wolf pack before setting out to hunt. The goal here is to become an active listener and attentive to God's words, for He wants to be heard: "Listen my people and I will speak . . . for every animal of the forest is mine . . . and I know all the birds in the sky."[152] Becoming present to rhythms like those of songbirds and rivers opens our hearts and enables us to hear Him humming the melody of the good; and becoming present to scenery like that found at the Grand Canyon or the Maroon Bells, opens our hearts and enables us to hear Him shouting the motif of glorious vistas, "See with what large letters I am writing to you with my own hand!"[153]

Silence in beautiful settings cultivates the practice of verse and response, for only a silent heart can enter into dialogue with the Most Holy Trinity. God speaks and we answer. We've included several examples already, but dialogue is the difference between seeing a spectacular cumulus cloud and merely commenting on its features (or the weather it foretells), and responding to it as a word of His ascension and second coming – perhaps with the prayer *Maranatha!*[154] Antiphons like those found in the Liturgy of the Hours or the responsorial psalm during mass can help us form an antiphonal habit with creation. In order to further develop this virtue, the principal verse and response of NOPS is repeated throughout the day as the Spirit wills: "Come behold the works of the Lord . . . 'Be still and know that I am God'".[155]

Another fruit of silence is priestly intercession on behalf of the cliffs, the meadows, the lakes, and all that is in them. And still another is what we at NOPS call a numinous fire, but this is difficult to explain without experiencing it and seems too sacred to write about here, "too deep

---

151 Mother Teresa, *Jesus: The Word to Be Spoken*, 136.
152 Psalm 50:7,10,11
153 Galatians 6:11
154 Aramaic for "Come Lord!"; 1 Corinthians 16:22 (cf. Chapter 16: *Clouds*)
155 Psalm 46:8,10

for words" as it were. I suppose we should also mention the element of duration which enters into the equation. A one day outing can be extremely valuable, and certainly a three day weekend can be even more so – but a week is much better. For on the third day, when the dust of distraction begins to settle, the heart enters a stage of openness which makes a wilderness retreat truly amazing, truly "theophonic" . . . as if one can hear the sun shining.

The Book of Yellowstone

July 15th has been an important date in my life for two reasons: first, because it marks opening day for fishing on the Yellowstone river; and second, because it is the feast of St. Bonaventure, the saint who explained the spiritual sense of creatures. Most of my solo retreats have revolved around this date, and perhaps the most recent serves as a good example, not because it was better than others but because it was typical and is fresh in my aging mind.

Over the course of ten days last summer, I rested in the beauty of one of God's most spectacular Yellowstone valleys. He led me to a river island that had a heron rookery with six nests and fifteen chicks; He led me to a canyon rim overlook from which I could look down into an osprey nest built on a spire of rock; He led me to a black wolf pup playing with his uncle at a rendezvous site, and to mature mule deer bucks drinking not thirty yards from the brink of the Lower Falls.[156] But the greatest gift was a fresh bison kill which I could safely observe from an opposing ridge.

This particular gift was extraordinary. Three times a day for five days I watched and listened as the creatures of the forest took turns feeding. Bears were run off the carcass by larger bears, coyotes were run off by wolves, ravens by eagles. One morning I prayed the whole rosary while a gray wolf howled from a hillside about a hundred yards away, summoning the rest of the pack. One evening I prayed until it was dark as a griz covered his prize with dirt and lay down to sleep on top of it. And one afternoon a bear larger than I had ever seen in the lower forty-eight came hurling down the mountain and scattered two other bears, which until then seemed enormous. The giant boar grabbed the bison in his jaws and pulled it twenty yards through the sage, trying to get out

---

156 In late spring or early summer, a wolf pack will move their pups from the den site to a rendezvous site, which is like a hunting base camp.

of the open meadow and into the trees. Seeing a bear that powerful made me question if I could ever be alone in the backcountry again.

I told a bear-management ranger about the carcass the very first day and she could not believe that hundreds of tourists had not flocked to the kill site. She was bewildered further when I saw her four days later and the crowds had still not come, because she didn't understand that I was on a spiritual retreat; and that anyone who devotes time to be alone with God receives special attention – like a boy on a fishing trip with his dad.

St. Francis of Assisi

Wilderness is charged with gift and mystery . . . but also with carefully nuanced deceptions. A proper relationship with the physical world should be grounded in the following verse from the Old Testament: "Look at the rainbow and praise him who made it, for majestic indeed is its splendor."[157] Regardless of the creature we are reading, this verse serves as a paradigm, "Look at the _____ and praise him who made it"; for if nature does not lead us into God, it will lead us into idolatry. Thus, it is vital that a wilderness retreat be guided by a reliable outfitter: a faithful spiritual director, a faithful commentary on Scripture, or a faithful daily structure like the one found in the *Liturgy of the Hours* or in the *Spiritual Exercises* of St. Ignatius of Loyola. But perhaps none of these is a more reliable guide than the patron saint of ecology, also known as *il poverello* (the little poor man).

Quite simply, St. Francis was the whole package. On account of his ability to read the words of God without gloss (*sine glossa*), he was comfortable counseling a wolf, preaching to birds, and embracing lepers as if they were Jesus himself.[158] He established the devotion of the *Stations of the Cross* for Lent, as well as the tradition of a manger scene for Christmas. He composed an incomparable song of appreciation for nature, and was the first to receive the wounds of Christ, the stigmata. Reflect upon that for a moment – creation, crèche, crucifixion – these things are the pillars of salvation history; and yet this one man influenced what it means to live within that history as a Catholic in every part of

---

157 Sirach 43:11
158 In the thirteenth century, some Bibles had commentaries written in the margins called *glossa*. St. Francis believed that rather than explaining the text, sometimes these notes explained away the text.

THE DAY OF FIRE

the world. It may be that no saint will ever again have a greater impact on the universal Church. It also may be that no saint will ever again compose a poem which better reflects the right ordering of nature to nature's Maker than his famous *Canticle of Creatures:*

> *Most High, all-powerful, good Lord, yours are the*
> *praises, the glory, the honor, and all blessing. To you*
> *alone Most High do they belong.*

> *Praise to you, my Lord, through all your creatures especially*
> *Brother Sun, who is the day and through whom you give us*
> *light, for he is beautiful and radiant with great splendor and*
> *bears a likeness of you Most High.*

> *Praise to you, my Lord through Sister Moon and the*
> *stars for you formed them clear and precious and lovely*
> *in heaven.*

> *Praise to you, my Lord, through Brother Wind, and*
> *through the clouds, and every kind of weather by which*
> *you give sustenance to your creatures.*

> *Praise to you, my Lord, through Sister Water, which is*
> *very useful and humble and precious and chaste.*

> *Praise to you, my Lord, through Brother Fire, through*
> *whom you light the night, for he is bright and playful*
> *and mighty and strong.*

> *Praise to you, my Lord, through our Sister Mother*
> *Earth, who sustains and governs us, and who produces*
> *various fruits and flowers.*

> *Praise to you, my Lord, through all those who forgive*
> *one another out of love for you, and bear sickness and*
> *tribulation; blessed are those who endure in peace, for*
> *you, Most High, will give them a crown.*

Praise to you, my Lord through Sister Bodily Death,
from whom no living being can escape. Woe to those
who die in mortal sin. Blessed are those whom death
will find in your most holy will, for the second death will
do them no harm.

Praise and bless my Lord and give him thanks and serve
him with great humility.[159]

St. Francis' canticle is an unrivaled song of thanks and praise, but notice how his love for creation flows seamlessly into a mindfulness of *"Bodily Death"*, *"mortal sin"*, and the peculiar phrase, *"the second death"*.

The Lake of Fire

The first death is that state of bodily death from which no man is excused, but "the second death, the lake of fire" is a state of permanent physical and spiritual death reserved only for those who have left God's family; that is, "the cowardly, the faithless, the polluted, the murderers, the fornicators, the sorcerers, the idolaters, and all liars".[160] Since bodily death is the inescapable doorway to eternity – either eternal life or eternal damnation – Sunday should be a day when we are particularly mindful of death and the judgment which awaits us: "For all of us must appear before the judgment seat of Christ, so that each may receive recompense for what has been done in the body, whether good or evil."[161]

When Jesus comes again to judge the living and the dead, those who are living in mortal sin or have died in mortal sin will hear the words, "depart from me into the eternal fire prepared for the devil and his angels."[162] (It is worthwhile, then, to be clear about what dying or living in mortal sin actually means.[163]) The lies of false teachers and the lusts of those who have become their own gods will all be exposed on the last day, a day when all will be revealed as suddenly as a thunderbolt: "For as lightning flashes and lights up the sky from one side to the other, so

---

159 St. Francis of Assisi, *The Canticle of Brother Sun.*
160 Revelation 20:14; 21:8 (The exceptions to the rule of death are the *Immaculata* and those who are alive when Jesus returns.)
161 2 Corinthians 5:10
162 Matthew 25:41
163 Cf. Chapter 31, Day of Light, *Physical life vs. Spiritual Life:* <u>Reconciliation and Anointing of the Sick.</u>

will the Son of Man be in his day."[164] This should not give rise to anxiety and paralyzing fear, however, for the signs of the times are intended as incentives to be vigilant:

> Though the Lord has described the signs of his coming, the time of their fulfillment has not been plainly revealed. He has kept those things hidden so that we may keep watch, each of us thinking that he will come in our own day.[165]

His second coming appears imminent so that we might consider whether we are ready to meet God face to face. As the first pope assures us, the re-creation of man and nature will be a day when "the elements will be dissolved by fire, and the earth and everything done on it will be found out"; therefore, we should "be eager to be found without spot or blemish before him, and at peace."[166]

There are some who make the error of thinking that our words and deeds go unnoticed, that somehow God does not see, but being aware that God is aware is an indispensable condition for being prepared. A healthy practice is to ask oneself, "Can he who made the ear not hear? Can he who formed the eye not see?"[167] The goal here is to look at things from the perspective of eternity; for after all is said and done, this is the only perspective that matters: "What a man is in God's eyes, that he is and nothing more."[168]

The *Canticle of Creatures* teaches us that a right relationship with creation segues into a right relationship with the last things: death, judgment, heaven, and hell. St. Francis links an appreciation of creation with giving thanks, humble service, and living in God's "most holy will", so as to remain free of mortal sin and eternal punishment. Thus, the book of creation (especially its chapters on death) should serve as a preface to the book of life; that is, as a prologue to St. John's vision of that final day, where "anyone whose name was not found written in the book of life was thrown into the lake of fire."[169]

---

164 Luke 17:24
165 St. Ephrem, *Office of Readings*, First Thursday of Advent.
166 2 Peter 3:10, 14.
167 Psalm 94:9
168 St. Francis of Assisi, *Admonitions*, 19.
169 Revelation 20:15

CHAPTER 35

The Day of Re-creation

The human person yearns not for temporary or half-hearted love, but permanent and whole-hearted love, and here on earth we occasionally glimpse a shadow of this perfect fulfillment. Some places in the physical world are so beautiful that they seem to anticipate the *eighth day* of perpetual tranquility. As the famous mountain man Osborne Russell wrote as he contemplated Yellowstone's Lamar valley: "I almost wished I could spend the remainder of my days in a place like this where happiness and contentment seemed to reign in wild romantic splendor."[170] Some places in the human heart are also so beautiful they seem to foreshadow the eighth day. Ask a faithful young couple on their honeymoon. In some way, heaven will be like a pristine valley of abundant game and fish, and a pristine consummation of love between man and woman. It will be a place where our deepest longings for beauty and communion will be fulfilled: "Heaven is the ultimate end and fulfillment of the deepest human longings, the state of supreme, definitive happiness."[171]

If our deepest desires cannot be satisfied, our lives are ridiculous and God is demented; because to have these desires be "unfulfillable" would be like Him creating us with hunger and thirst then placing us on a planet which lacked food and water. But the truth is that God has planted the *finality of fulfillment* in our hearts; so just as hunger is satisfied

---

170 Osborne Russell, *Journal of a Trapper,* entry for July 30, 1834.
171 *Catechism of the Catholic Church,* #1024

by food and thirst is quenched by water, our desire for unending joy is fulfilled by the reality of heaven:

> Lo, I am about to create new heavens and a new earth;
> the things of the past shall not be remembered or come
> to mind. Instead, there shall always be rejoicing and
> happiness in what I create ... No longer shall there be in it
> an infant who lives but a few days ... The wolf and the lamb
> shall feed together, and the lion shall eat hay like the ox.[172]

In the new heavens and earth, we will finally be free from the effects of sin, residing in a perfect home where "death will be no more; mourning and crying and pain will be no more," and the horror of losing a child will be no more.[173]

The Second Christmas

The liturgical season of Advent celebrates the first coming of Jesus as well as His promised second coming where all things will be made new. His first coming, when celebrated well, offers us another glimpse of eternity. Heaven will have all the joy of children on Christmas morning. Every child that ever dreamed of finding a puppy in their stocking or a fire truck under the tree will be satisfied. The joy of opening the gifts of the new heavens and earth are so far beyond our dreams and visions that even if all the splendors of the physical universe, past, present, and future, were gathered together in a single moment, they would be less than a drop in the ocean of what God has in store for his children: for "no eye has seen, no ear has heard, nor the human heart conceived, what God has prepared for those who love him."[174]

My little friend with special needs, Kyle Dockter, had a peculiar habit of needing to be reassured on dozens of occasions each day that the future promised great joy. For the first few months I knew Kyle, I followed his obsession modification program and directed him to talk about something else. Then I realized that he wanted to talk about his favorite things like every other kid; it was just that his favorite things were few in number and were thus repeated over and over, driving people

---

172 Isaiah 65:17-18, 20, 25
173 Revelation 21:4
174 1 Corinthians 2:9

crazy. But they were still what brought him most joy. A few of his favorite topics were simple declarations, such as "I like elk" or "I like your head"; but one was a hope-filled question: "Christmas is coming, right Lewer?" Doc would do anything to earn some time caroling or talking about Christmas morning, and after a couple years of rewarding him by singing Rudolph the Red-nosed Reindeer (which can be painfully out of place in mid-summer), my eyes opened to his wonderful perspective. He was right. There is only one day of the year when Christmas isn't coming, and as a person of tremendous joy and hope his focus in life was the coming of that great day.

Descending to the Dead

When we were still quite young, my parents took my brother and me to Carlsbad Caverns National Park; and just recently they took my brother's three little boys. The main attraction at the park is the twilight emergence of 100,000 bats which spiral out of a large cavern. This event, in a spiritual sense, is a sign of Holy Saturday – the day the Church recognizes that before Jesus rose from the tomb he descended to the dead and proclaimed the Good News.[175] As St. Peter assures us, "the gospel was preached even to the dead".[176] We should not take this to mean that all the dead were evangelized, however, only those who had lived according to natural law but as yet did not have the fullness of hope in bodily resurrection. The condition of these souls before they heard the Good News was similar to bats in a cave. They were imprisoned by the meaninglessness of bodily death, being unable to fathom how death would be overcome by the Messiah and the gates of heaven opened "for the just who had gone before him."[177] They remained in darkness, hanging upside down as it were. Nevertheless, obeying God's commandments had given them wings which predisposed them to the heavenly flight of faith. And when Jesus rose, they rose too.

Rising from the Grave

By rising from the dead, Jesus overcame sin and death, opening for us the doors to eternal life. Since the resurrection of the body is absolutely

---

175 Catechism of the Catholic Church, #632
176 1 Peter 4:6
177 Catechism of the Catholic Church, #637

essential to Catholic faith and hope, we might reasonably expect it to be a word often found in nature:

> My friends, look how regularly there are processes of resurrection going on at this very moment. The day and the night show us an example of it; for night sinks to rest, and day arises; day passes away, and night comes again. Or take the fruits of the earth; how, and in what way, does a crop come into being? When the sower goes out and drops each seed into the ground, falls to the earth shriveled and bare, and decays; but presently the power of the Lord's providence raises it from decay, and from that single grain a host of others spring up and yield their fruit.[178]

Appropriately, the annual celebration of the Lord's resurrection corresponds to the emergence of new life that we call springtime.

I have never experienced such a profound correspondence between the liturgical season of Easter and the explosion of new life and color in nature as I did just after I had begun this book. I was on retreat for the *Triduum* (the three days which precede Easter) after a long and lifeless winter. As I prepared for the Easter vigil mass on Holy Saturday, a poignant sign of the resurrection moved me to tears – the first butterflies of the year. Then, as if on cue, the great oaks began to leaf out on Easter morning. Little spring beauties and yellow trout lilies sprung up at the base of almost every tree. Violets carpeted the forest floor. Blue jays and mallards returned. Crows, robins, and squirrels eagerly sought a mate; and a pair of sharp-shinned hawks began to build their nest just outside my second-floor bedroom window. The whole created world seemed to be celebrating the coming of the risen Christ right along with the Church.

The following Easter I was home again in Jackson Hole and my good friend Stuart had invited me to have brunch with his family and some mutual friends. Because of what happened the previous year, I was expecting a theophany of some sort but certainly nothing that would compare to the year before. I was wrong.

Easter morning ushered in the third straight day of gray skies and drizzling rain, which, though not unusual for April, is always a cross.

---

178 Pope St. Clement of Rome, *First Letter to the Corinthians*, #24

The sun began to shine intermittently after mass as I began to drive from town to my friend's home just outside Grand Teton National Park. Along the way, I was captivated by some cloud formations that seemed as though they were being exhaled from the cliffs above the National Museum of Wildlife Art, which overlooks the National Elk Refuge. I immediately turned up the road which traverses the butte and pulled into the museum's empty parking lot. The strange shapes of mist spirating from the cliffs were mesmerizing, but after a few moments I turned around to survey the great plain of the refuge where 10,000 elk spend each winter. There on the valley floor, this peculiar combination of humidity and radiant heat had produced twenty or more cyclones, not descending from clouds but rather ascending from the earth. These small vortexes of vapor were slowly dancing across the flats as far as half a mile away. One of them (as tall as a two-story building) had risen above the others not more than hundred yards from where I was standing. Jesus was rising from the dead, and in the whirlwind of the Spirit was leading the souls of the just from their graves. When I arrived at brunch, a local artist and his wife told me they had seen the same spirations, but it didn't surprise me. Both are devout Catholics who cultivate a sacramental vision of reality by frequently reading from the book of Yellowstone and sacred scripture. Their attentiveness to God's words gives them eyes that see and ears that hear. She is writing a book which unveils the rich symbolism of our stained glass windows at Our Lady of the Mountains, and he is one of the premier painters of the most celebrated scenery in America. Neither they nor I had ever seen or heard of such a thing before.

Transfiguration

The scriptures state that Jesus was transfigured on "a high mountain", but one tradition holds that Mt. Tabor was the site while another says it was Mt. Hermon. In a certain sense, however, locating the Transfiguration on Mt. Hermon is more fitting because it forms the headwaters of the Jordan River, the river which brings life to the fifth gospel. The source and summit of the *temporal* Promised Land, then, is the place where Jesus, the source and summit of the *eternal* Promised Land, foreshadowed the luminous glory of resurrected creation: "Jesus took Peter, James, and John and led them up a high mountain apart by themselves. And he was transfigured before them; his face shone like the sun and his clothes became white as light."[179]

The Transfiguration is a sign of the renewal and *eternalization* of all temporal things, that infusion of light into all which comprises the new heavens and the new earth. It is an event which reaffirms the revelation that our resurrected bodies "will shine like the sun in the kingdom of their Father."[180] It also indicates what will happen to the physical world as it follows the human person into an eternal state: "What is sown is perishable, what is raised is imperishable. It is sown in weakness, it is raised in power. It is sown a physical body, it is raised a spiritual body."[181]

Certainly we can speculate about how the scientific theory of time standing still at the speed of light has something to do with temporal things being eternalized, or how the essences of individual types of non-human creatures may exist as eternalized archetypes, but how the universe will be transfigured is not something we should be too curious about; for as we've said, penetrating the mysteries of the sun is not for our eyes. We should instead remain hopeful that we will find out soon enough, trusting that He has "a plan for the fullness of time, to gather up all things in him, things in heaven and things on earth."[182]

What we do know is that regardless of how non-human creatures have *being* in heaven, they will follow a pattern of renewal similar to that of our own bodies, which will follow the pattern of the resurrected body of Jesus: "He will give a new form to this lowly body of ours and remake it according to the pattern of his glorified body, by his power to subject everything to himself."[183] The things of time and space will somehow be drawn into eternity. The finite will be subsumed by the infinite. And we can rest assured that every instance of true love, every kind word and good deed, and all that had been truly fulfilling for us on earth will be illuminated in our new home:

> We do not know when or how the universe will be transfigured. The world as we see it, disfigured by sin, is passing away. But we are assured that God is preparing a new dwelling place and a new earth. In this new earth

179 Matthew 17:1-3
180 Matthew 13:43
181 1Corinthians 15: 42-44
182 Ephesians 1:10
183 Philippians 3:21

righteousness is to make its home, and happiness will fill and surpass all the yearnings for peace that arise in human hearts. On that day, when death is conquered, the sons of God will be raised in Christ and what was sown in weakness and dishonor will put on the imperishable. Charity and its words will remain, and all of creation, which God made for man, will be set free from its bondage to decay. . . When we have spread on earth the fruits of our nature and our enterprise – human dignity, brotherly communion, and freedom—according to the command of the Lord and in his Spirit, we will find them once again, cleansed this time from the stain of sin, illuminated and transfigured.[184]

St. Paul reveals that on the last day "the trumpet will sound, and the dead will be raised imperishable, and we will be changed." This calls to mind a particular fall morning in Jackson when, as I was walking to work, a pair of swans began trumpeting as they flew up Flat Creek toward the elk refuge. Their sleek white bodies drifting in and out of the fog seemed to foreshadow that Day when Jesus shall return with all the clarity of a trumpet blast, yet for now remains obscure – shrouded in mystery.

Lumen Gloriae

The Lord reveals through the prophet Isaiah a simple truth: "As high as the heavens are above the earth, so high are my ways above your ways and my thought above your thoughts."[185] Our minds cannot grasp the ways of eternity or even picture things that are purely spiritual. Try imagining an angel without a body and inevitably you will insert size, shape, and color (or at least light), for these things are essential to creating a mental image with the intellectual power of imagination. That is why angels must take on physical form and make audible sounds when they come as God's messengers – so that we may see and understand.

Since our minds are not equipped to imagine eternal things, we can only reflect on what eternity is or is not through comparisons with things limited by time and space. The images of heaven provided by Scripture and the Church are somewhat abstract. We often speak of "beholding

184 Vatican II, *Gaudiem et Spes*, #39
185   Isaiah 55:9

the face of God" or "celebrating the eternal liturgy". It is no wonder, then, that some view heaven as boring when for them contemplation and mass are boring. To praise God, to do just that one thing for all eternity, seems static . . . unless that one thing is the perfect fulfillment of every fulfilling experience of God, neighbor, and creation that we've ever had on earth. But how can we think of timelessness as dynamic. How can all the things we find satisfying here in a world of motion and change be related to a place where there is no past or future, only a present? Perhaps the better question is to ask: how we can thank God for the goodness of this temporal and finite universe, and then not trust that the eternal universe He promised is not infinitely better?

A transfigured universe and a transfigured body awaits those who have assented to His truth, trusted in His goodness, and embraced His beauty, but in the end our minds fail when whenever we try to put God's eternal mysteries in a temporal box:

> But the ways of his providence are often unknown to us. Only at the end, when our partial knowledge ceases when we see God 'face to face', will we fully know the ways by which – even through the dramas of evil and sin – God has guided his creation to that definitive sabbath rest for which he created heaven and earth.[186]

We know, for instance, that the offering of creation to the Father can only be made through His Son, Jesus Christ – since He alone is both human and divine, He alone can eternalize temporal creation – but exactly how His human body exists within the divine Trinity is not something our minds can handle while we are living on earth. This is why St. Thomas Aquinas teaches that our resurrected intellects must receive a gift he calls the light of glory (*lumen gloriae*) in order to be fulfilled by such mysteries.[187]

At the end of *The Divine Comedy* (when Dante has completed his journey through heaven), he is confronted by this limitation of human intellect. He finds himself in the presence of Love, The Most Holy Trinity, which is represented by a circle. He then notices a human image painted within the circle, but his mind cannot grasp the mystery

---

186 *Catechism of the Catholic Church*, #314
187 St. Thomas Aquinas, *Summa Theologica*, I.12.2-5.

of God becoming man. Finally, even though his powers of imagination are found to be inadequate to his desire, he experiences a flash of the beatific vision:

> Like a geometer who sets himself to square the circle, and is unable to think of the formula he needs to solve the problem, so I was faced with this new vision. . . But that was not a flight for my wings: except that my mind was struck by a flash in which what it desired came to it. At this point high imagination failed; but already my desire and my will were being turned like a wheel, all at one speed, by the love that moves the sun and the other stars.[188]

---

188 Dante Alighieri, *The Divine Comedy*, "*Paradiso*", 33.

CHAPTER 36

The Day of Communion

There is perhaps no better example of beauty in nature than a waterfall. Though we have tried to harness their energy with inventions such as the waterwheel, they are not generally useful to us and have even less value in sustaining the health of a river. A waterfall, it seems, is primarily an artistic endeavor intended to draw us toward the satisfaction of communion.

In the *Grand Canyon of the Yellowstone*, the Lower Falls plummet over 300 feet and can be viewed from a number of vantage points. The cover photo depicts the view accessed by way of Red Rock Trail. From that perspective, forest, chasm, and sky, frame the falls in a way that is truly inspiring. As C.S. Lewis has noted, to call such a scene "beautiful" is not to offer an opinion (as if the matter where subjective), but only affirms an objective fact.[189] Anyone who does not think the Lower Falls are beautiful has a defect; for in this case, beauty is not in the eye of the beholder, it simply is.

Another vantage can be gained by hiking to the brink of the falls, though it is much less serene. There, the tremendous display of power is at first unsettling but then awe-inspiring. Grown men and women will often have there breath taken away and become mesmerized with mouth agape, which calls to mind the reflection of David: "Deep calls to deep at the thunder of your cataracts."[190]

---

189 C.S. Lewis, *The Abolition of Man*, I.
190 Psalm 42:7

Being thunderstruck is an appropriate posture when ambushed by beauty, for it cannot be fully anticipated; it is an unwarranted and superfluous gift – a sheer grace. Remaining thunderstruck, however, is a truncated response; for there is something inside us that wants to go deeper: "We do not want merely to see beauty . . . We want something else which can hardly be put into words – to be united with the beauty we see, to pass into it, to receive it into ourselves, to bathe in it".[191]

The beautiful in nature arouses a yearning for communion which goes beyond the art to the Artist. Since beauty can neither be known like the truth nor chosen like the good, it is soon discovered that this yearning cannot be fulfilled by intellect or will, and that any attempt to do so is like trying to bite a wall. Whenever we seek communion, intellect and will are still working to discern and decide, but since love is a matter of the heart, something more is required.

We've seen how the heart is primarily ordered to giving and receiving beauty – to loving and being loved. This is why we typically don't say: "I love you with all my intellect and free will", but rather: "I love you with all my heart". Notice, however, that since nothing in the physical world is able to reciprocate a gift of love, it is an error to attempt to commune with it. It is a deception to think that nature as a whole is a goddess capable of loving or being loved, or that one can enter into communion with the life-force of the universe. Communion can only be established between persons, because only a person (divine, angelic, or human) is capable of reciprocating with a gift from the heart. Therefore, communion with the Creator is the only loving response to beauty in the physical world. And this we call prayer.

When the Creator carves sea caves into the Hawaiian coastline, He sometimes collapses the ceiling at the back of the cave to make a hole in the ground above. When waves funnel into the cave, water is forced through the hole and shoots a geyser-like fountain into the air. A few years ago I was headed out for an early morning run near two of these "blow holes" along the cliffs of Kona. As dawn approached, I was drawn into what they were saying – it was a declaration of joy, the joy of simply being. I walked over and stood still. The next big set of waves thundered into the cove and exploded through the blow holes in exultations of existence. I walked through the lingering sea spray and was renewed. Then I noticed overhead that a citrus-wedge moon was keeping vigil over the slopes of Mauna Loa and when

---

191 C.S. Lewis, excerpt from his sermon, *The Weight of Glory*.

I turned toward the horizon the full spectrum of color was heralding a new day. Inspired by the beauty of it all, I then stepped into communion: "Lord, let your love fill our hearts as morning fills the sky."[192]

An encounter with beauty should be a captivating moment of hope, a moment to accept the proposal that life should be this good, that love should be this true. Words of beauty speak of transcendence – that eternal joy for which our hearts long. They are invitations to enter a heart to heart communion with the Father and the Son, in the Holy Spirit.

Sacred Heart of Jesus

A few summers ago, I found a sign of the Sacred Heart of Jesus in Jackson Hole. Near the center of the valley, there is a small circular refuge with seven distinct paths leading to it and proceeding from it – like the spokes of a wheel or rays of sunlight.[193] Similar to the Sacred Heart of Jesus, it is a safe haven, a place of peace. During Christmas of that same year, I returned there to pray before I began leading a retreat for a dance troupe of four young women. And as I plodded through the snow toward the refuge of the Sacred Heart, I began to think about how Sarah, Michaela, Bernadette, and Brooke are inspiring dancers who strive to be courageous Catholics; and about how their guardian angels had been so good to them. I then said a prayer of thanks to all guardian angels. These heavenly creatures are given to us as the perfect companion for our journey in becoming the person God wants us to be, for it's not as though they stand in line waiting to be assigned to the next child conceived; rather, He created them from the beginning with our particular gifts and shortcomings in mind. They are like editors of our personal stories, never imposing on free-will but making suggestions, presenting options, helping us to see the flow of God's narrative. And on that particular day, my own guardian angel helped me understand how the Sacred Heart of Jesus is the true center of the universe, the true *axis mundi*.[194]

In the classic western *Dances With Wolves*, the medicine man Kicking Bird takes Lieutenant John Dunbar to Jackson Hole and tries to convey the religious significance of *axis mundi* for many native cultures: "It is said that all the animals were born here and that from here they spread over the prairies to feed all the people. Even our enemies agree that this

---

192 Liturgy of the Hours, *Morning Prayer*, Friday Week IV.
193 The seven sorrows of Mary? The seven last words of Jesus?
194 Defined as the place where the spiritual and physical universe intersect.

is a sacred place."[195] That's how it is with the Sacred Heart of Jesus: all the graces were born there and from there they spread over the universe to redeem all the people. And even our enemies, the demons, agree that this is a sacred place. One could argue that Calvary is the true *axis mundi* for Christianity, but this would only show that the Sacred Heart of Jesus is a sacred space within that sacred place – just like my little sanctuary within the valley of Jackson Hole.

Since the "heart is the innermost core where one chooses for or against God, life or death, light or darkness", the *fiat* of Jesus was a choice that willed all the good His heart had to give (which was all the good in the universe) to the Father and to us.[196] Creation was redeemed, then, because He loved with all His Heart.

Immaculate Heart of Mary

In God's providence, Jackson Hole has been blessed with both the parish church of *Our Lady of the Mountains* in the town of Jackson, and the *Sacred Heart Chapel* in Grand Teton National Park. The meaning of the French word *teton* is "breast", and while most folks attribute this naming of the mountains to an overactive imagination on the part of early French trappers, anyone who has ever canoed the east shore of Jackson Lake can hardly deny the semblance. The original name of our parish church was *Our Lady of the Tetons*, but during the late sixties it was changed by some over-zealous parishioners who deemed it inappropriate, and were probably just over-reacting to the sexual revolution. Nonetheless, both Puritanism and promiscuity are extremist positions. Everything God created is good. Sex is good, breasts are good, but like any gifts not appreciated in accordance with His plan, they can become sources of evil. Consider that the prophet Isaiah does not hesitate to compare the joys of the heavenly Jerusalem to a baby nursing: "Oh, that you may suck fully . . . that you may nurse with delight at her abundant breasts!"[197] Consider also that the evangelist Luke recounts a woman unabashedly crying out to Jesus, "Blessed is the womb that bore you and the breasts that nursed you!"[198]

Mary is indeed blessed because she gave birth to Jesus and nursed Him, but even more so because she is obedient to God's will, as Our Savior's response to the woman makes clear: "Blessed rather are those

---

195 *Dances with Wolves*, Scene XXVII, collector's edition DVD.
196 *Catechism of the Catholic Church*, #2563
197 Isaiah 66:11
198 Luke 11:27

who hear the word of God and obey it!"[199] Even more than that special intimacy between mother and nursing child, Our Lady's distinct status is based on her surrender.

The Blessed Virgin is the perfect daughter of the Father, the perfect mother of the Son, and the perfect spouse of the Holy Spirit. No other human being has shared such intimate communion with the Most Holy Trinity. She is called the Seat of Wisdom (*Sedes Sapientiae*) because upon her lap Wisdom sat and learned wisdom, upon her lap the summit of awe and wonder played and nursed as she pondered Him in her heart. And if we apply our simple definition of wisdom as *the understanding of causes*, she is also the Seat of Wisdom because she understands what causes us to be freed from slavery in order to become the artist God wants us to be.

As the greatest human artist ever, Mary's heart overflowed with creativity, and her last words recorded in Scripture are a palate from which to paint every hue of wisdom and freedom: "Do whatever he tells you."[200] The Immaculate Heart of Mary is the archetype of true wisdom and freedom just as Lucifer is the archetype of false wisdom and freedom. She is the true light bearer, he the false light bearer.

The Two Hearts

Theologically, all paths of inquiry eventually lead to the Sacred and Immaculate Hearts of Jesus and Mary, for when one arrives at the creative love which His heart symbolizes, and the complete transparency to that love which her heart symbolizes, there is little left to say . . . but much to surrender. Precisely because these two hearts share the same blood and the same perfect conformity to our Father's plan, whenever we entrust our hearts to theirs, our lives become filled with light and creativity. The papal motto of John Paul II, *Totus Tuus*, underscores this act of entrustment, an act which is summed up in the following prayer:

Totus tuus ego sum,
Et omnia mea tua sunt,
Accipio te in mea omnia,
Praebe mihi cor tuum Maria,
Praebe mihi cor tuum Jesus.[201]

---

199 Luke 11:28
200 John 2:5
201 I am all yours, and all I have is yours, I bring you into all that is mine, grant to me your heart Mary, grant to me your heart Jesus.

The Marian Condor

Franciscan University is built upon a high cliff which overlooks the Ohio River valley. Conspicuously erected on that cliff is a giant steel cross. After mass one day, I was speaking with a friend who had just learned that he had a terminal illness and was wrestling with both acceptance and denial. He was twenty-one years old. During our conversation, we simultaneously noticed how two vultures were perched on the cross, one on each side of the crossbeam equidistant from the center. We both fell silent. Then this young man, who had such a keen mind and gentle heart, seemed to find peace in those harbingers of death, situated as they were on the great sign of meaning. Over the next few years, I became more and more aware of the ubiquitous turkey vultures of Steubenville; but knowing that God has made all things good I tried to see them as more than symbols of death. And in my darkest season, I finally did.

It may seem repugnant to associate an ostensibly ugly creature with the most beautiful creature in the universe, but the flight of vultures and condors speak of Mary, while their faces speak of how even when we consecrate ourselves to her, our sinfulness contrasts with her purity.[202] The California condor inhabits the canyons of the southwestern United States. With a wingspan of nine feet they are easily lifted up by spirations of wind and thermal energy to elevations unrivaled by any creature in America. From that vantage they seek carrion for sustenance and have the most deliberate and infrequent wing-beat of any bird. Upon returning to land, they often bask in the sunlight with wings outstretched. Similarly, by consecrating ourselves to Mary we open our arms in total surrender and become sensitive to how the Spirit generates lift. We acknowledge that the "Spirit blows where it wills" and "we abandon ourselves to that will together with her"; thus soaring to the heights of contemplation with the least amount of effort.[203] From that lofty vantage, our main concern on earth becomes to feed on His life-giving corpse. Those consecrated to Mary are naturally devoted to Eucharistic adoration and daily mass for a simple reason: "Where the body is, there the vultures will be gathered together."[204]

---

202 Because Mary was preserved from the effects of original sin at the moment of her conception, our imitation of her is limited by our status as sinners (whereas our imitation of her Son is limited also by our status as creatures).
203 John 3:8; *Catechism of the Catholic Church*, #2677
204 Luke 17:37 (An alternative translation here is "eagles" and indeed they too should evoke surrender. As the great I AM reminds us: "I bore you up on eagles' wings and brought you here to myself." Exodus 19:4; cf. Isaiah 40:31)

We not only learn how to pray and obey by entrusting ourselves to Mary, but also how to see God in all things. By taking her into our home, we enroll in the school of Mary, becoming home-schooled as it were.[205] She does not teach us the identity of creatures or how to read human words, as natural mothers do, but instead she teaches us the *meaning* of creatures: how to read colors, flowers, and birds. When it comes to reading the book of creation, she is an incomparable teacher because she did not inherit any of the myopia, astigmatism, or cataracts associated with original sin; that is, she can read as well as Adam and Eve did before the fall.

Seeing God in all things reaches its summit at Calvary, for if you can see love in the crucifixion of your only child, you can surely read it from all events and creatures. Consecration to Mary raises our reading level and our faith level, opening vast new horizons of literacy and elevating our ability to see Him and serve Him in nature and neighbor:

> For those who have faith, the entire universe speaks of the Triune God. From the spaces between the stars to microscopic particles, all that exists refers to a Being who communicates himself in the multiplicity and variety of elements, as in a symphony. All beings are ordered to a dynamic harmony . . . but only in the human person, who is free and can reason, does this dynamism become spiritual, does it become responsible love, in response to God and to one's neighbor through a sincere gift of self. It is in this love that human beings find their truth and happiness.[206]

If we offer our life to Mary, it becomes a prayer of "truth and happiness" in communion with her Son; because "Jesus, the only mediator, is the way of our prayer; Mary, his mother and ours, is wholly transparent to him."[207] In simplest terms, Jesus came to us through Mary and it is the Father's plan that we should to return to Him in the same manner.

---

205 Cf. John 19:27; "'Behold, your mother.' And from that moment the disciple took her into his home."
206 Pope Benedict XVI, *Angelus,* June 11, 2006.
207 *Catechism of the Catholic Church,* #2674

Furthermore, if our destination is life in Christ, both now and forever, we should follow the safest and surest means available to arrive at that destination. As a man of tremendous wisdom (and perhaps the greatest youth minister of all time), Pope John Paul II understood what caused young people to remain devoted to Jesus and His Church as well as what caused them to turn away. In his view, the method of Marian consecration established by St. Louis-marie de Monfort "marks out for us the path of true wisdom that must be laid open to so many young people who search for meaning in their lives and for an art of living."[208]

The "art of living" is the art of communion and the art of story-telling. Our words and deeds can either augment or diminish the story God wishes to write with our lives. By entrusting ourselves to Jesus through Mary, then, we are employing the creative genius of those who write best, those who let it be written according to the Father's word.

---

208 Pope John Paul II, *Letter for the 50th Anniversary of the Canonization of St. Louis-Marie de Montfort,* June 21, 1997.

CHAPTER 37

The Day of Story

It is fitting that when God wrote a second book it contained many stories, because part of our being created in His image and likeness is to have a gift for reading, writing, and responding to them. As one of the great authors of our time put it: "Man the story-teller would have to be redeemed in a manner consonant with his nature: by a moving story."[209]

The biblical account of creation, sin, and salvation is the prototype of story, or as some call it, the greatest story ever told. God is the great story-teller, and in a certain sense, all of our own stories borrow from this one inspired text. Our limitations as story-tellers are easier to see if we reflect for a moment on the elements of a good story and how the creative writing of Scripture cannot be outdone. For example: we cannot write a more surprising twist than to foreshadow the coming of a messianic figure, the Son of David, and then have Him turn out to be the Son of God as well; we cannot write a more powerful *dénouement* than to have that Son tortured and crucified by the men He is trying to save; and we cannot even imagine writing a more inspiring ending than to have Him rise from the dead, ascend into heaven, and return to recreate the universe so that we might live forever in paradise.

Scripture is the divine Revelation of what went wrong and what God has done to make it right by means of covenant, but we should always "recognize as a first stage of divine Revelation the marvelous book of nature".[210] For in spite of its deficiency when addressing questions of

---

209 J.R.R. Tolkien, *Letter #89,* (to his son Christopher).
210 Pope John Paul II, *Fides et Ratio,* #19

meaning, creation remains God's first story of covenant faithfulness: "In creation, God laid a foundation and established laws that remain firm [laws of nature and natural law], on which the believer can rely with confidence, for they are the sign and pledge of the unshakeable faithfulness of God's covenant."[211]

God reveals covenants through words. After Adam and Eve lost the ability to read His first words of His first covenant, He gradually gathered His family through human words by making covenants through Noah, Abraham, Moses, David, and Jesus. But notice that throughout these covenant-stories of Scripture, the covenant-story of creation is never suspended; rather, it is a subtheme which steadily expresses His love for us:

> Thus the revelation of creation is inseparable from the revelation and forging of the covenant of the one God with his People. Creation is revealed as the first step toward this covenant, the first and universal witness to God's all-powerful love.[212]

God's first book witnesses to His love from the moment we are born, though not primarily through the physical world. Instead, the first word we read is one of being in relation with a human person who nourishes us while looking upon us with kindness and joy. This first word is our mother's smile.[213] The revelation of our mother's smile is the foremost sign of God's tender love, for it is at our mother's breast where we first "taste and see that the Lord is good."[214] St. Paul confirms this idea when he reminds the Thessalonians that he proved his love by treating them as gently "as a nursing mother cares for her children."[215]

The story of our natural life is nurtured as we behold our loving mother. Since all grace flows from the cross, where Jesus asked us to see His mother as our own, so is the story of our supernatural life.

---

211 *Catechism of the Catholic Church*, #346 Cf. Hebrews 4:3-4; Jeremiah 31:35-37; 33:19-26

212 *Catechism of the Catholic Church*, #288.

213 Hans Urs Von Balthasar, *Love Alone is Credible*, 5.

214 Psalm 34:8

215 1 Thessalonians 2:7 (emphasis mine); Jesus also uses an example of maternal tenderness from the physical world when explaining to the Jews that He often desired to gather them together "as a hen gathers her brood under her wings" – Matthew 23:37; cf. Ruth 2:12, Psalms 57:2; 61:5; 91:4)

Accordingly, the story of becoming His mother's child should not only be one of growing strong, but also of growing young at heart.

Juvenescence

Throughout my life I have loved working with children, and have been able to find something to love about every kid I've taught (though with some you have to dig pretty deep). Children are my favorite words for two reasons: first, because they are so easily filled with wonder; and second, because time after time when I needed consolation, God has sent one of these little ones to comfort me. But the little gift I received in St. Peter's square – at the threshold of the apostles – was perhaps the most moving.

When I was studying for the priesthood, I often felt betrayed by the dissenting priests and seminary professors I encountered. They were openly hostile to most everything I had learned about the Church from the saints, popes, and councils. And while being opposed to the Magisterium was not an arrogance I possessed, I struggled with other types of pride and was careful not to look down on them. After leaving the seminary, my dad was generous enough to give me a ticket to Rome so that I could have a couple weeks to renew my love for the Church. It was glorious. I began each day with mass and the rosary at St. Peter's basilica, and then would walk along the Tiber river as far as I could on my way to another basilica or religious site. One morning, however, I decided to be first in line outside the Vatican museum and then proceed straight to the Sistine Chapel after it opened. I had been there before when the chapel was filled with tourists, but now there were only three of us. I knew it was the pope's private chapel, so I knelt down before the altar and Michelangelo's *Last Judgment* to pray. Soon, many others entered and joined me. Upon leaving the museum, I went and sat cross-legged on the ground in the middle of St. Peter's square and began praying the rosary again. There was a large gathering of bishops that day and I began to ruminate on what caused *some* of these apostles to be confused about the apostolicity of the Church. Why did some bishops not oversee what was being taught in their seminaries and colleges? How could they justify having professors who become stumbling blocks to young people as they conceal or distort what the Church believes? My head dropped and my eyes closed as I continued the prayer of peace, calling to mind the warning of Jesus: "If any of you put a stumbling block before one of these little ones who believe in me, it would be *better* for you if a great millstone were fastened around your neck and you were drowned in the depth of the sea."[216] When I looked up, the face a two year-old boy from Indonesia was just inches from my own. Without hesitation, he sat down on my lap – in complete trust – and began playing with my rosary beads. His father was at first concerned but then relented, and we exchanged smiles. God had spoken through my little friend and answered my questions. Negligence regarding Catholic education was the result of not having childlike faith in our Blessed Mother: "Amen I say to you, unless you turn and become like children you will not enter the kingdom of heaven."[217] Those bishops who allow the youth of their diocese to be deceived have become too sophisticated in their thinking, or too afraid. They may have big reasons and big concerns, but their blunder lies in having little faith. Pride, fear, and anxiety – stemming from that ancient distrust of God's plan – age the soul and war against juvenescence.

For those apostles who do trust, however, growing old physically is counterbalanced by growing young spiritually. As the bishop St. Paul reveals, "although our outer self is wasting away, our inner self is being renewed day by day."[218] Growing young again begins with prayerful surrender to the manifest will of the Father, so that we might "become like children" in our hearts.

The hearts of children are fascinated with nature – birds and bugs, sand and sticks, cows and kittens – anything that has *being* fills them with a sense of wonder. The greatest joys of my life have been to share this fascination, especially with my three nephews. When the middle child, Jack, was a two year-old, a butterfly was tickling his ear, so he just put out his finger for it to land on. He was not at all surprised when it did, but just smiled and looked contentedly at it for a moment. And when the two of them had finished talking, he announced in his tiny new voice, "Heee's . . . going . . . to fly!!" Sure enough.

For most of us, this innate sense of the sacred in nature becomes clouded as we allow the fears and anxieties of adulthood saddle us with heavy loads. The tendency to lose our bearings must be consciously corrected by setting a course toward rejuvenation, by becoming

---

216 Matthew 18:6 (emphasis mine).
217 Matthew 18:3
218 2 Corinthians 4:16

anchored in the Lord's Day as a day of youthfulness and levity, of awe and amazement before all that is; in other words, by making Sunday a day of reading well and writing well. For the past century, many of God's children have been moved by the story of a soul who never lost her ability to read and write with the heart of a child:

> Ah! How quickly those sunny years passed by, those years of my childhood, but what a sweet imprint they have left on my soul! . . . I still feel the profound and poetic impressions that were born in my soul at the sight of fields enameled with cornflowers and all types of wild flowers. Already I was in love with wide open spaces. Space and the gigantic fur trees, the branches sweeping down to the ground, left in my heart an impression similar to the one I experience still today at the sight of nature.[219]

The reason that God's first book had the same effect on The Little Flower when she was an adult was because she remained pure: "Blessed are the pure of heart, for they shall see God."[220] To see God in all things requires that we retain the heart of a child, a heart of purity, wonder, and trust. In the words of Thomas a Kempis, author of the renowned *Imitation of Christ*, "If your heart is right, then every created thing will become for you a mirror of life and a book of holy teaching. For there is no creature – no matter how tiny or how lowly – that does not reveal God's goodness."[221]

Joy

In the physical world, joy is expressed by simple declarations of being in possession of *being*. Whale spouts, dolphin acrobatics, magma geysers, and sea cave blow holes, for instance, are all exaltations of island joy: "Let the sea and all within it thunder praise; Let the land and all it bears rejoice."[222] In the human person, however, joy can be defined as being in possession of what we love (like the joy of a nursing mother). It must be distinguished from the feelings usually associated with it,

---

219 St. Therese of Lisieux, *Story of a Soul*, 29.
220 Matthew 5:8
221 Thomas a Kempis, *The Imitation of Christ*, II.4. (Historically, this book is said to be second only to the Bible in popularity.)
222 Psalm 96:11-12

for it is more than just being in possession of momentary pleasure or excitement. True joy means possessing peace even in times of suffering or apparent darkness. For example, those who are in possession of right reason and the answers to life's big questions have no reason to worry because they are in conversation with God and can see that creation and scripture tell a story that ends well; they continually choose love over fear, leaving little room for sadness, because their hearts are steady.

The most joyful group of people I ever met were *Poor Clares* from Mexico.[223] They were establishing a new convent in Denver and had made themselves available for a few weeks before becoming cloistered again. At the time, I was working at the Samaritan House homeless shelter and living at the House of Clare along with some other volunteers and the volunteer director, Dorothy Leonard. Dorothy was the first person in my life who could confirm what I had learned from St. Francis, for she too had learned to read him with simplicity. One evening she arranged for the Poor Clares to have dinner with us – and we were all captivated by their profound joyfulness. Being in possession of what they loved most, Jesus, their hearts were intent on becoming living psalms of joy: "This is the day which the Lord has made; let us rejoice and be glad".[224]

Living Letters

The first word we read from our mother is joy and the first word we write as newborns is joy. The challenge is to keep reading and writing that same story for the rest of our lives. As the saying goes, the way we live could be the only gospel our neighbors ever read. St. Peter teaches that love of neighbor begins by writing life well "so that any of them who do not believe in the word of the gospel may be won over apart from preaching.... They have only to observe the reverent purity of your way of life."[225] And St. Paul teaches that we are called to be "a letter of Christ . . . written not with ink but with the Spirit of the living God, not on tablets of stone but on tablets of human hearts."[226]

A reliable template for writing life well is to ask oneself, "Is this choice part of a good story? Does it imitate in some way the virtues found in the

---

223 Poor Clares are a religious order founded by St. Clare of Assisi, St. Francis' closest female friend.
224 Psalm 118:24
225 1 Peter:1-2
226 2 Corinthians 3:3

greatest story ever told? Am I choosing love over fear?"[227] We should not apply these questions only to big decisions, however, but to small decisions as well, because the little things, the daily things, comprise the flow of our personal narrative. As Mother Teresa teaches us, a well-written narrative is made up of small yet meaningful words: "Do small things with great love. It is not how much we do but how much love we put into doing it. To God there is nothing small. The moment we have given it to God it becomes infinite."[228] Presenting a small act of love to God it is like dropping a dry pine needle on a bed of red-hot coals: as soon as it is offered, the little puff of incense is drawn in and transposed by the eternal Spirit.

Nonetheless, extraordinary things like miracles continue to be a part of God's story, for in every age Jesus is asked the same question: "How long are you going to keep us in suspense? If you are the Messiah, tell us plainly."[229] And in every age Jesus responds in the same way: "I told you, and you do not believe. The works that I do in my Father's name, they bear witness to me; but you do not believe".[230] Jesus gives us evidence of His divinity by suspending the laws of nature with miracles, or suspending the natural law of justice with heroic mercy (i.e. loving one's enemies, praying for one's persecutors, or forgiving one's neighbor seventy seven times). The living letters of Jesus, His saints, submit evidence of both throughout the centuries, offering a living testimony that He truly is the promised Son of David.

My dearest friend, Sister Teresa of the Two Hearts, is a wonderful example of becoming a living letter. I could tell many stories of her as a young girl discerning her vocation, or of her trying to do even the smallest act (picking up trash) with great love, or even how the creatures of Grand Teton and Yellowstone rose up to greet her on her retreat into the wilderness. But I know her too well. I know that she desires to remain small, "a little pencil in God's hand" as her patron saint would say. So be it.

---

227 "Choose love or fear" (adapted from St. John's "love casts out fear") is a useful phrase to recall when writing one's story. But here we must reaffirm that true love is a willing of objective good which is guided by natural and supernatural wisdom.
228 Blessed Teresa of Calcutta, *Works of Love are Works of Peace*, 101.
229 John 10:24
230 John 10:25-26

But if I was compelled by obedience to write one thing about her, it would be that she is a person of great joy because she is in possession of the knowledge "that God makes all things work together for good, for those who love Him".[231] Even before she had graduated from Franciscan University, there was an unusual clarity in her of the value of trust. I remember one day introducing her to *The Teaching of the Twelve Apostles*, a first century book usually referred to as *The Didache*. She immediately opened it and read aloud what she saw, "Accept as good whatever experience comes your way, in the knowledge that nothing can happen without God."[232]

Deep within us, where we are free to accept whatever comes our way as good, where we compose our letters, poems, and songs for others, we make the choice. If we choose not to trust, acting *without* God, we become words of hypocrisy and scandal, impediments of light; but if we choose to act *with* God, we become words of beauty, diffusions of light. As our Blessed Mother shows us, the most illuminating story is always written by an author whose soul "magnifies the Lord" with joy.[233]

* * *

The story of our fallen universe is one of glory, distortion, and triumph. Objective truth is often contradicted, objective goodness is often mocked, and objective beauty is often rejected, yet evil does not prevail. It may at times seem to grab humanity by the throat, but its grip is inevitably broken by those who put confidence in the objective principles of right reason and are led by the objective light of faith. From the first source, thinking clearly, we can know with absolute certainty the first universal principles of being; and from the second source, the light of faith in Jesus Christ, we can know with absolute certainty what life and love are all about. Like the story of creation, either scientific or metaphysical, the story of our salvation is communicated by God through words of non-contradiction, that is, through words of objective truth:

---

231 Romans 8:28
232 *Didache*, 3.
233 Luke 1:46

This truth, which God reveals to us in Jesus Christ, is not opposed to the truths which philosophy perceives. On the contrary, the two modes of knowledge lead to truth in all its fullness. The unity of truth is a fundamental premise of human reasoning, as the principle of non-contradiction makes clear. Revelation renders this unity certain, showing that the God of creation is also the God of salvation history. It is the one and the same God who establishes and guarantees the intelligibility and reasonableness of the natural order of things upon which scientists confidently depend, and reveals himself as the Father of our Lord Jesus Christ. This unity of truth, natural and Revealed, is embodied in a living and personal way in Christ.[234]

The storyline of faith does not obstruct the storyline of reason. Instead, it develops it in light of the "unity of truth". Catholicism is the one religious story on earth which harvests this fullness of truth and, unlike other religious stories, contains no contradictions because it has not uprooted any of God's teachings. Thus, the more we read this story with reason guided by faith, and the more our faith is guided by humility, the more He is pleased to let us access the archives of His great library of creation.

God wants us to read every passing butterfly as a verse of transfiguration and every narcissist as evidence that "man can fully discover his true self only in a sincere giving of himself."[235] And he wants every creature to gather meaning as we learn how it is related to other words within a paragraph, page, chapter, or volume; because the more we learn about the content and unity of creation, the more we can discern the greatness of the Creator: "For God appears the greater to every man in proportion as he has grasped a larger survey of the creatures: and when his heart is uplifted by that larger survey, he gains with all a greater conception of God."[236]

---

234 Pope John Paul the Great, *Fides et Ratio*, #34. (cf. Ephesians 4:21; Colossians 1:15-20; John 1:14-18: Acts 17:23)
235 Vatican II, *Gaudiem et Spes*, #24
236 St. Cyril of Jerusalem, *Maker of Heaven and Earth, and of All Things Visible and Invisible*, IX.

For Catholics, who have received the keys for unlocking the fullness of His story, the universe as a whole should speak of hope. And if we can just go deep enough – if we can just become still enough to open the eyes of our hearts and form the habit of seeing well – we can read every day that God's first book is a story of courage under fire and of growing young again. And its pages are always open.

Epilogue

Divine providence is often perceived in hindsight, but during the four years I have been writing this book I have felt His hand almost daily. I remember, for instance, the day I returned to Jackson Hole after being gone for two years and how I was working out the idea of a nourishing mother when I was greeted by sunrise on the Tetons and a milk-mustached buffalo calf that had just finished his breakfast; or the day when I was trying to finish a section on evolution and was beginning to question what I had written when the Holy Father confirmed my efforts (see Appendix B).

Of course, God began writing words on my heart long ago through family and friends, islands and mountains, saints and scripture; but I began to put them on paper only recently, during a long solitary winter in Michigan. At that particular moment, it seemed that He had led me down dead-end roads and opened doors to rooms that seemed dark. The one and only thing I knew for certain about His plan for my life was that I had been commissioned to be a Godfather to my three nephews in order to help them "live a Christian life befitting the baptized and faithfully to fulfill the duties inherent in baptism."[1] These duties, which we pledge to fulfill every Easter, consist of little more than being devoted to God and the teachings of His Church, while rejecting Satan and "the glamour of evil".[2] To the best of my ability, I have designed this book to help them do just that.

For the most part, however, the story of my life has been a great squandering of grace. All too often, I have preached one thing then done another. I have blasphemed God's name in both word and deed,

---

1   *Code of Canon Law*, #872
2   Easter Vigil Mass, *Renewal of Baptismal Promises.*

becoming a stumbling block to others and contributing to their own blasphemy:

> Why is God's name blasphemed? Because we say one thing and do another. When they hear the words of God on our lips, unbelievers are amazed at their beauty and power, but when they see that those words have no effect in our lives, their admiration turns to scorn, and they dismiss such words as myths and fairy tales.[3]

All too often, I have also failed to exhort those closest to me. Some of my oldest friends and favorite students have invented their own version of Christianity. Others have fallen prey to the New Age: either becoming captivated by spiritualities that endorse moral relativism (some even going so far as promoting communion with creation rather than the Creator); or becoming duped by the well crafted lies of self-fulfillment found within the human potential movement. Still others have contracted spiritual leprosy by becoming overly concerned with wealth. I cannot help but think I had something to do with these lapses, for during my freshman year of college Jesus called me: ". . . sell your possessions and give to the poor, and you will have treasure in heaven; then come, follow me."[4] I refused. He called again and again, trying to reassure me: "Anyone who has given up houses or brothers or sisters or father or mother or children or lands for the sake of my name will receive a hundred times more, and will inherit eternal life."[5] But I had no courage. I thought of getting married and becoming an outfitter, a professor, or a special education teacher; I even tried to become a diocesan priest to avoid taking a vow of poverty like a religious priest, anything to avoid the call. But the hounds of heaven were unrelenting. So many times I have tried but failed. So many times I have been like the rich young man who walked away sad because of his many possessions. Still, I have reason to hope. For just the other day, our Holy Father encouraged me: "The sadness experienced by the rich young man in the Gospel story is the sadness that arises in the heart of all those who lack

---

3   From a homily written in the second century, *Office of Readings*, Thirty-Second Thursday in ordinary time
4   Matthew 19:21
5   Matthew 19:29

courage to follow Christ and to make the right choice. Yet it is never too late to respond to him!"[6]

So what prevents me from responding right now, from finally taking to heart all He has taught me? If the apostles and so many saints throughout history left everything to follow him upon hearing these words, why haven't I? I wanted to trust Him then and I want to trust Him now, but I can't seem to muster the courage. I am afraid. I want to begin writing more words with my life, but where will that strength come from? How will I be able to set my jaw and summon the grit to accomplish what he asks? The thought of it makes my heart feel like wax . . . and then there is His voice crying out over and over: "Take heart! Have courage! Do not be afraid!"

Domine, ut videam

My book is finished now and I have decided to withdraw into the mountains with some texts from World Youth Day in Denver and with the confidence that John Paul II's prayer from that day will be answered with an abundance of grace:

> Give these young people the courage and generosity of the great missionaries of the past, so that through the witness of their faith and their solidarity with every brother and sister in need, the world may discover the Truth, the Goodness, and the Beauty of the life you alone can give.[7]

The place I have chosen to set camp is just outside the Royal Village of the Holy Faith of St. Francis of Assisi; because there, at the southern tip of the Blood of Christ mountain range, what is arguably the largest living organism on earth sprawls across the western slope. This giant stand of quaking aspen trees is an eloquent sign of the mystical body of Christ and the familial nature of life in the Spirit. For just as an aspen grove is formed by many shoots that have cloned from a single root and grows leaves which reverently tremble or "quake" at the slightest breeze, we become one living organism in the Blood of Christ, cloned as it were

---

6   Pope Benedict XVI, *Message for the 25th World Youth Day*, March 28, 2010
7   Pope John Paul the Great, *World Youth Day: Vigil of the Assumption of Mary*, August 14, 1993; Cherry Creek State Park, Colorado.

from a single root, "the Root of David", and find our vocation within His Body by being sensitive to the breaths of the Spirit.[8] I am returning to that sacred place today seeking courage, having completed a novena to the Sacred Heart with a simple request: *Domine, ut videam* (Lord, that I may see).

As I begin my ascent, my thoughts turn to all the courageous examples set by parents, soldiers, and even some athletes. And as I settle into camp, I begin to reminisce about my Olympic dreams and my favorite Olympic moment when Billy Mills came from behind to win the 10,000 meters. And St. Paul's voice resounds in my mind: "Run so as to win."[9]

When I was young, I always ran to win, I always trained hard; yet as an adult I have been a poor Olympian for God and have often frustrated my family and friends. I want to cast off my lukewarm life and finally put on the new man, but maybe times have changed and God no longer wants us to follow him like "the great missionaries of the past". Maybe it has all been a ploy of the devil, a false light to lead me astray . . . . . . then again, maybe it was a harbinger of a call I was not prepared for. Maybe I needed to study and teach theology, maybe I needed to learn to read God's words and to be humbled with yellow roses from the Little Flower so I could learn the value of humiliation – just as she had: "Jesus knew very well that his little flower stood in need of the living waters of humiliation, for she was too weak to take root without this kind of help."[10] Maybe I needed to fall in order to rise.

My thoughts drift back to my trail above Cherry Creek and to the messages of John Paul the Great at World Youth Day – and there it is again. The man who had been appointed to update the gospel for the modern Church had encouraged us to read the words of Jesus without gloss:

> Do not be afraid to go out on the streets and into public
> places, like the first Apostles who preached Christ and
> the Good News of salvation in the squares of cities, towns,
> and villages. This is no time to be ashamed of the gospel!
> It is the time to preach it from the rooftops! Do not be
> afraid to break out of comfortable and routine modes of

---

8   Revelation 5:5
9   1 Corinthians 9:24-25
10   St. Therese of Lisieux, *Story of a Soul*, 206.

living, in order to take up the challenge of making Christ known in the modern 'metropolis.' It is you who must "go out into the byroads" and invite everyone you meet to the banquet which God has prepared for his people. The Gospel must not be kept hidden because of fear or indifference.[11]

It has been some time since I wrote what is above, and my fire is steady now. The great aspen family, *la familia de la Sangre de Cristo*, has given me repose. And as I watch their ballet, choreographed by the wind, I begin to see them as past and present members of His body – siblings who are nourished by His blood and support one another with an intricate root system, buried in humility. And St. Paul's voice resounds in my mind again: "Therefore, since we are surrounded by so great a cloud of witnesses, let us rid ourselves of every burden and sin that clings to us and persevere in running the race that lies before us."[12] The great cloud of witnesses! The great saints of the Church! I have always loved them! They have always given me hope! And now I am begging them for the courage to change and persevere. My guardian angel, St. Raphael, St. Noah, St. Abraham, St. Moses, St. David, St. Elijah, St. Susanna, Sts. Peter and Paul, St. Irenaeus, St. Athanasius, St. Richard, St. Martin, Brother Francis, Kamiano, The Little Flower, St. Katherine Drexel, St. Gemma, Mother Teresa, and JP II. If all these saints kept such great training schedules and now support us like we're running a race a stadium, what am I so afraid of? I begin to imagine them all cheering for us as we come down the final stretch, and I can almost hear them crying out like the commentator at the '64 Olympics, "Look at our brothers! Look at our sisters! The children of God are coming on!"

It seems painful that I have turned away so often, but at the same time it seems as if all things have led to this moment, as if it was His story from the beginning. Selling my possessions, giving the money to the poor, and following Him wherever He leads seems like the most natural and rational life I could live. Simplicity is not a path of misery (though the world might think so); rather, it is a path of peace. I have peace now,

---

11 Pope John Paul the Great, *World Youth Day: Feast of the Assumption of Mary*, August 15, 1993; Cherry Creek State Park, Colorado.
12 Hebrews 12:1

because I am prepared for war. And I ask my guardian angel to help me be content with food and clothing, ever mindful that "if I give away everything I own . . . but do not have love, I gain nothing."[13] This is what I desire with all my heart – to have everything I am be something in the eyes of God. And after the all the years of confusion and cowardice, after all the wasted time, talent, and treasure, I see now that all He ever wanted from me was just a simple yes . . . . . . a simple surrender to what the ravens and lilies have been saying all along.

---

13   1 Corinthians 13:3: cf. 1 Timothy 6:8

Appendix A

PROFESSION OF FAITH

I, Jon Lewer, with firm faith believe and profess each and every thing that is contained in the Symbol of faith, namely:

I believe in one God, the Father almighty, maker of heaven and earth, of all things visible and invisible. I believe in one Lord Jesus Christ, the Only Begotten Son of God, born of the Father before all ages. God from God, Light from Light, true God from true God, begotten, not made, consubstantial with the Father; through Him all things were made. For us men and for our salvation He came down from heaven, and by the Holy Spirit was incarnate of the Virgin Mary, and became man. For our sake He was crucified under Pontius Pilate, He suffered death and was buried, and rose again on the third day in accordance with the Scriptures. He ascended into heaven and is seated at the right hand of the Father. He will come again in glory to judge the living and the dead and His kingdom will have no end. I believe in the Holy Spirit, the Lord, the giver of life, who proceeds from the Father and the Son, who with the Father and the Son is adored and glorified, who has spoken through the prophets. I believe in one, holy, catholic, and apostolic Church. I confess one baptism for the forgiveness of sins, and I look forward to the resurrection of the dead and the life of the world to come. Amen.

With firm faith, I also believe everything contained in the Word of God, whether written or handed down in Tradition, which the Church, either by solemn judgment or by the ordinary and universal Magisterium, sets forth to be believed as divinely revealed.

I also firmly accept and hold each and every thing definitively proposed by the Church regarding teachings on faith and morals.

Moreover, I adhere with religious submission of will and intellect to the teachings which either the Roman Pontiff or the College of Bishops enunciate when they exercise their authentic Magisterium, even if they do not intend to proclaim these teachings by a definitive act.

Appendix B

ADDRESS OF HIS HOLINESS BENEDICT XVI TO MEMBERS
OF THE PONTIFICAL ACADEMY OF SCIENCES
(Clementine Hall, October 31, 2008)

Distinguished Ladies and Gentleman,

    . . . In choosing the topic *Scientific Insight into the Evolution of the Universe and of Life*, you seek to focus on an area of enquiry which elicits much interest. In fact, many of our contemporaries today wish to reflect upon the ultimate origin of beings, their cause and their end, and the meaning of human history and the universe.

In this context, questions concerning the relationship between science's reading of the world and the reading offered by Christian Revelation naturally arise. My predecessors Pope Pius XII and Pope John Paul II noted that there is no opposition between faith's understanding of creation and the evidence of the empirical sciences. . . . A decisive advance in understanding the origin of the cosmos was the consideration of . . . metaphysics with the most basic question of the first or transcendent origin of participated being. In order to develop and evolve, the world must first be, and thus have come from nothing into being. I must be created, in other words, by the first Being who is such by essence. . . . [T]he Creator founds these developments and supports them, underpins them and sustains then continuously. . . .

To "evolve" literally means "to unroll a scroll", that is, to read a book. The imagery of nature as a book has its roots in Christianity and has been held dear by many scientists. Galileo saw nature as a book whose author is God in the same way that Scripture has God as its author. It is a book whose history, whose evolution, whose "writing" and meaning, we "read" according to the different approaches of the sciences, while all the time presupposing the foundational presence of the author who has wished to reveal himself therein. This image also helps us to understand that the world, far from originating out of chaos, resembles an ordered book; it is a cosmos. Notwithstanding elements of the irrational, chaotic, and the destructive in the long processes of change in the cosmos, matter as such is "legible". It has an inbuilt "mathematics".

The human mind therefore can engage not only in a "cosmography" studying measurable phenomena but also in a "cosmology" discerning the visible inner logic of the cosmos. We may not at first be able to see the harmony both of the whole and of the relations of the individual parts, or their relationship to the whole. Yet, there always remains a broad range of intelligible events, and the process is rational in that it reveals an order of evident correspondences and undeniable finalities . . .

Experimental and philosophical inquiry gradually discovers these orders; it perceives them working to maintain themselves in being, defending themselves against imbalances, and overcoming obstacles. And thanks to the natural sciences we have greatly increased our understanding of the uniqueness of humanity's place within the cosmos.

The distinction between a simple living being and a spiritual being that is *capax Dei* [capable of understanding and desiring God], points to the existence of the intellective soul of a free transcendent subject. Thus the Magisterium of the Church has constantly affirmed that "every spiritual soul is created immediately by God – it is not 'produced' by the parents – and also that it is immortal." (CCC #366) This points to the distinctiveness of anthropology, and invites exploration of it by modern thought.

Distinguished academicians, I wish to conclude by recalling the words addressed to you by my predecessor Pope John Paul II in November 2003: "scientific truth, which is itself a participation in divine Truth, can help philosophy and theology to understand ever more fully the human person and God's Revelation about man . . ."

Appendix C

ST. PATRICK'S BREASTPLATE

I arise today:
Through a mighty strength, the invocation of the Trinity; Through the belief in the threeness; Through the confession of the oneness; of the Creator of Creation.

I arise today:
Through the strength of Christ's birth with his baptism; Through the strength of his crucifixion with his burial; Through the strength of his resurrection with his ascension; Through the strength of his descent for the Judgment Day.

I arise today:
Through the strength of the love of Cherubim; In obedience of angels; In the service of archangels; In hope of resurrection to meet with reward; In prayers of patriarchs; In predictions of prophets; In preaching of apostles; In faith of confessors; In innocence of holy virgins; In deeds of righteous men.

I arise today:
Through the strength of heaven; Light of sun; Radiance of moon; Splendor of fire; Speed of lightning; Swiftness of wind; Depth of sea; Stability of earth; Firmness of rock.

I arise today:
Through God's strength to pilot me; God's might to uphold me; God's wisdom to guide me; God's eye to look before me; God's ear to hear

me; God's word to speak for me; God's hand to guard me; God's way to lie before me; God's shield to protect me; God's host to save me; From snares of demons; From temptations of vices; From everyone who shall wish me ill; Afar and anear; Alone and in multitude.

I summon today all these powers between me and those evils: Against every cruel merciless power that may oppose my body and soul; Against incantations of false prophets; Against black laws of pagandom; Against false laws of heretics; Against craft of idolatry; Against spells of witches and smiths and wizards; Against every knowledge that corrupts man's body and soul.

Christ to shield me today:
Against poison, against burning; Against drowning, against wounding, so that there may come to me abundance of reward. Christ with me, Christ before me, Christ behind me, Christ in me, Christ beneath me, Christ above me, Christ on my right, Christ on my left, Christ when I lie down, Christ when I sit down, Christ when I arise, Christ in the heart of every man who thinks of me, Christ in the mouth of everyone who speaks of me, Christ in every eye that sees me, Christ in every ear that hears me.

I arise today:
Through a mighty strength, the invocation of the Trinity; Through belief in the threeness; Through confession of the oneness; of the Creator of Creation.

Appendix D

ST. ANSELM, OFFICE OF READINGS,
FEAST OF THE IMMACULATE CONCEPTION

Mary is the Mother of the New Creation

Blessed Lady, sky and stars, earth and rivers, day and night -everything that is subject to the power or use of man- rejoice that through you, they are in some sense restored to their lost beauty and all are endowed with inexpressible new grace. All creatures were dead, as it were, useless for men and for the praise of God, who made them. The world, contrary to its true destiny, was corrupted and tainted by the acts of men who served idols. Now all creation has been restored to life and rejoices that it is controlled and given splendor by men who believe in God.

The universe rejoices with new and in definable loveliness. Not only does it feel the unseen presence of God himself, its Creator, it sees him openly, working and making it holy. These great blessings spring from the blessed fruit of Mary's womb.

Through the fullness of grace that was giving you, dead things rejoice in their freedom, and those in heaven are glad to be made new. Through the Son who was the glorious fruit of your virgin womb, just souls who died before his life-giving death, rejoice they are freed from captivity and the Angels are glad at the restoration of their shattered domain.

Lady, full and overflowing with grace, all creation receives new life from your abundance. Virgin blessed above all creatures through your blessing all creation is blessed, not only creation from its Creator, but the Creator himself has been blessed by creation.

To Mary God gave his only begotten son, whom he loved as himself. Through Mary God made himself a son, not different but the same, by nature son of God and son of Mary. The whole universe was created by God, and God was born of Mary. God created all things, and Mary gave birth to God. The God who made all things gave himself form through Mary, and thus he made his own creation. He who could create all things from nothing would not remake his ruined creation without Mary.

God, then, is the Father of the created world and Mary is the mother of the re-created world. God is the Father by whom all things were given life, and Mary the mother through whom all things were given new life. For God begot the son, through whom all things were made, and Mary gave birth to him as the savior of the world. Without God's Son nothing could exist; without Mary's son, nothing could be redeemed.

Truly the Lord is with you, to whom the Lord granted that all nature should owe as much to you as to himself.

Made in the USA
Charleston, SC
13 December 2010